Women Characters
in Baseball Literature

Women Characters in Baseball Literature

A Critical Study

KATHLEEN SULLIVAN

McFarland & Company, Inc., Publishers
Jefferson, North Carolina, and London

LIBRARY OF CONGRESS CATALOGUING-IN-PUBLICATION DATA

Sullivan, Kathleen, 1969–
　　Women characters in baseball literature : a critical study / Kathleen Sullivan.
　　　　p.　　cm.
　　Includes bibliographical references and index.

　　ISBN 0-7864-2170-3 (softcover : 50# alkaline paper)

　　1. Baseball stories, American — History and criticism.
2. Feminism and literature — United States.　3. Women and literature — United States.　4. Baseball in literature.　5. Women in literature.　I. Title.
PS374.B37S85　2005
813.009'357 — dc22　　　　　　　　　　　　　　2005007423

British Library cataloguing data are available

©2005 Kathleen Sullivan. All rights reserved

No part of this book may be reproduced or transmitted in any form or by any means, electronic or mechanical, including photocopying or recording, or by any information storage and retrieval system, without permission in writing from the publisher.

On the cover: background ©2005 Artville; baseball ©2005 PhotoSpin

Manufactured in the United States of America

McFarland & Company, Inc., Publishers
　Box 611, Jefferson, North Carolina 28640
　www.mcfarlandpub.com

For Connor

Acknowledgments

I am thankful for Professor Cordelia Candelaria, a true baseball goddess, whose expert guidance during the dissertation process made this work possible. To Professors D. G. Kehl, Duane Roen, and Mark Harris, all at Arizona State University, I extend my deepest gratitude for their help.

Pat Sullivan, my father, fabulous research assistant, and fellow Texas Rangers fan, and Tim Morris of the University of Texas at Arlington read and edited drafts of this work. Thank you to both of them, though Tim's fondness for the Yankees makes him suspect in my father's eyes.

Thanks Mom and David, for all of your support, especially for the computer and for the care and feeding of Natty Bumppo. I couldn't have done it without you.

Other significant contributions to this work were made by my M.A. thesis committee at Baylor University, Professors Robert Collmer, Greg Garrett, and Nancy Goodloe.

Thank you to my son Connor, whose kitchen table and summer vacation was littered with drafts of this work. I hope you had a good time anyway, sweetie.

And thank you to my friends and family for their kind words and support during this process: Margaret "Nonnie" Sullivan, Jane Sullivan, Tom and Stacy Sullivan, Patrick, Savannah, and Sera, Sue and Tom Johnson, Mary Johnson, Amy and Shawn Hughes, Lorraine and John Lamb, Sebastian Francis, Chris and Rania Saidi Combs, Ryan and Sarah, Lisa Landrum and Julian, Terelyn Hepple and D. J., Karmon

ACKNOWLEDGMENTS

Runquist, Jan Kullman, Jared, Kayleigh, and Ty, Brad and Erica Gottschalk, Henry and Ethan, Jane Schneider, Lisa Scogin, Shana Cannon, Ashley and Cory, my friends at St. Andrew's United Methodist Church in Arlington, and all the super folks in the Sports Literature Association, especially Judy Hakola and David McGimpsey.

Finally, thank you to Brian Karnes, a good sport and my favorite Aggie.

Contents

Acknowledgments vii
Preface 1
Introduction: Taken Out of the Ballgame 3

One: Mount Olympus in the Majors 13
Two: Gods and Goddesses at the Plate 29
Three: Absent Mothers and Mothering Men 57
Four: Substitute Mothering in *The Southpaw*
 and *She's on First* 91
Five: The Transformational Goddesses 115
Six: The Compound Goddesses 149

Chapter Notes 175
Bibliography 181
Index 191

Preface

This work extends the examination of women characters within the discourse of sports literature by applying feminist frameworks to some of the previously overlooked roles of women characters in baseball literature. It employs a variety of theories and approaches from literary criticism, particularly archetypal analysis. Using Robert J. Higg's *Laurel & Thorn: The Athlete in American Literature,* Cordelia Candelaria's *Seeking the Perfect Game: Baseball and American Literature,* and Deeanne Westbrook's *Ground Rules: Baseball & Myth* as inspiration for the archetypal analysis of baseball literature, this study first explores both the absence of biological mothers and the presence of heightened maternal qualities in both the men and women characters of baseball short stories, novels, and plays.

Following the examination of motherhood in baseball literature is a brief historical overview of a unique subgenre of baseball literature: stories about female ball players (both girls and women). These stories, first written by both men and women in the mid-twentieth century, began to show greater sophistication as they evolved from literature written predominantly for children into literature written for adults. By the 1970s, the real-life influence of legislation like Title IX helped authors imagine increasingly complex characterizations of women playing baseball and allowed for more fully realized characters in the late twentieth and early twenty-first centuries.

Such characters may be analyzed through the use of Jean Shinoda Bolen's *Goddesses in Everywoman: A New Psychology of Women.* Bolen's popular psychological study calls attention to the patterns of behavior often found in women. The women characters of baseball literature may act similarly, applying Bolen's work to these characters illuminates the importance of such patterns. The patterns that recall the Greek goddesses Demeter, Hestia, and Hera are here labeled "transformational goddesses" because the women characters who can be viewed as these types most often contribute to the development or transformation of those characters nearest to them. Other women characters, those whose attributes embrace more than one goddess and whose personal development does not necessarily guide or instruct those around them, are here termed "compound goddesses."

An examination of the contributions of these goddesses cannot be understood without a thorough appreciation of what Candelaria describes as the "gender exclusivity" that characterizes the sport of baseball, its literature and criticism. This study pushes the boundaries of existing criticism beyond the overtly male cultural practice of sport by furthering scholarly recognition of how women characters, the feminine, and the feminist imagination inhabit baseball and its literary representations.

Introduction: Taken Out of the Ballgame

I am limiting "sport" to exclusively human games: organized competitions involving tests of physical skill, pitting men against men, without extraordinary means of locomotion.

Every sports novel begins with a hero.
— Michael Oriard (5, 25)

In his influential study *Dreaming of Heroes: American Sports Fiction, 1868–1980* (1982), Michael Oriard uses the terms "men against men" and "hero" to define sport and its novels, excluding women from both his theories and literary analysis. More recently, David McGimpsey's *Imagining Baseball: America's Pastime and Popular Culture* (2000) claims that "the women are, with some notable exceptions, in the background of the texts that form the body of baseball fiction" (13). Who the exceptions are and why they are exceptional receive minimal attention in his work.

While Oriard's definitions and McGimpsey's observations may have once adequately depicted the literary landscape surrounding them, new works of fiction and a culture that more readily accepts women's involvement in the game demand a reexamination of the roles of women characters in baseball literature. The shift in baseball's cultural landscape is easy to see: Compare Jimmy Duggan (Tom Hanks) sneering, "There is no crying in baseball" in *A League of Their Own* (1992) with Jean Hastings Ardell's well-received *Breaking into Baseball: Women in the National Pastime* (2004). Similarly, "You play like a girl" is the ultimate insult to a boy in *The Sandlot* (1993), but only a few years later

Karen Joy Fowler gives us *The Sweetheart Season* (1996), a thoughtful novel of women joyfully play the game.

The old habit of removing femininity from baseball is hardly limited to grumpy coaches, little leaguers, and sophisticated literary analyses. Although everybody sings "Take Me Out to the Ball Game" in the seventh inning, few of those stretching in the stands know that the familiar tune is sung by a woman who is "baseball mad." Jack Norworth and Albert Von Tilzer's ode to Katie Casey was a smash in 1908. Ninety-six years later, the Smithsonian displayed the original draft of Norworth's lyrics in the exhibit "Baseball as America," which was held during the 2004 baseball season and featured in the magazine *Smithsonian*. The article "Baseball's Anthem for All Ages" mistakenly labels the song "a pitcher's song" based on "the one, two, three strikes you're out" lyric (47). The Katie Casey verse appears only in the image of Norworth's manuscript and in its caption is called "a forgotten first verse" (48). Despite the ongoing neglect of her first verse, Katie's chorus, her request to be taken out to the ball game, is played daily in nearly every professional ballpark across America.

Similarly taken out of the ball game is little Bridget White (Donna Corcoran) of the 1951 movie *Angels in the Outfield,* whose visions of baseball-playing angels inspire hope among those around her. The 1994 Disney version featured an eleven-year-old boy, Roger (Joseph Gordon-Levitt), instead of a girl. How could a little girl, the executives at Disney seem to be saying, pay careful enough attention to baseball to see anything special, particularly angels, at a ball game? Although Disney attempted to make amends by casting Brittney Irvin as thirteen-year-old Laurel Everett in *Angels in the Infield* (2004), Bridget White and Katie Casey occupy the same seats in the stands as onlookers who have been sadly overlooked in the "boys only" club that seems to be baseball literature.

Real Grass, Real Dirt, Real Women

In the 1980s sports writers like Susan Fornoff started knocking on clubhouse doors, and her coverage of baseball for the *Sacramento Bee*

Introduction

shattered the restrictions against women reporters in Major League Baseball's locker rooms. Her journey resulted in the insightful *Lady in the Locker Room: Uncovering the Oakland Athletics* (1993), a painful reminder of women's past journalistic outsider status to the sport. The famous "Kong the Rat" incident, in which ballplayer Dave Kingman sent her a corsage box containing a live rodent with the nametag "Sue" during a game, reveals the ridicule she endured as well as how low Kingman and his cohorts could sink in disparaging a colleague (83–84). If the rat weren't bad enough, Fornoff's only friend on the team, Moose Haas, supported Kingman afterward, which was "the only time I got upset to the point of tears" (86).

Also claiming space in professional baseball, and probably a few real tears in the process, though she has not yet written about them, left-handed pitcher Ila Borders played for the Northern Independent League with the St. Paul Saints (1997), Duluth-Superior Dukes (1998), and Madison Blackwolf (1999).[1] Although she posted an understandably rookieish ERA of 7.50 during her first season, she pitched twelve scoreless innings of baseball for the Dukes and had a 1.67 ERA in Madison (Ardell 1–2). However, the numbers don't reflect the hardships she faced. She reported, "I've been spit on, had beer thrown on me and been sworn at and was hit 11 times out of 11 at-bats while in college.... But the memories I have are the ovations when I would run in from the bullpen" (Ardell 1). Borders walked away from professional baseball on June 30, 2000, and, in spite of the abuse she suffered, fondly recalled playing the game. Now that the clubhouse doors are slightly ajar, they will open fully for future generations of women baseball players, perhaps without men admonishing them to stop crying.

The historical re-establishment of the roles of women in baseball started in the 1990s, especially in accounts of the All-American Girls Professional Baseball League (AAGPBL). After *A League of Their Own* hit the screens, works such as Barbara Gregorich's *Women at Play: The Story of Women in Baseball* (1993), Susan E. Johnson's *When Women Played Hardball* (1994), and Gai Ingham Berlage's *Women in Baseball: The Forgotten History* (1994) began hitting the bookstore shelves. These historical accounts of women playing baseball, which reflect our general acceptance of revisionist history — because it really happened — tend to be more readily accepted than feminist readings of traditionally masculinized baseball fiction.²

Elinor Nauen continued the mid–1990s trend of establishing the connection between women and the game in her collection of sports literature, *Diamonds Are a Girl's Best Friend: Women Writers on Baseball* (1994). Nauen was initially concerned that her project would suffer from lack of quality entries. She was wrong: "At first as I researched *Diamonds* I worried that I'd have to use every little scrap I could lay my hands on; I was delighted and surprised at how much material there turned out to be" (xiii). Nauen admits to including her favorites from the large number of possibilities, and similarly, the women characters I have chosen for this work are the ones I find significant and compelling, most often from novels and short stories, and even children's literature. Yes, there were many to choose from, and I am certain there will be more.

Like Katie Casey and Bridget White, who represent women as fans of the game and as victims of cultural amnesia, the women characters of baseball literature make significant contributions to the genre as catalysts for change in the lives of others and as players in their own right. Katie sings her song solo, and Bridget is the only person in the original *Angels in the Outfield* who sees the angels. They join women characters in the works of literary heavyweights Mark Harris and August Wilson in necessitating the inclusion of women in discussions of sports literature, particularly baseball fiction.

The Game of Life

In the first book of Mark Harris's popular Henry "Author" Wiggen tetralogy (*The Southpaw, Bang the Drum Slowly, A Ticket for a Seamstitch,* and *It Looked Like For Ever*), Holly Webster visits her steady boyfriend, a baseball "hero" who has just thrown an illegal spitball. She tells him: "It is a beautiful game, clean and graceful and honest. But I will be damned if I will sit back and watch you turn into some sort of low life halfway between a sour creature like Sad Sam Yale and a shark

Introduction

like Dutch Schnell" (*The Southpaw* 307). With these words, Holly initiates Henry Wiggen's growth from an insolent spitballer into a man who can manage a professional baseball career, a marriage, and a family. Unlike the aging, cynical pitcher Yale or the hostile, pedantic manager Schnell, Wiggen will become a caring and careful spouse, who, while not perfect, outshines the other players on his team. Holly's notions of responsibility and maturity push Henry across the threshold of the playing field and into the "real" world as Harris represents it in the early 1950s.

Additionally, strong women characters have continued to appear in more recent baseball literature, deepening the need for their inclusion in any literary analysis of sport. In August Wilson's Pulitzer Prize–winning *Fences* (1986), an aging Troy Maxson, unlike the young Henry Wiggen, is already the head of a twentieth-century American household, but Troy's anger at being excluded from white, organized baseball and his marital infidelity cause him to fail in this role. Troy cannot conceptualize a changing world that had seen African Americans playing major league baseball for ten years and witnessed the desegregation of American schools through the Supreme Court's 1954 *Brown v. Board of Education* decision. Like the truly oxymoronic term "deliberate speed" used by the court to describe the desegregation process, Troy remains fenced within his past. Troy's wife Rose, however, moves with the changes in her life. She becomes a gate, and as society swings from segregation to integration, she also remains anchored in the family home while opening its doors to accept responsibility for the child her husband fathered yet cannot raise alone.[3]

In Act Two, Scene Three of the play, standing quietly on the front porch of their home, Rose listens to Troy's pleas for assistance in raising his lover's newborn child. After a moment, she speaks haltingly to him, a baby in his arms: "Okay, Troy ... you're right. I'll take care of your baby for you ... cause ... like you say ... she's innocent ... and you can't visit the sins of the father upon the child. A motherless child has got a hard time" (79). She reaches for the child, and with the baby now firmly in her arms, Rose then speaks the play's pivotal lines: "From right now ... this child got a mother. But you a womanless man" (79).

Introduction

One cannot deny the tragedy of Troy's situation — yet when I saw this play, I witnessed women in the audience almost jumping out of their seats, fists raised, in a "you-go-girl" salute to a woman who would no longer suffer the abuses of a raging, self-serving, cheating husband. Instead, Rose will provide a nurturing home for herself and her adoptive daughter, thereby resisting the oppressive marriage that had stifled her growth as a woman and embittered her sons.

In contrast to these scenes of conflict and accountability, many narratives about sports heroes depict strong male athletes in their prime (Janeway 264). These heroes succeed in both their professional and personal lives as they conquer baseball rivals and enjoy the attention of adoring female fans. Such achievements, as represented in literature, often conflate sporting events and sexual fulfillment (264). "Getting to first base," "striking out," or "hitting a homerun," as we know from overhearing the conversations of many American teenagers, replay more than the action of the previous day's baseball game. In fact, in Robert Coover's *The Universal Baseball Association, Inc., J. Henry Waugh, Prop.* (1968), baseball becomes sex as characters Henry Waugh and Hettie Irden "ran the bases, pounded into first, slid into second heels high, somersaulted over third, shot home standing up," ... and then they "run them all again" (29). Later, Waugh sees Hettie not as a woman, but as metaphor for sex itself, with baseball as its vehicle: "Hettie had invented her own magic version, stretching out as the field, left hand as first base..." (206).

How did "scoring" become a term for sex, particularly with its one-base-at-a-time references in literature? This situation, according to Elizabeth Janeway's *Man's World, Woman's Place: A Study in Social Mythology* (1971), occurs when men, who once proved their strength through activities that ensured their people's survival, now have few opportunities to display their physical abilities. No longer needed for hunting animals or protecting the family from enemies, "men's skills and prowess have degenerated into sport" (265). Men may pursue superlative athletic skill in much the same way they pursue sex, while neglecting their own moral growth.

In *The Southpaw* and in *Fences*, athletes face difficulty in life off

Introduction

the diamond and inadequacy in relationships due to their stunted ethical development. Harris's Henry Wiggen, at the beginning of his career, cannot meet the emotional demands of the woman he wishes to marry. She wants a mature, responsible man, one who can share her home and help her raise a family. On the other end of the career spectrum, Wilson's Troy Maxson is old and broken-down, having lost his home and family. His wife cannot trust him after his extramarital affair, even though she nurturingly accepts his child.

Harris and Wilson provide increasingly difficult complications to these characters' situations by showing them at home rather than exclusively at home plate. Henry Wiggen's excitement over winning a close game fades as he realizes that throwing a spitter may cause him to lose the woman he loves. Although the cheers of the fans have long faded for Troy Maxson, his lost chance at a career in white organized baseball pales in comparison to the loss of his family as his wife banishes him from their home and he slumps into the darkness. To emphasize the significance of family in these narratives, Harris and Wilson remove Henry and Troy from the glory of the sports arena and confront them with strong women characters. Henry, in danger of sacrificing his future over a spitball, and Troy, in losing his present home to his infidelity, receive stern reprimands from Holly and Rose, respectively. Harris and Wilson create woman-centered scenes in sports literature by giving women characters such key roles.

The nurturing, edifying qualities of Holly and Rose expand the boundaries of sports literature and contest literary representations of the self-centered, frustrated athlete. Such well-rounded characterizations of women underscore the developmental challenges of male protagonists, providing ethical substance to each work. These men must overcome their personal limitations, in some cases generated by the very nature of being professional athletes, to become good mates and parents. Men often learn to follow the lead of their partners, who generally have better social skills. Such feminist readings of Harris and Wilson uncover previously overlooked implications of women's crucially significant roles in baseball literature.

These roles may, of course, vary in their importance to a text.

INTRODUCTION

Some women characters have been totally erased from the narratives, especially the mothers of baseball players, yet their absence has tremendous consequences for those players. In addition, many women characters, like the memorable Miss Paris of *The Natural* fame, have been appropriately labeled distractions from athletes' focus on their profession. Other women support the players' game as fans, girlfriends, or wives. These stereotypes have roots in the early and mid-twentieth century, when women were seen as troublemakers, spies, possible sexual conquests, fans (on Ladies' Day), and as ball-playing publicity stunts (Crepeau 160–161). There are, however, numerous women characters who pursue their own lives and achieve their own professional goals apart from the typical roles in which they have been historically and fictionally cast.

From Absent Mothers to Goddesses

The evolution of women characters from total absence, most notably the many missing mothers of baseball players, to key figures in narratives can be traced through the application of archetypal studies and myth criticism to baseball literature. References to mythology are found throughout cultural representations of baseball and most notably explored in Deeanne Westbrook's comprehensive *Ground Rules: Baseball & Myth* (1996). From Ivy Keller, who sports "hair done in a curly Greek effect" and adores "a blonde god standing on the pitcher's mound" in Edna Ferber's "A Bush League Hero" (1912) to the slobbering bulldog Hercules, who gnaws a Babe Ruth–autographed baseball in the movie *The Sandlot*, myths translate baseball tales into serious literature and exuberant films. As Ferber reminds us, "Any man who can look handsome in a dirty baseball suit is an Adonis" (58).

Many previous mythological approaches to the characters of baseball literature exclude any discussion of women characters (Potter, Higgs, Murdock, Oriard) or mention only their supporting roles (Wasserman, Bjarkman, Candelaria, Solomon, Westbrook).[4] However, these early works lay important groundwork for further explication of women characters as deserving their own categories in myth criticism.

Introduction

These new categories represent a significant shift from the most frequently erased women characters in baseball literature, who Westbrook terms the "absent mothers."[5] Not only are the mothers absent from the traditional father-son catch, "a durable trope in all representations of baseball" (McGimpsey 131), but they are also missing from their children's lives in other ways.

A surprising number of fictional ballplayers, hearkening back to the ultimate fiction of Babe Ruth's status as an "orphan," do not have mothers. Lack of maternal attention precipitates adult crises for Roy Hobbs of *The Natural* (1952), Roy Tucker of John R. Tunis's *The Kid from Tomkinsville* (1940), and the Russell brothers, Spike and Bob, of Tunis's *The Keystone Kids* (1943). Irini Doyle of Karen Joy Fowler's *The Sweetheart Season* lacks both a mother and a father, one lost in childbirth and the other to alcoholism. Additionally, some mothers become emotionally absent from the lives of their children, as in Bruce Brooks's *What Hearts* (1992), which chronicles the struggle of an only child, Asa or "Ace," through his mother's psychological and physical collapse as she inexplicably divorces his biological father and marries her abusive, immature old flame, only to divorce him as well.

However, not all characters respond identically to the physical or emotional absence of their biological mothers, especially when they enjoy the guidance of surrogate mother figures. Substitute mothers, men and women characters who gently offset the void left by absent biological mothers, appear in the Mark Harris tetralogy and in Barbara Gregorich's *She's On First* (1987). Harris's Henry Wiggen and Gregorich's Linda Sunshine need the unconditional support and encouragement of substitute mothers to achieve professional and personal success.

The presence of the feminine in baseball literature gradually evolves from the absent mothers into the substitute mothers and finally into strong women characters who can be categorized in their own right. They recall the Greek goddesses Demeter, Hestia, and Hera. Rose Maxson, of Wilson's *Fences*, and Consuelo and Carlota, of Lamar Herrin's *The Rio Loja Ringmaster* (1977), possess the qualities of Demeter, a maternal goddess who nurtures those around her. Harris's Holly

Webster Wiggen resembles the goddess Hera, who is, according to myth, attracted to a powerful yet immature man. Finally, the home fires of the domestic goddess Hestia burn brightly in Iris Lemon of *The Natural* and Annie Kinsella of W. P. Kinsella's *Shoeless Joe* (1982). Because these women help men become better people rather than just better ballplayers, I term them "transformational goddesses."

Displaying increased complexity, some women in baseball literature have attributes that embrace more than one goddess type and are devoted to their own personal development. These fascinating characters, the "compound goddesses," have qualities that recall traits associated with several goddesses. Possessing the athletic and artistic characteristics of Artemis and Aphrodite, Clare Bishop of Nancy Willard's *Things Invisible to See* (1985), Rachel Sonnshein of Silvia Tennenbaum's *Rachel, The Rabbi's Wife* (1978), and Irini Doyle of Fowler's *The Sweetheart Season* have physical and creative talents. Instead of using their gifts to serve others, however, the compound goddesses focus on their own personal and professional development, showing the multiple interactions of women and sport.

The contributions of the compound goddesses to literature cannot be understood without recognizing the "gender exclusivity" (Candelaria 13–15) dominating baseball fiction and its criticism.[6] The sport itself and its literary representations can be viewed as cultural practices, and these practices are often highly masculinized. But by examining exceptional women like Clare, Rachel, and Irini, we can show how women strike back, claiming their rightful places in baseball literature.

Play Ball!

Thanks to Katie Casey, Bridget White, Susan Fornoff, and Ila Borders, who show the boys how women enjoy, watch, write about, and play hardball. May we never stretch in the stands again without knowing that a woman's voice sings "Take Me Out to the Ball Game." And, I am proud to say, before games in Arlington during the Texas Rangers' 2004 season a recording of the song, sung by a woman, was played in its entirety.

ONE

Mount Olympus in the Majors

Past attempts at applying myth criticism to baseball literature may have necessarily erased or marginalized women characters due to the fact that the genre was almost exclusively written by men about men. When the traditional canon of baseball literature was dominated by men, women stood outside the foul lines or sat dutifully in the stands, cheering their heroes, whose exploits often reach Herculean proportions. However, some women have dared to enter the game, and their behaviors suggest exciting and new patterns of representation. The resulting major league Mount Olympus features the baseball goddesses standing proudly beside the traditional gods, providing us a positive, feminist view of sports literature.

Integration of critical approaches is nothing new to feminists who are generally pluralistic in their study of women in our culture. Over a decade ago, Elaine Showalter declared that "there are far too many internal differences of race, ethnicity, and theoretical affiliation to make the idea of a monolithic American feminist criticism meaningful. Taking refuge behind such a banner in the 1990s would be intellectually indefensible, and politically retrograde" (6). For example, American feminist theorists have used Marxist criticism to argue that the material conditions of women as a class evidences their marginal position in society, *l'écriture féminine* to propose that women's bodies are the primary source of feminist inspiration, and feminist dialogics to emphasize women's voices in texts.[1] These are just a few of the multiple strategies feminist critics employ to examine relationships between men and women.

Despite the attractiveness of using many approaches to explore literature, some women writers, like Annette Kolodny, also admit that "the search for patterns of opposition and connection [is] probably the basis of thinking itself" (185). The development of such patterns, as in the association of women characters with Greek goddesses, evidences shared structures of language and mind. Thus, proponents of pluralism in feminist criticism should not automatically distrust categorizing women characters into goddess types. Rather, this system reveals "the shared metaphors, phases, tropes, and myths" that are significant to the human experience (Showalter 7). Our commonalities help us establish connections to one another through shared literary experiences. Moreover, these categories may expose systems of domination and subordination, assisting feminist theorists in their struggle to reread various genres of literature. This gender inclusive analysis enables us to hear women's voices in baseball literature that would otherwise be muffled or silenced by the roars of the crowd, the chatter on the field, or the gloating of heroes after they run the bases.

The human experience as revealed through mythic figures may represent our societal beliefs about gender, power, status, and division of labor. During the formation of mythic criticism, scholars like C. G. Jung discussed the forces that shape relationships between men and women, particularly the forces that determine women's roles in society.[2] Jung defined these features through dichotomies such as sensitive (female) / tough (male); emotional / distant; caring / indifferent. He also believed that men and women could bridge these psychological gender gaps when men expressed feminine qualities and women masculine ones.

Such growth equipped individuals to function effectively and ultimately to achieve better relationships with others. Jung considered this development a key part of the individuation process — the external journey to join society and the inner journey to self-reliance and harmony. These journeys, Jung argued, can be seen in a progression of archetypal figures: "the Shadow, symbolizing our 'other side,' our 'dark brother,' who is an invisible but inseparable part of our psychic totality (Jacobi, *Psychology* 109). As Luke Skywalker must resist the "Dark Side" in the *Star Wars* films, he must also reconcile himself to the dark nature that is a part of his psyche, represented in his biological father, Darth Vader. For Skywalker, his father is a form of the Shadow; however, Jung saw mothers as a form of the Shadow, a "dark mass of experience that is seldom or never admitted to our conscious lives and bars the way to the creative depths of our unconscious" (112).

The (M)Others

When biological mothers are absent from baseball literature and/or are substituted with other characters, the substitutes belong to an (m)other category apart from the goddesses. Most notably described as the "Great" and "Terrible" mothers by Earl R. Wasserman in his article "*The Natural*: Malamud's World Ceres," Iris Lemon and Memo Paris are Roy Hobbs's "substitute mothers because Roy's biological mother abandoned him" (446). Deeanne Westbrook extends Wasserman's work on the "Great" and "Terrible" mothers by identifying additional characters in baseball literature whose mothers have left them.[3] Westbrook argues that the absent mothers are evidence of men's intolerance for women on the baseball field. While the field itself may be feminine, an enclosed garden or *hortus conclusus*, like the Garden of Eden, men desire exclusive access to it, hearkening back to Adam's carefree existence before the original mother joined him and caused sin and death to enter their lives (120). In the world of baseball literature, additionally, women are often excluded before the men arrive at the field of play so that the narrative focuses exclusively on a male environment. This setting encourages the development of boys into ballplayers, uninterrupted by calls to dinner or by chores around the house.

Ironically, although the mothers are absent from the text, the search for a maternal presence often consumes the protagonists. The ballplayer must fulfill his maternal quest by successfully developing a romantic relationship, ensuring his personal happiness off the playing field once his career has ended. While they lack the autonomy and authority of the baseball goddesses who are able to speak for themselves, the absent mothers are included here to read their absence in the same way that we read the presence of the goddess characters. The absent mothers are "silent bearers of meaning," emphasizing that although women often "have not yet been accepted as makers of meaning" in certain types of literature, their silence and the cultural processes that silence them have meaning (Bauer, "Gender" 709). In the absent mother category, the mothers' absence may be the unconscious impetus for the ballplayers' searching for maternal figures as well as a social commentary on the perceived incompatibility of women characters and sports literature.

Yes, Virginia, there is a Cooperstown

When A. G. Spalding created the myth of baseball's immaculate conception in a New York pasture, he was not too far off base in giving baseball a mythic quality, perhaps explaining our eager acceptance of Cooperstown. The very origins of games are often described in ethnographic studies as derived from ancient rituals found in the cultural and religious activities of primitive societies: "These were contests with sticks and stones; sometimes stone throwing only; sometimes a tug of war between contending forces.... In certain places, the ritual combat was accompanied by a wedding, held in a ploughed field, a custom replete with symbolism related to the idea of fertility" (Henderson 8). Baseball has its roots firmly planted in such ritual activity, and game theorists, such as Johan Huizinga and Roger Caillois, as well as anthropologists, such as Margaret Mead, argue that the bounded ritualized activity of play and leisure forms culture, and, therefore, play continues to develop and change along with the culture. From the baseball-obsessed fans of the 1950s to the more diversified sports aficionados of today, we see — and perhaps sometimes lament — the changes in sport culture. While our gaze is often clouded by nostalgia for the game as we believe it was once played, we must also realize that as culture changes, sports inevitably must, too.

One. Mount Olympus in the Majors

Ethnographic studies of the ritual places associated with the origins of ball and stick games, such as the ploughed field, connect baseball to our agrarian past and explain the lines on playing fields. In addition, the baseball season begins in spring, a time of renewed vegetation, which is another reason why chalk lines and intricate mowing patterns appear on a ball field. By applying the same kind of scrutiny to the patterns of characterization present in baseball literature, we may discern clues to the origins of larger societal patterns and gender roles. Thus, as the physical landscape of ball fields reveals hints about the ritualistic roots of baseball, characters who watch or participate in the sports may also represent deep structures of a communal past.

Students of the Game

As a teacher of baseball literature, I have often enjoyed hearing students joke about me as "Dr. Baseball." To me, this term of endearment proves their acceptance of the topic and their willingness to take the study of popular culture seriously. While we do have fun, and interesting guest speakers ranging from a local actor who was a ballplayer in the movie *The Rookie* to the president of the Ft. Worth Cats Baseball Club, we read and read and read, eight novels and one play. How baseball literature became an undergraduate English class at the University of Texas at Arlington, granted its close proximity to the Texas Rangers ball club, may be understood through an examination of the development of popular culture studies, particularly in the work of Mikhail Bakhtin.

Scholarly attention to popular culture gained wide acceptance with Bakhtin's revolutionary *Rabelais and His World* (1968). Bakhtin was among the first scholars to identify the intellectual benefits of studying mass social activities. In his work, Bakhtin divides the medieval folk practices represented in the literature of François Rabelais into ritual spectacles, comic verbal compositions, and various genres of billingsgate (5). Historians and sociologists had previously ignored these folk practices and the ritual spectacle of the carnival in the work of Rabelais in favor of examining the culture of the elite, such as the opera or symphony. The same privileging of certain cultural practices exists today; however, Bakhtin opened many fields, such as sports literature, for scholars in his writing about non-elite discourses, especially in the various forms of language used by the masses.

For example, Bakhtin applied his theories of language use to the novel, then thought of as a popular rather than elite cultural expression. In his essay "Discourse and the Novel," Bakhtin defines the novel in terms of dialogue, "a phenomenon multiform in style and variform in speech and voice" (261). The novel, for Bakhtin, records the discourses of not only the author but also the larger world around him or her: "Authorial speech, the speeches of narrators, inserted genres, the speech of characters are merely those fundamental compositional unities ... [that] can enter the novel; each of them permits a multiplicity of social voices and a wide variety of their links and interrelationships (always more or less dialogized)" (263). Bakhtin examines these sources of dialogue both individually and for their influences upon one another. In baseball literature, this strategy can be valuable for identifying the institutional voices of the sport, as represented by owners, and the individual voices of players, with their numerous interactions with others, both inside and outside the game. Moreover, both the individual speakers and the institutions contributing to the discourse within the novel include members of elite and non-elite social classes. They are, for example, the traditionally wealthy characters who own teams and the uneducated, poor characters who play the game in early baseball literature. Although the player of today is just as rich, if not more so, as his boss, the fascinating rube voices Ring Lardner recorded in *You Know Me Al* (1914) show just how effective and revealing the representations of non-elite characters in literature can be.

Bakhtin further argues that the conflict of such cultural forces shaped the emergence of the novel as various groups were forming literary responses to their worlds in the middle ages. During this time "the clown sounded forth, ridiculing all 'languages' and dialects; there developed the literature of the *fabliaux* and *Schwänke* of street songs, folk-sayings, anecdotes, where there was no language-center at all, where there was to be found a lively play with the 'languages' of poets, scholars, monks, knights and others" (273). Within Bakhtin's analysis of language, the novel represents the voices in and around its creator, voices whose complexity and variety may defy general description and categories. However, Bakhtin also recognizes the historical and social backgrounds of the novel. These settings may assist readers in understanding many layers of dialogue. Additionally, the reader may use his or her knowledge of the author, his or her other works, the time and place of the novel, and the novel's chronology as clues for further understanding of characters' actions.

A Book for Every Season

Just as texts have pushed the limits of categorization by using numerous voices, they have also helped critics develop highly systematic literary studies, such as Northrop Frye's *Anatomy of Criticism* (1957). By revealing archetypes and archetypal patterns in various literary genres, Frye's survey is useful in establishing the presence of archetypes in baseball literature. According to Frye, literature's objective laws form a system based on the archetype, or "a typical or recurring image" (99). The activities of these archetypes generate narrative patterns, or "*mythoi*," in four categories, the comic, romantic, tragic, and ironic, which correspond to the seasons or spring, summer, autumn, and winter, respectively (160). Frye shows that narrative patterns tend to progress from spring (comedy) through winter (irony).[4] As literature makes this shift, we see that "the fundamental form of process is cyclical movement, the alternation of success and decline, effort and repose, life and death..." (158).

Similar cyclical patterns recur in baseball literature through authors' reliance on a narrative structure based on seasonal changes. Many stories begin or are born in spring with a new season and the hopeful start of a young player's career. The approach of the season's end in autumn signals the literal or metaphorical fall of a player, a victim of accident, illness, or old age. For Frye, the changing seasons, the life and death of nature, represent how the *mythoi* of literature moved from the mythology of the ancients to the irony of the twentieth century, a pattern that will ultimately return to myth and start anew. Thus, as Terry Eagleton summarizes Frye, authors are recycling the "collective subject of the human race itself, which is how it [literature] comes to embody 'archetypes' or figures of universal significance" (93).

In his focus on archetypes, Frye was not concerned with individual authors, who were, after all, just re-presenting what was on all of our minds. However, Annis Pratt recognized women writers as unique, and she sought to extend Frye's work in mythic genre studies to include discussion of gender in her *Archetypal Patterns in Women's Fiction* (1981). Pratt examined three hundred and twenty-eight novels according to the archetypal roles of women in literature, including such roles as a green-world archetype, like Medusa, Medea, Daphne or Persephone (9); an archetype "antithetical to the virgin goddess — the mad wife" (45); "the witty, sartiric virgin [in] in the role of Virtue" (59); and the doomed lover, Isolde (75), among others. In addition to categorizing characters, Pratt grouped novels into five types: the female *bildungsroman* (or story of individual, personal growth), the novel of marriage, the novel of social protest, novels of love between men and women, and novels of love between women. Pratt demonstrated how some of these patterns allow characters less freedom and fewer choices as they become trapped in marriage.

Correspondingly, in baseball literature, marriage to a baseball player often requires a loss of freedom for women characters as they become the sole care-givers to children when their husbands travel. For example, Holly Wiggen, left at home for much of the Henry "Author" Wiggen series of novels, anxiously awaits the return of a full-time husband so that they can spend time together at the vineyards she plans on purchasing for his retirement. On the other hand, some women characters, like Annie Kinsella in *Shoeless Joe*, thrive in such an isolated environment, eager to make sacrifices for their husbands. For all the baseball Annies in literature, Pratt believes that these kinds of characters draw their strength from emotional bonds with other women. Holly spends time with her four daughters, and Kinsella's Annie has daughter Rachel and the comfort of knowing her husband's journey will end soon, not to be repeated the following baseball season. Pratt writes,

"These women draw strength from sharing. In many novels of this type, in fact, there are passages that duplicate the experience of being mother, daughter, sister, friend, and lover all at once..."(108).

In addition to her study of archetypes in novels, Pratt explores English poetry in *Dancing with Goddesses: Archetypes, Poetry, and Empowerment* (1994), describing the recurrent figures of Medusa, Aphrodite, and Artemis. Pratt argues that the origins of the mythological figures, though remote in time and geography, are nevertheless deeply embedded in our psyche: "[T]hey [archetypes] clearly embody suggestions about feminine power to which ... both men and women respond at a profound psychological level" (xi). As ancient representations of feminine power appear English poetry, so may they also be found in baseball literature.

While Pratt makes her case for powerful women characters, some generic studies have been critical of the roles of women, most notably in African American literature. Barbara Christian argues that early representations of African American women were stereotypes of the "mammy," the "concubine," the "conjure woman," and the "tragic mulatta" (3). Alice Walker categorizes these same kinds of women throughout *In Search of Our Mothers' Gardens* (1983). For Walker, an African American woman is "the '*mule* of the world,' because we have been handed the burdens that everyone else — *everyone* else — refused to care" (237; emphasis hers). Also, African American women, according to Walker, have been labeled "Matriarchs," "Superwomen," "Mean and Evil Bitches," "Castraters," and "Sapphire's Mama" (237). These stereotypes still hold cultural power because they are "images germinated in the white southern mythology and enhanced and enriched by film, television, and social programs even up to the present" (Christian 16). One only has to picture the face of "Aunt Jemimah" smiling down from grocery shelves full of syrup to recognize the weight that advertisers continue to place on such stereotypes.

Despite the popularity of media images of African American women, authors also struggle to present characters who are not stereotypes. According to Christian, "the black woman herself had to illuminate her own situation, reflect her own identity and growth, her relationship to men, children, society, history, and philosophy as she experienced it" (16). Such stories offer us characters whose complexities defy easy categories. Thus, in the critical analyses offered by Pratt, Christian, and Walker, increasingly complex characters emerge, which may be useful to examining the women of baseball literature.

Goddesses in the Outfield

As suggested above, mythic frameworks in psychology, ethnography, history, and literature can enhance feminist inquiries into texts. These examinations are generally concerned with issues of gender equality and empowerment. The world of organized baseball, as a male-dominated institution, can also provide significant representations of women's experiences. The interactions of the characters in baseball literature show that women become increasingly complex, often following numerous options in their private lives, including, for some, athletic competition.

Layered beneath the ideal of domesticity, the women of baseball literature initially appear to be simply good or bad characters: the affectionate wife and mother or the destructive temptress. In early baseball literature, women characters were often stereotypes of a seducer, like Circe. This first set of characters, who possess the characteristics of a single goddess type, were generally created and explicated by men. However, in later works of baseball literature, written and critiqued by women, the numbers of women characters who have a positive relationship with sport increase. The stereotypical categories of temptress or unsophisticated baseball fan no longer satisfied women writers. Instead, culturally rich characters began to represent more accurately the developments of women in the sports world. Such characters are instrumental in fleshing out the roles of women by giving them the attributes of multiple goddesses.

These characters become powerful not only in the home but also in scenes of recreation or the workplace, which may be conflated in the ballpark if they are baseball players, allowing them more opportunities to be heard. They are no longer silently waiting at home for their ballplayer boyfriend or husband to return at the end of the season. Once they have greater interactions, they become stronger characters with more numerous roles (fan, wife, mother, lover, player) than the ones strictly associated with the home (wife, mother). These variations in roles are heard in the multiple goddess voices. As they express themselves more freely, women characters begin to show feminine strength within the traditionally male-dominated dialogue of baseball literature. For example, a character may be considered an Aphrodite-Artemis woman, who has qualities of both goddesses that assist her in achieving her personal and professional goals.

These multi-goddess characters show the need for multiple frames of reference within a categorical system, allowing overlap and inclusion in several categories. Although the single-goddess categories are useful, the movement from single to multiple goddess characters does not imply an inevitable organic movement. Instead, the development shows writers' increasingly serious attention to women characters.

Haven't I Seen You Somewhere Before?

Popular psychology, particularly Jean Shinoda Bolen's *Goddesses in Everywoman: A New Psychology of Women* (1984), has suggested that women may be empowered by recognizing the goddess(es) within themselves. For the benefit of her clinical patients, Bolen reconciled her work as a psychologist with her goals as a feminist. She reworked the Jungian dichotomies (sensitive/tough; emotional/distant; caring/indifferent) into a classification system of personality types based on the Greek goddesses. Bolen proposes that women can embrace their existing goddess(es) or emulate ideal goddess models for self-improvement purposes. Bolen's work is among what the narrator of Fowler's *The Sweetheart Season* ironically labels the "be-your-own-goddess books" (28). Yet far from the prideful Cassiopeia, talented Minerva, or maternal Latona the narrator describes (28), Fowler's women ballplayers often stumble around each other, men, and even the ballpark, and may have benefited from a few goddess books themselves.

These ballplayers are more closely aligned with the women characters Christian K. Messenger describes in *Sport and the Spirit of Play in Contemporary American Fiction* (1990) than with Bolen's goddesses. Messenger notes that women characters fight within and against the sports world because the female athletic form often becomes a marketable commodity, just as Fowler's women ballplayers, the Sweetwheat Sweethearts, promote a breakfast cereal. These forces may be oppressive or empowering to women characters who are athletes, depending upon their reactions to them (157). In the face of oppression, women athletes may use language to gain strength by verbally supporting each other, being socially inclusive, and cooperating with teammates and coaches (377). Messenger's work also reveals that women athletes often resort to using masculine language with male athletes and members of the sports industry, such as coaches and trainers, to be understood or gain power (246). Despite their best efforts, Messenger believes, women characters will continue to be dominated by male dialogue in sports literature (174).

This domination may also be mistakenly generated by a "goddess" classification system, with women perceived as subordinates in an ancient world view. However, we must remember two things. First, the term "goddess" is not necessarily a reference to the Greek goddesses, and second, the women in baseball literature are ultimately not confined to one "goddess" category. In fact, matrilineal cultures that worshipped a supreme female deity or a number of powerful goddesses predate the worship of the Greek pantheon (Pratt, *Archetypal* 4; Motz 1; Graves 11). Pratt notes that "the term archetype derives from the Greek *archi*, a beginning or first instance, and *typos*, a stamp, and denotes the primordial form, the original, or a series of variations," including pre–Achaean goddesses (3). After all, at 25,000 years old and one of the world's oldest fertility symbols, *The Venus of Willendorf* is a figure of a very matronly woman. For ancient Egyptians more than three thousand years ago, Isis "was a powerful mother goddess and protector. She brought [her husband] Osiris back from the dead and then cared for their son, Horus" (Murdoch 38). Thus, acknowledging the power of goddess literary archetypes does not necessarily recall male-dominated Greek myths.

Similarly, Lotte Motz's *The Faces of the Goddess* (1997) describes the historical and present powers of several non–Greek goddesses, among them Cybele of Anatolia, Amaterasu of Japan, Mother Saule of Latvia, Sedna of the Eskimo, Nintur of Mesopotamia, and various Mexican divinities (1). Such non–Greek goddesses extend into American literature as well. Alice Walker notes that Phillis Wheatley's writing includes references to "'the Goddess'—as she poetically called the Liberty she did not have" (236). For the slave Wheatley, Liberty became a "Goddess," representing the freedom of the white owners she served. This historical meaning of the term "goddess" reveals that not all literary uses of the term refer to the Greek goddesses. The multiple meanings of "goddess" show the possibilities of critically interpreting them from many perspectives. These multiple views of women are especially notable in the characters of baseball literature that are so complex they overlap into several goddess types, resisting the notion that this taxonomy is necessarily narrow.

(Not) Another Baseball Book

The multitude of books by and about baseball originates in the sport's required recording of itself and its subsequent inclusion in the record of the American experience (Candelaria 13–15). Alexander Cartwright led the formation of the first official baseball team, the New York Knickerbockers Base Ball Club, on September 23, 1845, and by 1857 they and fifteen other teams played according to a rule book written by him (Ward and Burns 4–7). Henry Chadwick, a former shortstop for the Knickerbockers, later suggested that *The New York Times* publish the results of ball games. Chadwick was soon named baseball editor for the New York *Clipper* and created the newspaper box score (Ward and Burns 7–8). The written history of baseball's scores as well as player and team achievements provided a seed for the development of baseball literature (Candelaria 14). These game scores and records also eventually took the form sports stories in weekly or daily newspapers, and *The Baseball Encyclopedia*. Sports writers like Ring Lardner and Heywood Broun turned to literary forms like the short story and novel to record further the impact of the game on America, its people and culture.[5] Baseball's nonfiction and fiction reveals that certain players have been left out of sports histories and literature.[6] Unofficial histories, often oral or encased in literary form, are frequently a record of peripheral players and show that the racial, commercial, and gender exclusivity of baseball was often recorded in marginal forms.

After the 1947 inclusion of Jackie Robinson in professional white baseball, the Negro leagues were no longer the only place for black baseball players, and the racial divisions they represented practically disappeared from the sports pages. Members of the media, once concerned with stopping Major League Baseball's exclusivity, started championing other causes (Andreano 11). Consequently, for most white fans, "the long struggle for equality and the intensity of the resistance to Negroes in baseball has now been expunged in the memories of those in the game" (11).

As early as 1977, Mark Harris noted that most of his students, who were on average twenty years old, were unable to identify the first black man to play major-league baseball when asked, "What does the name 'Jackie Robinson' mean to you?" (*Diamond*, 159). How did a generation so quickly forget Robinson and his accomplishments? Perhaps it was our embarrassment that he played such a role. In his introduction to William Brashler's novel *The Bingo Long Traveling All-Stars and Motor Kings* (1973), Peter C. Bjarkman reminds us the "if baseball maintains a skeleton in its closet — an hour of national disgrace — it's the exclusionary treatment of its black-skinned citizens throughout the first half of the present [twentieth] century and much of the second half of the previous one as well" (xix). Brashler's fine novel along with many histories of the Negro leagues, such as Robert W. Peterson's *Only the Ball Was White: A History of the Legendary Black Players and All-Black Professional Teams* (1970), revived our memories of them, but for some fans, baseball's history of racial tension disappeared along with organized baseball's color barrier.[7]

The history of exclusion in organized baseball also extends to gender. In *Women in Baseball: The Forgotten History*, Gai Ingham Berlage traces the participation of women in American baseball from the mid-nineteenth century to the end of the twentieth century. As the title of

One. Mount Olympus in the Majors

her work implies, Berlage uncovers a previously ignored yet complex and detailed record of women who played the game, from college students to professionals (xi–xii). Berlage's work was published in 1994, three years before Ila Borders became to first woman to join men's professional baseball and almost fifty years after Jackie Robinson's major-league debut. Just as Robinson set the precedent for the acceptance of black players in major-league baseball, the inclusion of Borders in men's baseball may someday lead to women playing in the major leagues. Many authors have already dared to imagine such a situation through fictional accounts of the first woman major-league baseball player, though some of their stories exploit rather than explore the topic.[8] These developments in real-life and fictional baseball show the limitless possibilities available to sport and gender in literature.

Two

Gods and Goddesses at the Plate

Since the early twentieth century, American writers have scrutinized the popularity of sports by recording and fictionalizing the real life activities of great players. These writers often divide players, both real and fictional, into classification systems that reflect players' physical and psychological attributes. The texts and their systems offer useful frameworks for disclosing patterns of the treatment of gender in fiction. For the most part, these patterns reveal that baseball attempts to exclude women. However, in the 1990s and into the first decade of the twenty-first century, women writers have worked to represent the contributions of women in baseball's history, and, perhaps more significantly, works by men have begun to reflect language that is gender inclusive. For example, when Richard Skolnik writes, "what these players do, we too have done, men and women alike" (17) in *Baseball and the Pursuit of Innocence: A Fresh Look at the Old Ball Game* (1994), the nod toward women as ballplayers may be underappreciated without a thorough understanding of baseball's exclusively male past.

Histories for All Americans

Historians were among the first writers to introduce baseball as a subject of academic study. They often used highlights from the careers of talented ballplayers, accomplished coaches, or successful owners to chronicle the game in the United States.[1] According to these early histories, white players, coaches, and owners were the only great men of organized baseball history until the major-league debut of Jackie Robinson. Within the racial boundaries defined by the sport until Robinson joined the Brooklyn Dodgers, such historians deemed only the achievements of organized baseball's greatest players — Christy Mathewson, Babe Ruth, Lou Gehrig, and Joe DiMaggio — worthy of recording. Thus, highlighting the careers of selected men has been the dominant style baseball histories until the 1990s, when Barbara Gregorich, Gai Ingham Berlage, and Susan E. Johnson wrote about the players of the All-American Girls Professional Baseball League (1943–1954).[2]

Harold Seymour, the first academic historian of baseball, wrote three volumes about the sport, and his approach is partly responsible for the exclusivity of subsequent histories. His publications, though less than inclusive, span an impressive four decades (1960 to 1990), making Seymour a major contributor to the validation of baseball as a mode of academic inquiry. *Baseball: The Early Years*, covers from 1845 to 1903; *Baseball: The Golden Age*, from 1903 to 1930; and *Baseball: The People's Game*, from 1930 to 1990, all three from the prestigious Oxford University Press. Seymour's doctoral dissertation, the first on baseball accepted by Cornell University's History Department, later became the first published scholarly history of baseball by a professional historian (*People's* v). As indebted as current academics are to Seymour's groundbreaking work, he, however, set a precedent of racial and gender exclusivity that recurs in other baseball histories. The first two volumes of Seymour's history present a thorough account of baseball from the codification of its rules in 1845 through its tremendous popularity in the 1920s in America. Seymour presents those years solely in terms of organized baseball, a white, male professional institution.

By 1990 Seymour attempted to rectify his omissions by dedicating his third and largest volume to all the individuals and groups he previously ignored, for example, "college players, members of the armed forces, industrial players, and softballers" (v). But three decades of historians had already emulated Seymour's first two volumes and established the dominant canon of baseball histories. His approach, which focuses on the most extraordinary participants of organized

Two. Gods and Goddesses at the Plate

baseball and either omits or postpones discussions of other players, has been copied by numerous historians.[3] As a result, those players who are not white and male are anomalies in the history of baseball, placed at the end of chapters, in footnotes, or in separate volumes, as afterthoughts.

More recently, Benjamin G. Rader's *Baseball: A History of America's Game* (1992) draws heavily on Seymour's work and continues the practice of gender and racial exclusivity through its organization. Rader mentions women and minorities toward the end of each chapter, treating them as extras to the major players, white and male, of baseball's grand professional history. More significantly, he calls baseball "America's Game," but when he does so, he describes a white, male America: "Long before 1839 ... American boys played a large variety of informal bat-and-ball games, all of which probably had direct or indirect origins in England" (2). By noting that ball games appeared in America before 1839, Rader, like Seymour before him, unmasks the Abner Doubleday's Cooperstown myth and describes early forms of the sport like "old-cat, one-old-cat, barn ball, rounders, town, base, and base ball" played in the early nineteenth century (2).

These activities, in Rader's accounts, involved only boys and men, while women and minorities receive no mention as participants in early versions of the sport even though they were, in fact, playing them. In a letter dated November 14, 1748, Lady Mary Hervy included a description of both men and women playing an indoor version of early baseball in England (Henderson 134). Also, in *Northanger Abbey* Jane Austen's Catherine finds more pleasure in "cricket, base ball, riding on horseback, and running about the country" than in reading (39). The 1818 reference to "base ball" in Austen's novel is the first time the words appear in English literature, but the game she mentions is not our American baseball. Her version is an English precursor; however, Catherine's fondness for it is important in light of history's omission of these games as played by women. Rader repeats these kinds of oversights, especially in his description of the benefits of baseball: "Unlike other sports, only baseball encouraged 'manliness,'' of self-control, the opposite of boyishness or uninhibited behavior" (10). Rader's remarks, particularly the use of the word "manliness," restrict the game to men, where it will remain for the majority of his history.

Wanted: Baseball Heroes

Ralph Andreano focuses on professional baseball's economic history rather than attempting a complete history of "America's game" in the tradition of Seymour. Andreano notes the decline of baseball's popularity during the ten years preceding his work's publication, 1955–1965. In *No Joy in Mudville: The Dilemma of Major League Baseball* (1965), Andreano discusses economics as the driving force behind the institutionalization of baseball and its recurrent labor conflicts. He adds to these observations a discussion of the "folk hero factor," which determines the rise of a ballplayer to wealth and celebrity and ensures a team's profitability. Baseball dominance as a cultural and business practice was caused, according to Andreano, by "America's need for symbolic characters, myths, and legends," or folk heroes and their accomplishments (4). The folk hero, in his account, is an extraordinary man whose actions fans want to imitate because the hero's physical skills are far superior to their own. Our inability to find heroes worthy of such emulation is, according to Andreano, responsible for the decline of baseball's popularity as a spectator sport during the late 1950s and early 1960s. This loss is the scope of Andreano's test, which laments baseball's fall from being the "National pastime," defined as what "all America stands for in the popular imagination" (5–6), to what he believes is its current existence, another part of America's entertainment industry.

Only the rejuvenation of the folk hero, with his combination of colorful personality and controversy both on and off the field of play, will, Andreano argues, restore baseball to its preeminent place in American sports culture (4). Although he offers a valuable insight into both the history and folklore of baseball, Andreano's discussions are limited to only male folk heroes, the players of organized baseball. Such a focus ignores the diversity and multiple imaginations possible within America during the mid-twentieth century. Perhaps baseball in the late 1950s

Two. Gods and Goddesses at the Plate

and 1960s was failing to engage an increasingly diverse America, which began turning to professional football and basketball for its popular heroes. Regardless of his limited focus, Andreano recognizes a human need for heroes of tremendous physical stature and emotional appeal, and he successfully shows hero worship at work in baseball.

The ritual origins of such hero worship can be discerned in Robert W. Henderson's *Bat, Ball and Bishop: The Origin of Ball Games* (1947) as he extends baseball research into the deep roots of the game's ancient history (3). Contemporary ball games, according to Henderson, are distant descendants of pagan agricultural and fertility rites practiced in ancient Egypt, Greece, Rome, Babylon, and Persia, which were later integrated into Christian rituals. Two transformations, from pagan rites to Christian rituals and from those rituals to secular pastimes, result in our sports and sports heroes. As Will Irvin notes in the introduction to Henderson's work, "the boy who kicks a football or catches a baseball does not suspect that he is honoring the dead Osiris," Egyptian god of agriculture (xvi), which is the anthropological source of ball and stick games.[4]

Football and baseball, two of the many sports Henderson examines, are "vestigial remains of religious rites of ancient times, designed to influence the pagan gods that they might make the crops grow, and so ensure the continued existence of a grateful people" (3–4).[5] Henderson's observation that these sports are "vestigial remains" does not diminish their value; rather, their continued popularity testifies to the power of the original rites that have mutated and survived countless centuries. In fact, Henderson argues that "all modern games played with bat and ball descend from one common source: an ancient fertility rite observed by Priest-Kings in the Egypt of the Pyramids" (4). The ancient Egyptians believed that if they assisted the statue of the god Osiris, "the god of all things that grew," in his ceremonial procession to the Temple of Papremis in Egypt, the growing season would return (4, 8). The success of this procession, the Egyptians felt, would determine their ability to produce food and to survive (4). When the statue approached the temple's entrance, a group of men pushed it through the priests who were defending the temple (8–9). Both sides, if you will, used clubs to either defend or attack. Later, the statue of the god was reduced to the most powerful part of his body, his head, now represented by a ball (17–18).

Although only men participated in Osiris's temple procession, Henderson notes evidence of women's involvement in other early ball ceremonies and in the spread of modern sport. He writes, "one of the earliest representations of a ball ceremony is found on ... Tomb 15 at Beni Hasan, which was built before the year 2000 B.C. It shows semi-nude women, in pairs ... throwing balls" (19–20). Among the first to discuss women and sport, Henderson describes women's early participation in sports and their later contributions to the global expansion of sports, most notably introducing lawn tennis to the United States: "The honor of introducing the game of lawn tennis to America goes to Miss Mary E. Outerbridge.... In the winter of 1873–74, while on vacation in Bermuda, Miss Outerbridge observed some British Army officers playing lawn tennis. From them she obtained a set, which ... she brought with her to the Port of New York" (127). In addition to bringing tennis to the states, she was the first person to set up a game at the Staten Island Cricket Club (127).

Tennis was not the only sport women helped establish in America. As early as 1621 American colonists played stoolball and most often included women as participants, making the sport an opportunity for courtship (75–76). These formerly ritualized activities, first practiced by ancient peoples to assure the return of the growing season, would later ensure the health and growth of their communities by providing a place for men and women to meet. Athletes and sports fans now understand the scientific regularity of seasonal change, and they continue playing or watching sports, anticipating winter through football season and rejoicing at baseball's return in the spring. By including women's involvement in the origins and development of organized sport, Henderson reveals the often overlooked roles of women in the world of ball games.

Literary Heroes

While the scholarly study of the ritual ceremonies behind sport helped initiate its acceptance in universities, other writers have more recently focused their work on baseball's heroes as literary types. Tristram Potter Coffin, Eugene C. Murdock, and Christian K. Messenger analyze folk practices, such as exaggeration in the story-telling of tall tales and yarn-spinning, and show how these practices make baseball heroes into legends of immense proportion. With the exception of Messenger, who includes women characters in his text, the majority of their writing focuses on male sports heroes.

The first of these three authors to organize heroes into literary categories was Coffin in *The Old Ball Game: Baseball in Folklore and Fiction* (1971). Coffin describes sports heroes as "prowess, trickster, and ethical heroes," based on real-life players and the folklore associated with them. According to him, Babe Ruth best exemplifies the "prowess hero," whose "batting was Titanic, in the mythological sense of the world — smooth, but memorable for raw, sheer power, nothing if not overwhelming" (81). The prowess hero conquers adversaries, consumes large amounts of food and sometimes alcohol, and satisfies his sexual appetites, traits traceable to the historical activities of Ruth (82–83). The prowess hero, also identified by his "mass of strength, of crude power, courage and determination" (79), suggests heroes like Ajax and Achilles from *The Iliad*, who would stop at nothing to achieve success (79–80). Although Babe Ruth remains the best specimen of the prowess hero, other baseball players Coffin notes for their strength are Lou Gehrig, Ted Williams, and Willie Mays (80). More recent prowess heroes, I suggest, would be Albert Belle of the Baltimore Orioles and Frank Thomas of the Chicago White Sox, also known as "The Big Hurt." Although allegations of steroid use among major-league baseball players have tarnished the image of prowess heroes during the 2004 baseball season, bulky players like St. Louis's Mark McGwire, who "looked like Paul Bunyan" even as a minor-leaguer (Morris and Engel 98), and the Cubs' Sammy Sosa seem to capture our imaginations as they send homeruns sailing out of ballparks.

Strength alone, especially in a mental game like baseball, may not adequately describe an athlete. Coffin's "trickster hero" represents the intellectual side of the game, though his antics may not always benefit the team. The trickster's behavior allows him to become "a culture hero, creating and ordering the world, instructing humanity how to behave; but he may also be a fool or clown, demonstrating what man should not do, acting out silly, stupid roles often harmful to himself and his own..." (88). Whether assisting others, instigating pranks, or suffering from the disastrous effects of such jokes, the trickster "is nearly always without brawn, living by his wits and resourcefulness" (88).[6] Coffin argues that there has been only one baseball trickster: Ty Cobb (89). An enormously talented man with a foul temper and great dedication to the game, Cobb often ignored the rules of the game to win (91). This tenacity and seriousness made him what Coffin calls a "non-comic trickster," and also "amoral, antisocial, a model of what not to do as often as of what to do" (93). Thus, although his behavior on the ball field was paradoxically condemned and celebrated, many consider Cobb the greatest ballplayer after Babe Ruth (89).

Coffin identifies a third and final type of hero in baseball, the "ethical hero," a player better behaved than Ruth and Cobb but less successful on the ball field because of his aversion to cheating. The ethical heroes in literature, who create "codes of conduct" for themselves, are capable of "inviting respect and emulation" (93). Coffin explains that examples of these figures are also found in religion or politics: Christ, Moses, Abraham Lincoln, and Judge Roy Bean, the nineteenth-century Texas lawman (95). Although Coffin considers these heroes a rarity in baseball, the ethical hero finds a model in Judge Kenesaw Mountain Landis, whom he describes as "a Latter-Day Roy Bean" (95). Landis, appointed the first commissioner of professional baseball following the 1919 Black Sox scandal, restored the country's faith in the national game after eight members of the Chicago White Sox reportedly received money in a scheme to lose the World Series intentionally. Landis banned the players from the sport for life although each one had been acquitted from the charges brought against them by the city of Chicago. Coffin describes Landis's effect on the return of baseball to its former glory: "To the average American, Landis is simply the man who told baseball how it should act, proclaimed and exercised his own list of commandments, spoke sermons from the mount of the Commissioner's office, and guided the game off the primrose path that was leading it straight to Hell" (100). Ethical baseball heroes of the twentieth century may be identified by impeccable behavior in their public and private lives. Nolan Ryan and Cal Ripken, Jr., are ethical heroes for their dedication to their families, teams, and communities. These men enjoy enormous popularity in their home states as well as across the country. No one would argue their places in the Hall of Fame, and their exemplary qualities, as contrasted with the prowess and trickster heroes, explain their enduring appeal.

Casey's Big K

Perhaps enjoying the most prominent status among baseball's literary heroes has been Casey of the Mudville Nine, from Ernest L. Thayer's 1888 poem "Casey at the Bat." In *The Annotated "Casey at the Bat"* (1967), Eugene C. Murdock offers an exhaustive historical and literary analysis of the poem, whose full title is "Casey at the Bat: A Ballad of the Republic, Sung in the Year 1888." It was first published by the *San Francisco Examiner* on June 3, 1888. Although the poem's origin was disputed for many years, its tale of an overconfident hitter who strikes out, loses the ball game, and disappoints an entire town has inspired hundreds of variant poems (some of which include women players), numerous songs, art work, reenactments, and even an opera.

Our fascination with "Casey at the Bat" derives partly from its mysterious origin, the real-life identity of Casey, the location of his team's hometown, Mudville, and its American theme of an individual struggling against great adversity. Confusion over the origin of the poem arose because Thayer had signed the poem with his usual pseudonym, "Phin." Inquiries into the poem's source started after the poem gained national exposure and fame when the actor De Wolf Hopper added its recitation to his regular traveling performances in 1892 (6). Although the identity of the author was disputed until 1938, the name of the real Casey continues to be a point of controversy.

Murdock suggests that 1880s baseball hero Mike "King" Kelly, whose athletic feats were recorded in the song "Slide Kelly, Slide," was the inspiration for Casey (25). Other nominees include Patrick Parnell

Cahill, Daniel Maurice Casey, O. Robinson Casey, and Dennis Patrick Casey, all ballplayers from the late nineteenth century (22). Our fascination with the literary character Casey extends to where he played. Thayer wrote that the poem was not based on fact, but speculations about the location of the real Mudville include Stockton, California; Mudville, Kansas; Boston and Philadelphia.

Perhaps the geographical diversity of these locations represents the transcendent nature of the poem — an individual's struggle against adversity — that is a feature of both baseball and the American dream. However, the poem itself approaches this theme with a hint of parody: the hero's overconfidence, a quality that initially charms the crowds who have come to see him, ultimately harms his team's record and disappoints his fans as he watches two perfectly good pitches and then strikes out on a third. Casey fails the Mudville nine and his supporters while perhaps doing exactly what they want him to do — heightening the drama and enlarging his reputation and the spectacle of his performance.

Variant poems have explored the themes of the pitcher's perspective, Casey's redeeming himself, Casey's later exploits, Casey's family members (including his younger sister, daughter, and wife) and other parodies (vii; 37; 85–93). Murdock's work contains about seventy-five examples of variations on the poem as well as a description of the 1953 one-act opera *The Mighty Casey*, written by William Shuman and Jeremy Gury (138). In "Casey at the Bat" and its many artistic progeny, the paradox of an individual's struggle for personal success versus the sacrifice for the group play itself out daily in the game of baseball.

The Hero Classifieds

While Casey may have struck out, Christian K. Messenger examines the success of our literary heroes in his *Sport and the Spirit of Play in American Fiction: Hawthorne to Faulkner* (1981). Messenger identifies three hero types — the Ritual, Popular, and School Sports Heroes — based on historical figures and literary characters. The earliest of the

Two. Gods and Goddesses at the Plate

heroes, the Ritual Sports Hero, is "an Adamic figure who seeks self-knowledge" and "competes to learn what he is capable of against self or natural adversaries" (8). Highly individualistic, "he is a figure of both surpassing skill and great dignity and is only incidentally defined by a community or society with which he is most often in conflict" (8). He regards sport as a "revelation" (9). Examples of the Ritual Sports Hero are James Fenimore Cooper's Natty Bumppo and Henry David Thoreau.

In Hawthorne's *The Scarlet Letter*, Hester Prynne and her daughter Pearl also find sanctuary in isolation and in play, which Messenger believes makes them heroic (32–37). Both a source of income and delight, Hester's needlework is an outlet for creative play while Pearl "projects dreams and games in the free play of the child's imagination" (35). Though Hester and Pearl are not traditional athletes, Elaine Showalter suggests that women often use alternate expressions of artwork for play and community, including the patchwork quilt (21). Excluded from Boston's community and forced to rely on each other, on inventive play, and on nature for happiness, Hester and Pearl are Ritual Sports Heroes (Messenger 36–37).

While the Ritual Sports Hero enjoys seclusion and nature, the Popular Sports Hero competes for others who can reward him with "money, fame, [or] records" (9). Born during the westward expansion of the American colonies during the early nineteenth century, the Popular Sports Hero took the skills that were a part of everyday life and turned them into modes of competition. According to Messenger, "his sport grew out of his work with horse, rifle, and riverboat. Gradually, the Popular Sports Hero was refined and scaled down to fit into the modern arena of industrial society where he played for a team before huge crowds" (8). Thus, "popular" refers not to the hero but to the origin of the sport, "activity which evolves out of the daily life of the culture which is captivated by it" (9). Sport then becomes neither a child's game nor an adult recreational activity but a national pastime followed by millions. F. Scott Fitzgerald's *The Great Gatsby* (1925) includes the highly competitive golfer Jordan Baker, which Messenger believes is "the first serious portrait of a female American Athlete" (194).

For the Popular Sport Hero, sport is a "contest," enacted for the benefit of the team's hometown and often for tremendous salaries (9).

The inclusion of sports within the American educational curriculum produced a third type of hero, the School Sports Hero. At the university level, sport became a training ground for future corporate and political leaders (9). The School Sports Hero, therefore, "not only competed for personal victory but for a larger self-discipline and the approbation of an admiring society which then christened him as a potential leader" (9). Authors often interrogate the practice of crowning business and civic leaders on the gridiron or in the boxing ring by creating characters whose past glory days serve as a foil to their now questionable morals. Fitzgerald's Tom Buchanan was a former football hero at Yale in *The Great Gatsby*, and Ernest Hemingway's Robert Cohn was a middle-weight boxing champion at Princeton in *The Sun Also Rises* (1926). In these and other works, sports serves as a test of moral character, much like the tests encountered in other university courses. Performance on the field of play, or even on the sidelines as cheerleader-turned-president George W. Bush proves, indicates how successful a person may become upon graduation.

Natural Women

Malamud's *The Natural* has probably been the most celebrated portrayal of an American athlete, which reveals the continued relevance of hero worship in our culture. Malamud's women characters, though less well examined, have also garnered critical attention. For example, in her 1983 article "Women in Bernard Malamud's Fiction," Barbara Koenig Quart illustrates the similarities among several of his protagonists and the women they pursue. Although Quart does not mention *The Natural* in her study, Roy Hobbs, like the protagonists she describes, is "deeply isolated" and "suffer[s] intensely"; he has a "fear of love and human involvement" (138). Quart's descriptions of Malamud's women also apply to the women of *The Natural*, Harriet Bird, Memo Paris, and Iris Lemon: "Women are set at a curious distance in Malamud's fiction, despite the intense passion, lust, [and] yearning directed at them" (138). In fact, Quart notes that "Avis in *A New Life* has a 'sick breast'" (140), which is reminiscent of Memo's sick breast in *The Natural*.[7]

Why Quart omits Roy Hobbs is unclear, yet the recurrent patterns she identifies in Malamud's portrayal of women are significant. She concludes that while "women characters remain peripheral to the power of Malamud's work, they are certainly not peripheral to his characters' dreams, fantasies, [and] longings" (148). Indeed, although women may remain at the edge of the action in *The Natural*, in terms of Roy Hobbs's development, Harriet, Memo, and Iris are key to his becoming a mature adult, particularly in his ultimate rejection of the greedy Memo and acceptance of Iris's unselfish love.

Lucio Ruotolo's article "Bernard Malamud's Rediscovery of Women: The Impact of Virginia Woolf" (1994) follows Quart's practice of closely examining Malamud's male protagonists' interactions with women characters. Ruotolo identifies several recurrent themes in Malamud's treatment of women: "death and his [the protagonist's] mother"; the incapability of "dealing with, much less loving, women"; and "a sense of separation" (329). These characters reveal a distancing, a discomfort that Malamud attempted to overcome by studying Woolf's writings. In fact, he taught a course on Woolf at Bennington College in 1979, the same year that his novel *Dubin's Lives* was published (329).

Ruotolo claims that the women in *Dubin's Lives* are more fully realized than Malamud's previous women characters, for Woolf "was filling a void in his own experience" (329). With the help of Woolf's work, Malamud created women who were less marginalized and less eroticized than in his previous texts (329). Thus, Dubin, the protagonist of *Dubin's Lives*, is better able to succeed in life, becoming "more wisely open to others" (336). Had Malamud read Woolf before he wrote *The Natural*, Roy Hobbs may have been better suited for life as a professional ballplayer as well as a more accomplished person, but that may have made him a less memorable character. Hobbs and his associated shortcomings are, after all, far more famous than Dubin.

Not Even in the Same Ball Park

As we have seen, critical studies of sports literature have described characters based on recurrent behaviors in numerous narratives. The early hero classification systems adequately show the struggles of men characters as players and deepen reader awareness of heroes' roles in society as either models to emulate or as objects of pity. In relation to the ballplayers and their stories, the women characters are found remotely in the grandstands, or perhaps they are not even in the same ball park. For example, Eric Solomon, Michael Oriard, and Peter C. Bjarkman describe women characters in baseball literature as mindless cheerleaders or as distractions to men's sporting careers (Solomon 19–20; Oriard, *Dreaming* 179–82; Bjarkman 81), though Solomon seems the most sympathetic to their plight. Bjarkman writes that from the first juvenile sports novels to sophisticated adult fiction, women are portrayed as "creatures totally foreign to baseball's world ... the protective mother, virtuous girlfriend, or silly pigtailed classmate" or "cardboard symbol[s] for insidious forces of good and evil" (81). Bjarkman also notes a third category: the first woman baseball player. She is generally portrayed as a talented player who breaks the gender barrier of organized baseball, becoming an anomaly in an all-male world (81).

These limited roles for women characters initially existed because men were, of course, the heroes of the traditional canon and only men played the professional game. Examples of women who function only to distract players are easily found in Ring Lardner's short story "Women" (1925). As ballplayers Young Jake and Mike Healy sit on the bench, he tells the rookie Jake how women have pursued him and how romance has ruined his playing career. Healy repeatedly grouses to Jake, "Women!... And the more you have to do with 'em the better chance you've got of spendin' your life on this bench" (456). At the end of his story, Healy fails to heed his own warnings and accepts a note from a woman fan. Sophisticated readers see Lardner's signature irony at work and realize that the players are actually bushers unwilling to recognize themselves as such.

Damon Runyan's "Baseball Hattie" (1936) describes a fan more

Two. Gods and Goddesses at the Plate

dangerous than Lardner's scapegoats. The short story opens with Hattie as old woman admiring the players at the Polo Grounds and then flashes back to the start of her romance with New York Giants pitcher Haystack Duggeler. They meet after she protects him from a mob of angry Philadelphia fans. With her large frame, Hattie knocks out a member of the mob and "takes Haystack Duggeler by the pitching arm and personally escorts him" (84). They fall in love, and the manager attempts to separate them. In a line reminiscent of Lardner, she says to the manager, "You know me, Mac.... You know I will cut off my nose rather than do anything to hurt your club" (86). Haystack and Hattie marry, have a child, and quarrel over his drinking and gambling habits. He accepts a bribe to lose a game, and for this anathema to her sport, Hattie shoots a bullet into his pitching arm. Unlike Harriet Bird, who ends Roy Hobbs's pitching career with a bullet in *The Natural*, Hattie partially redeems herself at the end of the story by supporting her son's major-league career. Lardner's and Runyon's stories both emphasize what Bjarkman calls "the always irreconcilable incompatibility between women and the game itself" (85).

A less sinister plot involving distracting women appears in John R. Tunis's *The Rookie* (1944): Jane Andrews, girlfriend of Dodger Clyde Baldwin, is used in a plot to get rookie pitcher Bones Hathaway in trouble, and veteran pitcher Fat Suff's wife falls ill before the big game, forcing the player to return home. As demonstrated by Lardner, Runyon, and Tunis, Solomon, Oriard, and Bjarkman accurately describe a motif of baseball literature written roughly between 1888 and 1952 that emphasizes an incompatible polarity between women and the game.

Nevertheless, many narratives reveal that during this same time period women characters often also function as contributors to the success or failure of sports heroes, aiding in the heroes' transformations from immature, self-centered player to mature adults. For example, Florrie Keefe, wife of ballplayer Jack Keefe in Ring Lardner's *You Know Me Al* (1914) and Judith Winthrop Tyler, wife of ballplayer Tiny Tyler in Heywood Broun's *The Sun Field* (1923), although not ideal marriage partners, force Keefe and Tyler to take responsibility in their roles as spouses. As young husbands, Keefe and Tyler develop added dimensions to their characters when they confront marital problems and elect to stay married and work through them.

Nunnally Johnson gives a more lighthearted approach to the theme of ballplayers and marriage in his short story "Miss Gulp" (1933). Perhaps the first story of a woman who becomes a professional baseball player, Johnson describes a young woman who develops her catching abilities, specifically brides' bouquets at weddings. After being informed that whoever catches the bouquet will be the next bride, Miss Mildred Gulp makes daring, outfielder-like attempts to seize the bride's flying bouquet at every wedding she attends. Johnson writes of Miss Gulp's wedding antics in baseball terms: "Mildred was taking them against the wall, down the foul lines, directly behind the best man. Now and then she failed, of course, but she always gave the crowd a run for its money. 'Whatever happens,' they said, 'Mildred's always in there trying, always on her toes'" (49). Her athleticism results in a contract offer from the Giants: "Today, of course, you know Mildred as Old Gray-Eagle Gulp, the Giants' ballhawk in center, one of the keenest judges of batters in the big leagues, and an all-around good fellow at that" (51). Johnson's "Miss Gulp" is unique because Mildred finds baseball before she finds love. Usually, women characters in early baseball literature find love first, or they find it on the baseball field.

One such story is Edna Ferber's "A Bush League Hero," which appeared in her 1912 collection *Buttered Side Down*. Ivy Keller returns home from school for the summer and reluctantly joins her father at a local team's game. Her sudden admiration of pitcher Rudie "Dutch" Schlachwieler dismays her family, but she persists in her devotion toward him. Ivy's obsession with Dutch's playing soon interferes with her ability to appreciate him as a regular person. In fact, he often wants to talk about different subjects when they are together: "Oh, forget baseball for a minute, Ivy! Let's talk about something else. Let's talk about — us." To this suggestion, Ivy responds, "Us? Well, you're baseball, aren't you?.... And if you are, I am" (69–70). Ivy lacks an identity apart from being his fan, and the inability of their relationship to grow beyond hero worship causes her ultimate rejection of him when she sees him selling shoes in November. Ivy's stunted development is ironic considering

Two. Gods and Goddesses at the Plate

her name. As a garden-variety fan, she contrasts sharply to the richer characterizations of the baseball goddesses Iris, Holly, and Rose.

It is rare to find a love story that develops both on and off the field of play. Even rarer still is one that is depicted with sensitivity and an appreciation for the difficulties of mature relationships, compounded by the time and space baseball often puts between a couple. Perhaps that is why real-life ballplayer and oldest rookie Jim Morris's story is so compelling. He ultimately recognizes the value of his marriage when he concludes *The Oldest Rookie* (2001) by writing, "I'll smile because I won't have to regret losing my wife and family to a dream that I learned didn't mean as much to me as they did" (276). The Disney movie version of his story, *The Rookie* (2002), did not portray the Morris' struggling marriage, including a year-long separation and ongoing financial difficulties that required his wife Lorri Morris to work full time to support her husband as he finished college and attempted a professional baseball career at the extremely unlikely age of 35.[8] Also, we may want to consider that Morris only found his wife and family more important than baseball after he fulfilled his dream of pitching in the majors. Another historical example of a wife's providing unceasing support to her ballplayer husband is Lou Gehrig's wife, who helped him face a terminal disease, depicted in *The Pride of the Yankees* (1942), starring Gary Cooper and Teresa Wright. Often as strong as the real-life baseball wives, the women characters in baseball literature provide opportunities for ballplayers' personal growth. Such powerful women characters are not recognized within the existing categories developed by Solomon, Oriard, and Bjarkman.

Their categories also fail to accommodate the increasingly complex characterization of women in more recent texts — Iris Lemon in *The Natural*; Holly Webster Wiggen in Harris's series of novels; Rose Maxson in Wilson's *Fences*; Consuelo and Carlota in Herrin's *The Rio Loja Ringmaster*; Annie Kinsella in *Shoeless Joe*; Rachel Sonnshein in Tennenbaum's *Rachel, The Rabbi's Wife*; Clare Bishop in Willard's *Things Invisible to See*; and Irini Doyle in Fowler's *The Sweetheart Season*. Some of these women characters, relegated to a "none of the above" if we tried placing them in Oriard's and Bjarkman's categories, serve as muses for the development of ballplayers, such as Holly's editorial advice during Henry's novel writing, notably chapter 11A, and her reaction to his spitball (*The Southpaw* 105–15; 305–08). In addition, they often civilize the men who must return to their homes after playing a game for extended absences. There they learn to share the responsibilities of raising a family, as Roy Hobbs does when he reunites with Iris Lemon and their unborn child at the end of *The Natural* (205–06). That three of the women, Iris, Holly, and Rose, bear flower names further emphasizes their symbolic value, suggesting the evolved beauty and growth that is possible for the men in their lives.[9]

Women characters in baseball literature become catalysts in the evolution of the ballplayer from athlete to husband, father, and community servant. When women characters are mentioned in past literary criticism, they are sometimes named as limited representatives of goddesses or mythological figures. For example, Earl R. Wasserman, Michael Oriard, Cordelia Candelaria, and Deeanne Westbrook touch on the roles of women as they use mythology to organize their readings of baseball literature.

Baseball's First Myths

The earliest example a woman character labeled as a "goddess" is found in Earl R. Wasserman's article "*The Natural*: Malamud's World Ceres" (1965). Wasserman closely examines Malamud's work in the context of its numerous connections to Arthurian and Greek mythology. In addition to comparing the plot and the setting of Malamud's novel to those in myth, Wasserman aligns protagonist Roy Hobbs with the legendary medieval King Arthur, the Celtic myth of the Fisher-King, and the Greek hero Ulysses. Wasserman argues that "by drawing his material from actual baseball and yet fusing it with the Arthurian legend, Malamud sets and sustains his novel in a region that is both real and mythic, particular and universal" (440), American and global.

Wasserman also borrows from Jungian psychology to describe Roy Hobbs's relationship with his mother and his need to separate from her in forming a bond with his wife. Roy's continual struggle with his love interests during the majority of *The Natural* is emphasized by Wasserman's labeling Harriet Bird the Jungian "terrible mother," a role she shares with Memo Paris, while Memo is also called Morgan (the Arthurian witch), a Siren, Circe, and Charybdis (442; 446; 453). Wasserman draws further parallels between the women in *The Natural* and Arthurian legend by comparing the roles of Memo and Iris to Morgan and the Lady of the Lake: "Arthurian scholars have claimed they [Morgan and the Lady of the Lake] were originally one. Correspondingly, of Roy's two women, red-haired Memo is customarily clad in black, and black-haired Iris, complementarily, in red; and it is Iris who knows Lake Michigan intimately and whose presence restores the power of Wonderboy, his [Roy's] Excalibur" (442). Opposing the destructive forces of Memo, Iris Lemon is associated with the positive forces of the Jungian "great mother," Aphrodite, a mermaid, and the Lady of the Lake (442; 446; 455).

Wasserman ties Iris and Memo together as positive and negative forces, enabling him to extend his analysis to include Jungian psychology. Central to the struggle of Hobbs is his inability to reconcile his image of his mother, recurring in the destructiveness of Memo, to a positive maternal image like Iris. Without overcoming this conflict, Roy will never be able to gain the benefits of a healthy love relationship. According to Wasserman, "Unlike Memo and Roy's own mother — the terrible seductive mothers whom Roy identifies as whores — the Great Mother is the matrix of psychic powers; and through her, to use Jung's terms, the libido is redirected from its inward, ennervating [sic] prison to flow outwardly to the real world..." (454). The gift of Iris, in Jungian terms, is her restoration of Roy to a healthy image of woman and mother, crucial to Roy's acceptance of her as a mother to his child and her status as a grandmother.

The strength of Wasserman's article is his recognition of the balance between positive and negative representations of women characters in *The Natural*. Although Harriet and Memo are powerful psychological challenges to Roy's happiness during the majority of the novel's action, the presence of a "great mother" figure, Iris Lemon, minimizes their destructive behaviors. Iris holds the promise of providing Roy with the home and family he never had by sharing her life with him and their child. She also heals the psychic wound that the absence of Roy's biological mother inflicted, which is meant to explain his difficulty in trusting women. Wasserman's article is a valuable first step toward the critical recognition of women as positive mythological figures in baseball literature.

Wonder Boys

Mythology also serves Oriard in describing men characters in *Dreaming of Heroes*. Oriard's work focuses almost exclusively on the heroes, meaning the male protagonists, of sports literature. Oriard believes that the deep need for early American writers to produce literary heroes of their own grew out of our fledgling democracy's need "for reassurance that, in breaking from Europe, we had not lost more than we gained" (26). Although this need for heroes can be traced back through literary history to Ulysses and even Beowulf, American writers of the nineteenth century felt a great urgency to develop specifically American heroes, and the sports hero was readily available for their use. To build his case for the dominance of the hero's role in sports novels, Oriard refers to Joseph Campbell's work on the monomyth, the narrative pattern associated with mythology's male heroes.

According to Campbell's *The Hero with a Thousand Faces* (1949), these heroes always undergo separation, initiation, and return during their lives. As heroes progress through this pattern, we may also see several of the following themes develop: country versus city, innocence versus experience, youth versus age, and history versus myth (Oriard, *Dreaming* 38). These themes unfold as the hero leaves the city to prove himself, faces an initiation that usually results in a loss of innocence, and then he reenters regular life or retires when he is too old to participate in extraordinary events. Although Oriard does not name any specific mythological heroes, Ulysses and Gilgamesh readily come to mind as examples of the separation, initiation, and return motif in literature. As he retires, the hero must pass through the final theme: history versus myth. Will he become "other-centered" (39) and return to his non-heroic life, or will he fight against his age and remain trapped within the historical boundaries of the heroic ideal? Becoming "other-centered" means rejecting solipsism and reconciling with a father figure and/or becoming attached to a female character (39).

When Oriard applies the monomyth to sports literature, he proposes that the sports hero only transcends the game he plays (a game with no meaning outside of itself) by bonding with another person, a meaningful connection with humanity (38). The relationships with the father figure and with a woman become the "two great tasks" set up for the sports hero's ultimate success or failure in gaining maturity (38). His ability to bond with a father figure and a woman, who may often function as a surrogate mother, determines if the hero will be able to transcend the game and become mythical, that is, heroic in both his private and sporting life. Once he has reached this stage of development, he then wisely chooses to leave sports behind for further personal growth.

Despite the comprehensiveness of Oriard's text and its useful application of the monomyth, his analysis leaves no room for the subtle complexities of the women characters in baseball literature. In fact, in his 1983 article "On the Current Status of Sports Fiction," Oriard makes no mention of women authors or characters such as Harris's Holly Webster Wiggen (1953, 1956, 1957, 1979) and Tennenbaum's Rachel Sonnshein (1978). His system allows no recognition of women's roles in helping the hero become a mature individual. The monomyth, from beginning to end, is the hero's story, and its presence increases the difficulty of discussing women. In Oriard's interpretation, the building of love relationships is reduced to a "task," with no acknowledgment of the individual gifts that partners in the experience, whether women or father figures, demonstrate. However, Oriard's use of the monomyth continues the precedent Wasserman set by incorporating myth criticism into the study of sports fiction. It also allows for further interpretation of baseball literature through mythological figures, narratives, and images.

Following Wasserman and Oriard, Cordelia Candelaria proposes another mythological approach to classifying baseball heroes: *Seeking the Perfect Game: Baseball in American Literature* (1989). Extending the work of Robert J. Higgs in *Laurel & Thorn: The Athlete in American Literature* (1981), Candelaria identifies three categories of heroes in baseball literature: the Apollonian, the Dionysian, and the Adonic (20). Many heroes of sport in America literature fit these patterns: "The athlete in literature comes in a wide variety of splendid shapes and it is not an easy task to find a common thread. Even to begin the search it is first necessary to gain some understanding of the major myths that surround and motivate the athlete in his time off the field as well as on" (Higgs 7–8). In connecting this view of the athlete with baseball literature and popular culture, Candelaria remarks that "these and countless other similar 'hero-archical' views of supposedly peerless human icons lie at the heart of twentieth-century apotheosis of baseball players and other sports celebrities" (20).

Fans of sports may recognize the three mythological archetypes Higgs and Candelaria explore. The Apollonian hero reflects the beauty and order of the god who is his namesake. He applies himself to a fixed, rigid code that exemplifies the unity of body and soul (Candelaria 20), such as Casey from Thayer's "Casey at the Bat." Conversely, the Dionysian hero is a sensualist drawn to hedonistic indulgence and unrestrained revelery (21). A natural athlete, he accepts his body without reservation and is often narcissistic in his approach to life. The Dionysian heroes Roy Hobbs in *The Natural*, Louis Keystone in Brashler's *The Bingo Long Traveling All-Stars and Motor Kings,* and the historical Babe Ruth revel in food, wine, and women.

The third hero is a synthesis of the first two. He has learned from his mistakes and is muted in self-awareness and reason as he leads a double life, like the god Adonis, who lives six months of the year on the surface of the earth and six months in the Underworld with Persephone. The Adonic hero is thus both hero and mortal, who suffers in the pain of the non-sports world, yet retains hope in the consolation of human companionship (21). Both sportsmen and gentlemen, Harris's Henry "Author" Wiggen and Eric Rolfe Greenberg's Christy Mathewson of *The Celebrant* (1983) function well on the playing field and in the world of home and family through their mature awareness of the struggles, successes, and failures possible in life.

Two. Gods and Goddesses at the Plate

In the introduction to her work, Candelaria admits she limits herself to the male characters of baseball novels, a practice that also reveals the cultural tendencies of the sport's practice and its literary representations. Higgs's work also reflects the long history of limiting discussions of sport to men: "Who is the athlete? In Greek and Roman antiquity, he was 'one who competed for a prize in public games,' especially games requiring strength and stamina, and the definition is as relevant today as in classical times.... Who is this *one*? He is one, like all men, with a body *and* a self" (1, emphasis his). While Higgs does not acknowledge the limits of his gender-specific language, the exclusive use of masculine pronouns such as "he" concerns Candelaria. She writes, "I am keenly aware of the inadequacy of such an approach in acknowledging the major contributions of Black, Latino, Caribbean, and other excluded participants, including women, filling out a truer, whole picture of the baseball universe" (4). By understanding her work's role as one solar system within the "baseball universe," Candelaria allows for the expansion of myth criticism in sports literature into gender studies. Additionally, she often includes discussions of women characters, especially Holly Wiggen (85–88) and Iris Lemon (68–72). Candelaria's sensitivity to their presence adds another dimension to *Seeking the Perfect Game*'s predominately male character focus, revealing an aspect of baseball literature that Higgs and Oriard omit.

More Baseball Mythology

More recently, Deeanne Westbrook provides the most comprehensive exploration of baseball literature through myth criticism to date. Westbrook uses the Tower of Babel as the controlling metaphor of her work. The Tower of Babel, according to Westbrook, symbolically represents humanity's struggle to know all, to face the unknowable, and eventually to accept the limitations of human knowledge (52). Once we recognize these limits, we understand that glimpses of the unknown, of our origins, for example, appear in the gaps between the unconscious and the conscious. These glimpses then manifest themselves in myths, the shards of the past that become symbols, figures, and narratives and are passed from one generation through the written word.

Although Westbrook's work is extensive and inclusive — providing a section on baseball's absent mothers, "Mothers and Sons: Separation" (247–54) and a discussion of the recurrent "mutilations and handicaps" women in baseball literature suffer (72–75) — her analyses stress women as negatives. She focuses either on the absence of women, the torment they inflict upon others, or the mental and physical humiliations they suffer. While Westbrook provides ample evidence to support this negative reading of the representation of women in baseball literature, she largely ignores positive characters who are nurturing mothers, attentive wives, devoted fans, or successful players. For example, Holly Wiggen barely appears in Westbrook's text, except to give birth to a child in Harris's *Bang the Drum Slowly* (91). In addition, Westbrook omits Tennenbaum's Rachel Sonnshein, primary care-giver to a well-adjusted son in *Rachel, The Rabbi's Wife*.

Further, Westbrook grudgingly acknowledges that August Wilson's Troy Maxson in *Fences* is the exception to the "good-guy" father motif she identifies, without recognizing Rose Maxson's dedication to her son and step-son, Cory and Lyons (255). Westbrook writes, "One motif that stands out in the narratives is that of filial devotion revealed in the son's detailed early memories of a close, loving relationship with the father. No similar mother is *ever* mentioned" (255; emphasis added). While there are many genuinely caring fathers in baseball literature, as noted in Westbrook's chapter "Father and Sons, Blessings and Baseball's Myth of Atonement" (244–65), Rachel Sonnshein and several other nurturing mothers do not receive Westbrook's attention. For example, Lamar Herrin's *The Rio Loja Ringmaster* includes the protagonist Dick Dixon's pregnant wife (Consuelo) and her mother (Carlota), who are as supportive of children, both born and unborn, as Westbrook's "good guy" fathers. Contrastingly, Dick's father, Sarge, gets drunk at a baseball game and loses his then ten-year-old son in the stands (Herrin 55–57). Sarge is not a "good guy."

Also failing in the Dad department are the biological and step-fathers of Bruce Brooks's Asa in the Newbery Honor Book *What Hearts*

Two. Gods and Goddesses at the Plate

and the step-father of Scotty Smalls (Tom Guiry) in *The Sandlot*. While written for a juvenile audience, Brooks's work is far from childish in its superb treatment of a young boy's struggle against the fallout of a broken home. Asa's father, never named, loses touch with his seven-year-old son after Asa's mother remarries. Step-father Dave inflicts emotional and physical damage upon Asa, most notably in a large baseball-shaped bruise, the result of a friendly "father"-son batting practice gone awry in which he purposefully pitches to the boy's ribs (120). In *The Sandlot* Scotty also receives a bruise when his emotionally distant step-father Bill (Denis Leary) tries to teach him how to play catch. Bill tells Scotty to "keep his eye on the ball," an instruction that results in a black eye. Perhaps the emotional appeal of the father-son catch sours when step-fathers attempt to replace biological ones. The catch, though astoundingly exploded in *What Hearts* and subverted by *The Sandlot*, captivates writers and blinds them to mothers' roles in baseball literature.

So strong is this image of the father-son catch that David McGimpsey devotes an entire chapter to it, "Is that Good Enough for You, Pop? The Generational Question" (*Imagining Baseball*, 129–57), as recurrent motif in baseball literature. He writes, "*Fathers playing catch with sons* is a durable trope in all representations of baseball" (131; emphasis his). McGimpsey recognizes the limitations of a human relationship based solely on tossing a ball back and forth, saying that fathers often "fail to step aside from these myths and toward their sons" (140). There is a distance between the players as they catch the ball that no father, no matter how much of a "good guy" he is, bridges adequately. Although a game of catch may begin closing the gap in a father-son relationship, as it does so movingly at the end of the movie *Field of Dreams* (1989), it is only their initial contact. We are comforted in thinking that Ray Kinsella and his father, a catcher with the 1919 Black-Sox dream team turned Iowa corn-field regulars, will now share games of catch and also future conversation, once the lumps in their throat have cleared.

White Moms Can't Pitch

The exclusive nature of such father-son catches not only appeals to us emotionally but also by definition prohibits the participation of women.[10] Examples of women playing catch with their sons or even daughters are rare in baseball literature. Even when they are depicted, it is usually done to highlight the woman's ineptitude as a substitute in the almighty father-son catch. Again, in Brooks's *What Hearts*, Asa's mother tries valiantly to prepare her son for an upcoming tryout after step-dad Dave discontinues their practices following his brutal "purpose pitch." She's terrible: "Her first pitch was six feet outside and ten feet high. Her second was lower, but farther away. Her third arrived near the plate on the second bounce, and he gave it a tap into right field. 'See,' she yelled, gleefully. 'Hooray for us!'" (123). Rather than disappoint his mother's efforts, Asa thoughtfully decides to play defense: "In a few minutes she had learned to toss it, grip the bat, wait for the ball to come down, and chop at it with a short stroke. He moved out to the shortstop spot, and for almost an hour she pounded it at him, slow, high-bouncing balls sprayed all over the infield" (124–25). Asa's accommodation of his mother's abilities shows his sensitivity toward her and her willingness to take part in their own version of a father-son catch. Although she is far from ideal, Asa's mother and the stronger, more nurturing mothers of baseball literature like Consuelo Dixon, her mother Carlota, Holly Wiggen, Rose Maxson, and Rachel Sonnshein balance the negative images of women in baseball literature.

Square Roots

Perhaps Messenger best anticipates the inclusion of women in a mythology-inspired classification system in his second work about sports, *Sport and the Spirit of Play in Contemporary American Fiction* (1990). Messenger offers a structural approach to the sports hero's journey by applying Algirdas Julien Greimas's semiotic square to the sports hero's progression through different realms of experience.[11] Messenger's use of Greimas's semiotic square is significant because the life cycle

Two. Gods and Goddesses at the Plate

represented by the square can be applied to both men and women characters. For instance, each corner of the square represents a point in the life of the character: lower left is "play" (originally Greimas's "Play Drive"), upper left is "individual sports heroism" (the "Sense Drive"), upper right is "collective sports heroism" (the "Commodity Drive"), and lower right is "anti-heroism" (the "Form Drive") (Messenger, *Contemporary* 14). Messenger argues that "these roles represent the most significant points in the lives of sports heroes and comprise a life cycle that touches sports heroes at every stage of their development" (14).

The square thus represents the hero's life in a succinct visual form. A hero generally begins life in the lower left corner by enjoying simple "play" for the sake of play, but soon the hero's talent is recognized, and the player develops through "individual" practice and coaching (the upper left corner) to become a part of a "collective" team (the upper right). After playing for a team, which is generally used for the creation of profit in a market economy, the hero realizes that the initial carefree play that once produced his or her personal enjoyment is lost; the hero becomes cynical, the "anti-hero" (the lower right).

This progression can even be reflected in an entire team. For example, in John Alexander Graham's *Babe Ruth Caught in a Snowstorm* (1973), the Wichita Wraiths begin their first season as a non-profit organization whose team members play for the love of the game. The successful Wraiths are soon asked to join the National League but then begin to lose their idealism and their games as their pay increases and as they discover that the team's management is dishonest. Brashler's Bingo Long and his traveling All-Stars possess the same initial optimism as they begin their barnstorming tour. They later resign themselves to defeat by owner Lionel Foster and to the teams' subsequent dispersal as Foster offers more lucrative contracts than Long could afford. More importantly, Long himself finally recognizes the injustice of being "born too quick" to play for white organized baseball, and he settles down "to ride out the miles" of the rest of his life (244). Some stories vary this cycle by starting the narrative at different points on the square, but the hero or heroes almost always complete the same life cycle. According to Messenger, the square represents a shared "ideological consciousness common to authors of sports fiction," the hero's necessary participation in an exploitative market economy (14).

Through Greimas's square, Messenger addresses sports fiction written by women, which is characterized by "the mode of cooperation, of interaction and support among teammates" (377). Although the hero's life cycles around the square, her often tortuous experiences as a marginal member of the sport are buffered by the nature of the game as well as the presence of supportive teammates and family members: "Baseball appears to be the team sport most congenial to women athletes with its lack of aggressive physical contact and premium on attributes other than size and strength. Competition and heroic striving are present in the fiction but integrated with the team's other potentials: nurture, family, growth" (377). Thus, women's baseball fiction often focuses on the cooperation and interaction among women, whether they are teammates, family members, or friends outside of the sport. These characterizations integrate competitive play with an ability to nurture, generate family bonds, and explore personal growth. Women may then succeed in several capacities, as athlete, mother, sister, wife, or friend. Or, they may be seen as baseball goddesses, possessing the nurturing qualities of Demeter, the commitment of Hera, the domesticity of Hestia, the affection and artistry of Aphrodite, or the independence and athleticism of Artemis.[12]

Before we can read the presence of women characters in baseball literature, we must examine the absence of women, especially mothers, in numerous texts. Players' mothers are often absent from the narrative; either they died when the player was young, or they abandoned the player as a child. As a result, characters in the player's immediate or extended family may become their substitute mothers, who, by choice, nurture unconditionally. Despite the support of their substitute mothers, characters who suffer the loss of their biological mothers may experience trauma at her absence during their childhoods and even into adulthood. In particular, we shall see that their romantic relationships may suffer from unresolved anger at the loss of their mothers.

THREE

Absent Mothers and Mothering Men

The heroes of baseball literature often possess a "universal maleness," in Timothy Morris's terms, and their prodigious masculinity may erase many of their feminine qualities (91).[1] These qualities continued to be erased by what Candelaria calls the "gender exclusivity" in historical baseball, our cultural expectation that only men play baseball (13). Westbrook argues that the mothers are removed from baseball literature because of men's need to preserve the all-male sanctity of the baseball field, an Edenic first garden that should not allow women because of the past disastrous consequences of Eve's behavior (115). Our expectation that ballplayers be male limits not only the feminine qualities of male characters but also the mere presence of women characters, especially the mothers of sports heroes. The absence of biological mothers in baseball fiction and the presence of substitute mothers, characters who exhibit maternal qualities by unconditionally nurturing those around them, reveal both the rejection of women in sport and the underlying necessity of their qualities as caregivers.

Without their biological mothers, the protagonists of sports literature often possess questionable origins and uncertain parentage, aligning them with traditional mythic heroes and contributing toward their special status within the narrative. In *Mythology: The Voyage of the Hero* (1981), David Adams Leeming examines the life cycle of the hero and contends that an unusual birth contributes to heroic stature. According to Leeming, the events surrounding the conception and/or birth of heroes often "are miraculous or unusual in the extreme.... For the hero will burst through the limitations of the local and historical, the first event, like all the events in his life, must be special" (7). Leeming identifies numerous mythological figures whose births are unusual, such as Helen, Theseus, Buddha, Quetzalcoatl, Zoroaster, Siegfried, Karna, Maui, Horus, Dionysus, and Adonis (11–49). In addition, Biblical narratives often include characters who have unknown or mysterious origins. The infant Moses floats downstream in a reed basket and is found and adopted by Pharaoh's daughter, and the Virgin Mary's conception of Christ makes him both divine and human (Leeming 26–27; 42–46).

Even after heroes are born, mystery may continue to surround their adult lives. For example, Oedipus enters Thebes as a stranger, desperately attempting to hide his past so that he will not fulfill the terrible prophecy of killing his father and marrying his mother. The parental conflicts inherent in the Oedipus myth and in the Oedipus process defined by Freud hold great significance for the "suffering, self-sacrificial, crusading hero" of American baseball literature (Westbrook 79–80). The mysterious and godlike qualities of heroes, such as *The Natural*'s Roy Hobbs, suggest that questionable parentage, specifically the absence of a biological mother, whose presence would identify the would-be hero as a common person, has its roots in mythology as well as in ancient Biblical narratives. An "absent mother" is, then, the missing mother of the protagonist, whose character flaws and foibles are often an implied result of her absence. The missing mother may be dead or disappeared, or the maternal presence may have vanished without explanation.

Like their literary forebears, American writers also attempt to make their heroes extraordinary by omitting their heroes' origins, thereby creating impressive characters who had an aura of mystery (Ruland and Bradbury 179). Typical of much canonical American literature, the lone American hero, such as James Fenimore Cooper's Natty Bumppo, Washington Irving's Rip Van Winkle, Herman Melville's Ishamael, allowed no room for strong women characters.[2] These writers effectively omitted women while creating protagonists of heroic proportions.

Three. Absent Mothers and Mothering Men

Super Heroes and Stay-at-Home Moms

The dominance of such male characters in early American writing also appears in the male heroes and masculinity of mid twentieth-century American baseball literature. According to Morris, the process of making the team, by which he means becoming a member of a baseball team as well as a fully functioning member of the dominant culture of the United States, means that "all marked categories sink into the default categories: universal maleness (typed as a lack of gender), universal American ethnicity (typed as a lack of group identity [outside the new group]), universal language (as it has always been, English)" (91). Morris worries that these "default categories" represent the "maximum erasure" of a character's uniqueness as he or she struggles to become accepted in a ball club, and, ultimately, in America (91).

Ironically, characters' desire for acceptance in a new team and culture may lead them to abandon the qualities that once made them individuals. The struggle and humor of molding troublesome outsiders into productive team members, meaning persons who place the team's winning record ahead of their own lives, form the basic plots of numerous works of baseball literature and movies. Piney Woods, a rebellious young catcher in Mark Harris's *A Ticket for a Seamstitch* (1957), rides his motorcycle without a helmet, placing his life in danger and causing the team's management tremendous worry. In the *Major League* series of movies (1989, 1994, 1998), players from different ethnic backgrounds unite after many disagreements and play better baseball although they lose some of the individuality in the process. Most importantly, however, is the "universal maleness" necessary for acceptance on the team. As characters achieve "maleness," women and all of their associated roles, including mothering, are typically excluded from their fictional world.

Probably the most famous victims of absent motherhood, Roy Hobbs and Henry Wiggen share an interesting feature. They are both main characters in the first novels of then young writers Malamud and Harris (*The Natural*—1952, and *The Southpaw*—1953). In a personal interview, Harris commented that he felt he was "not competent to handle" writing about Henry's mother at that time though he "now would add that dimension" to his character.[3] Malamud may have excluded Roy's mother for the same reason. It was simply easier for them to leave out women characters early in their careers.

As a mythic type, the absent biological mothers have a role in hero formation because their absence makes heroes enigmatic and potentially godlike. As a mysterious stranger, the hero represented in literature is a part of humanity's collective mind (Westbrook 80). This feature of the heroes' backgrounds has consequences for the representation of male characters in popular culture, who become the Lone Ranger, Shane, Dirty Harry, Rambo, Superman, and Captain James T. Kirk (Westbrook 79). As universal males, they lack feminine influence and become hypermasculinized, feared and admired, treated as and behaving as misfits. They become "to some extent socially dysfunctional, that is, one who is isolated or shunned or who refuses to participate in society's normal human relationships" (Westbrook 79).

The isolated heroes in literature, television, and the movies become almost godlike in their separation from mere mortals. Such an unapproachable quality extends to America's cult of celebrity as it continues into the early twenty-first century. The highly paid stars of the entertainment (including sports) industry pursue lifestyles not available or even imaginable to ordinary citizens. We can hardly understand a world in which young women have never heard of Wal-Mart or think "Chicken of the Sea" is actually chicken, but Paris Hilton and Jessica Simpson provide us with proof that such a world exists. In fact, it is both fascinating and disturbing that we want to see how such women would function when dropped into reality-based television programs. Hilton's struggles with life outside the world of five-star hotels in the highly-rated "The Simple Life" and Simpson's attempts at solving real marital problems in the show "Newlyweds" are palatable only with the knowledge that once the show is over the stars can return to their lavish homes.

Such an insular existence, however, can have devastating emotional consequences that are far from glamorous because regular homemakers and even highly paid stars may find motherhood exhausting.

Three. Absent Mothers and Mothering Men

According to Jane Swigart's *The Myth of the Bad Mother: The Emotional Realities of Mothering* (1991), the new mother at home with her infant should be, according to societal expectations, enjoying a blissful life (3). Instead, the non-stop caring for her child may drain her emotionally and make her feel as if she is in solitary confinement, depressed from lack of adult company (22).

Swigart contends that instead of representing the often severe difficulties facing an isolated or single mother, writers glorify the independent child, typically a son, who has left her to pursue his own life (4). Writers ignore the previous dependence of the son on the mother. In fact, to write supremely independent characters, authors ultimately ignore the contributions of biological mothers toward their sons' development. Swigart writes, "Huckleberry Finn is the embodiment of the desire to run away from the cloying world of the care-giver toward independence. The mother figure in Twain's novel represents, among other things, our more or less slavish tie to someone who curbs, thwarts, and makes demands which curtail our autonomy" (4).

Literary Orphans

Precursors to Huck Finn who are independent from their mothers at an early age are Henry Fielding's *Tom Jones*, Charles Dickens's *David Copperfield* and *Oliver Twist*, and the orphan Pip in Dickens's *Great Expectations*. These types of lovable, lonely waifs also appear in early English and American sport literature, as they often live apart from their mothers in boarding schools or at college, such as Thomas Hughes's Tom Brown (1857; 1861), Gilbert Patten's Frank Merriwell and Dick Merriwell (1896–1913), and Owen Johnson's Dink Stover (1911).[4] One possible source for the numerous orphans in later baseball literature is found in the "orphan" Babe Ruth, who was not really an orphan but sent to a boy's home to correct his delinquent behavior. Through men such as Babe Ruth and characters such as Roy Hobbs, who was also placed in an "orphan home" while his father worked, the attractiveness of the lost child turned successful ballplayer story remains with us. In this tradition of independent heroism, the missing mothers reflect the notion that the hero's exceptionality, pluck, and talents derive from his solitary self-reliance.

With the development of feminist approaches to literary criticism, the consequences of the absent mother have been a source of concern for critics of many genres, such as lesbian fiction, Native American literature, and the plays of Shakespeare. In her essay "'This Is Not For You': The Sexuality of Mothering" (1991), Judith Roof writes, "In a number of lesbian novels, the lesbian protagonist has no mother nor is she likely to be a mother" (167). In addition, in her essay "Adoptive Mothers and Thrown-Away Children in the Novels of Louise Erdrich" (1991), Hertha D. Wong describes the many "orphans, thrown-away children, adoptive (by choice or circumstance rather than by law) mothers, and quests for or denials of one's mother" in Native American literature (180). Shakespearean critics have also concerned themselves with the absence of biological mothers in *King Lear* and other plays.

For example, in her essay "Where Are the Mothers in Shakespeare? Options for Gender Representation in the English Renaissance" (1991), Mary Beth Rose writes, "Mothers are conspicuously absent from *The Tempest, King Lear, Othello, The Merchant of Venice*, and *Measure for Measure*. Even more striking, in the six most celebrated romantic comedies (*Love's Labor's Lost, The Taming of the Shrew, A Midsummer Night's Dream, As You Like It, Much Ado About Nothing*, and *Twelfth Night*) no mothers appear at all" (292). To this list Coppélia Kahn adds the comment, "In the crucial cataclysmic first scene of his play [*King Lear*], from which all its later action evolves, we are shown only fathers and their godlike capacity to make or mar their children" (35). Thus, absent mothers help elevate and heroize male characters by adding to their special talents the appearance of being powerful and independent. Continuing in this tradition is J. K. Rowling's wildly popular orphan Harry Potter. However, Harry and the other heroes suffer psychologically, emotionally, and socially from the very means used to achieve their superhuman qualities, the removal of their biological mothers.

Three. *Absent Mothers and Mothering Men*

The Importance of Having a Mother

Nancy Chodorow's study of developmental psychology, *The Reproduction of Mothering: Psychoanalysis and the Sociology of Gender* (1978), reveals the crucial role of the biological mother's presence in her children's lives, a concept we may apply to the characters of baseball literature. Chodorow defines "biological mothers" as women who give birth to children (3). Although recent reproductive technologies complicate this definition, we will assume that the woman who bears the child is also the child's genetic mother. Chodorow suggests that biological mothers' care for their children will resonate throughout their psychological development and into their adulthood. The amount of nurturing children receive from the biological mothers has, according to Chodorow, profound effects on children's psychological development, physical well being, and later ability to provide mothering to others (5).

Chodorow identifies the mother-son relationship as particularly significant and a source of psychological turmoil especially if the son's preoedipal phase, lasting from approximately birth until ages two or three, ends too quickly (96). In Freudian terms, the preoedipal and oedipal phases of development are determined by the familiar oedipas/electra complex during which a child competes with one parent for the affection of the other.[5] The complex begins with the child's emotional attachment to the mother during the preoedipal phase (96). Girl infants generally remain attached to their mothers for a longer period, perhaps five or six years, because mothers and daughters identify more easily with one another than mothers and sons do (97). Daughters may also then better emulate their mother and her nurturing skills, which sons learn as something that women do (93). As a result, sons may later be less able to nurture their own children if they have not practiced these valuable skills (93).

These limitations to sons' nurturing abilities may begin in their early infancy because mothers sometimes see their sons as "a definite other — an opposite gendered and –sexed other" (105). Their differences are further emphasized through our society's assignment of gender roles.

We have seen that it is fathers, not mothers, who are expected to take sons to baseball games and play catch with them. Thus, the psychological boundaries between mothers and their sons are more definite that between mothers and their daughters (104).

As mothers distance themselves from their sons, sons may be pushed too quickly into an oedipal stage of development, possibly as early as two years of age, when issues of sexuality start clouding the preoedipal issues of separation and individuation. For example, in countries like the United States, which are "male-dominated but have relatively father-absent families," mothers may turn to sons for the affection and attention not available from working husbands (106). Additionally, the necessity of having two incomes to support a household may force mothers back into full-time employment while the children are very young, even as small as six weeks old. Single mothers may also be forced to use full-time child care to provide a home-away-from-home for their children. As a result, a mother may experience a rapid distancing from her son, which then speeds his emotional development as he learns to fend for himself during the eight or more hours a day she is away from him. In this accelerated oedipal phase, a son, according to Chodorow, reacts very strongly to his mother's absence. He develops a "heavy emotional investment" in his mother and "projects his own fears and desires" on her, whose behavior he then gives that much more significance and weight" (105).

As they grow, sons fully emerge into the oedipal phase of psychological development. This phase necessitates the presence of their biological mother so that they may eventually resolve the emotional conflicts associated with it (128). Without a biological mother, sons may not resolve the oedipal phase. In addition, the process becomes increasingly difficult if the father is missing. Mirroring Chodorow's psychological description of such situations, Malamud portrays a convincing portrait of parental neglect and a grim father-son catch as Roy Hobbs's father sees him only during the summers to teach him how to throw a baseball (*The Natural* 14, 25).

Although the infrequent appearances of Roy's biological father contribute to Roy's later difficulties to some extent, he fixates more on his absent biological mother than he does on his father. She is the underlying object of his confused desires, and her absence is the origin of his psychological distress, especially concerning women, romance, and love. The quality of a son's future relationships is dependent on the presence of his biological mother and completion of the oedipal process (Chodorow 128). The resolution of this rivalry forms children's, especially sons', later ability to have "emotional commitments and possibilities for love and emotional satisfaction" with other adults (128). Thus, while the absence of biological fathers may be a factor in a character's psychological development, the absence of the biological mother is more significant due to its profound implications for personal relationships.

Fathers are Fair Game, Too

We should quickly note, however, a few examples of baseball fiction in which a woman character's biological father is missing. In Celia Cohen's *Smokey O: A Romance* (1994) and W. P. Kinsella's *Shoeless Joe*, biological fathers are lost to such tragic circumstances that their demises border on the darkly comic. Brenda Constance O'Neill, nicknamed "Smokey," is not yet born when her father, a minor-league pitcher, dies: "He was expecting to be called up any day to the big leagues, when he unleashed a mighty fastball from the mound and toppled over dead from a freak brain aneurysm" (11). In *Shoeless Joe*, Annie, wife of protagonist Ray Kinsella, lost her father to a farming accident: "When Annie was nine, he [her father] found his way into the whirling gears of a John Deere harvester. Annie's mother relishes telling the story of how it took the threshing crew over four hours to recover all the parts of him from the clanking machine" (148). The violence of these deaths is unusual, very different from the circumstances of absent biological mothers. Perhaps Cohen and Kinsella found it easier to inflict horrible deaths upon fathers than mothers, who have typically gentle natures.

Most often a result of dying during childbirth, a biological mother's absence may lead young men on searches for maternal figures who have difficulty fulfilling the men's images of their mothers (Chodorow 113). This situation involves more than an inability to reproduce the absent mother's chicken and rice recipe. Instead, the son's image of his absent mother is so great or terrible that his love interest has no chance of achieving such perfection or the son is terrified that she may become the evil mother he remembers. In addition, sons may see these maternal women as desirable yet forbidden (108). This conflict may result in psychological disorders ranging from "preoccupation to mild neurosis to psychosis" (108). In such patterns, sons continue their search for their absent biological mothers as they pursue failed romantic relationships or experience immature behaviors and psychological turmoil.

These behaviors may be explored in the context of the absent mothers of baseball literature and their replacements — substitute mothers who are often men. As women were historically not members of men's baseball teams, male mentors, such as scouts, coaches, and older players often provide substitute mothering — nurturing, guidance, unconditional love — to young characters. Some of the characters who receive support from substitute mothers include *The Natural*'s Roy Hobbs, *The Kid from Tomkinsville*'s Roy Tucker, and *The Keystone Kids*'s Bob and Spike Russell, who enter the all-male work world of baseball players.

Substitute Motherhood Defined

Chodorow's and Swigart's works provide definitions of substitute mothers that can be applied to baseball literature. According to Chodorow, substitute mothers do not give physical birth but choose to invest significant amounts of time and emotion in nurturing children (3, 32). Swigart notes that these maternal relationships are formed freely, without the substitute mothers' expecting anything in return (25). The term "substitute mothers" is especially fitting because of its multiple connotations in the language of sports. "Subs" are "replacement players," ones who are less skilled than their "regular" or "starting" counterparts. Additionally, the term also brings to mind the word "subterranean," which describes the substitute mothers' previously hidden maternal functions in these narratives. When applied to the male characters, the term "substandard" may be applied their psychological states, particularly Roy Hobbs's, as a result of his biological mother's absence and the infrequent presence of his substitute mothers.

The idea of substitute motherhood has appeared in philosophical as well as literary studies. Sara Ruddick's *Maternal Thinking: Toward a Politics of Peace* (1989) and her later essay "Thinking Mothers/Conceiving Birth" (1994) offer one definition of substitute mothers and their goals. Ruddick writes that "all mothers are 'adoptive'" or substitute mothers because they ultimately must choose to care for an infant (*Maternal* 51). In Ruddick's terms there are "birthgivers" and mothers, and sometimes these are not the same people. Ruddick later softened these terms, stressing that a connection between birthgiving and mothering does often exist and that there is "a downside, a misogynist twist in the disconnection of mothering from birth" ("Conceiving" 38). Her more recent work underscores that substitute mothers' goals may be the same as biological mothers', whose "three-fold aim [is] to protect, nurture, and train" (34).

Brenda O. Daly and Maureen T. Reddy, in their "Introduction" to *Narrating Mothers: Theorizing Maternal Subjectivities* (1991), agree with the concept of substitute motherhood: "One 'adopts' the child — whether one has given birth to that child or not — when one chooses to care for that child. We think this notion of 'adoption' may serve as the foundation of a transformation of motherhood, as it is predicated upon the necessity of choice and thereby rejects essentialist views of women" (3–4). Such a transformation challenges the view that only women can mother and allows for the existence of maternal qualities in substitute mothers, including the sometimes male substitute mothers in baseball literature. These characters often behave maternally when they are responsible for developing young players into major-league professionals.

Adrienne Rich's *Of Woman Born: Motherhood as Institution and Experience* (1976) promotes such nurturing relationships as being the key to successful childrearing (xv). Building on Rich's work, Daly and

Reddy offer a new definition of motherhood: "Rather than seeing motherhood as biologically predetermined and central to all women's lives, we, like Rich, see motherhood ... as a choice essentially *separate* from biology, drawing a distinction here between the ability to give birth and the decision to care for children.... [C]aregiving *defines* the act of mothering, and caregiving is a choice open to those who give birth and to those who do not" (3–4; emphasis theirs). Moreover, in *Inventing Motherhood: The Consequences of an Ideal* (1983), Ann Dally writes, "Fathers can be as influential as mothers, can act as mothers and can be maternal" (246). Dally's observation illuminates the maternal potential in men and offers an especially useful way for certain male characters in baseball literature to be "substitute mothers."[6] In composite, the existing analyses of mothers and caregivers show the maternal qualities of those who have not given birth. Substitute mothers are caregivers by choice, and their presence allows for the recovery of maternal voices in baseball literature.

Those voices have for too long been mum, a word meaning both "silent" and "mother." "Mum" also recalls the word "mummy," a wrapped and preserved corpse which is buried and forgotten unless it is recovered and analyzed. Psychological studies of mothers often fail to examine them as subjects in their own right, rendering them, like the unwrapped mummy, silent. Sara Ruddick writes, "Not only is a mother's voice virtually absent in psychoanalytic tales; worse, the child that psychoanalysts reveal is often a stranger to her mother" ("Conceiving" 32). The same is true of the absent mothers in baseball literature, who are found in characters' conversations, vocalized memories, and internal thoughts about their absent mothers or in characters' maternal or attention-seeking behaviors. In fact, Philip Roth comically suggests a baseball team's psychological need for their absent mothers in *The Great American Novel* (1973) by having the players visit a "pink and blue district," where they are mothered for a fee.

The Silent Mums

An examination of such a need for absent mothers attempts to "read the woman's voice ... back into the dialogue in order to reconstruct the process by which she was read out [eliminated] in the first place" (Bauer, "Gender" 710). The absent mother is not separate from the world of baseball, but because she cannot speak for herself, she may be easily overlooked. Her dismissal represents a greater struggle against the language of sports literature and its criticism, typified by male critics' examinations of only male characters. These assessments ignore the maternal and create the expectation that only men's voices should appear in texts about baseball. Adding to this expectation is the widespread cultural belief that only male characters, like their real-life counterparts, may play certain sports, such as football, hockey, and baseball. In the shadow of this lively activity rests the idealized feminine qualities of silence and servitude, both fulfilled by women characters through absent motherhood.[7]

The absent mothers in baseball literature represent a presence made emotionally tangible through the hero's angst. The absent mothers leave a legacy in their children, who often speak of them and whose actions may be influenced by their absence. Thus, the characters who suffer the effects of their biological mothers' absences offer an insight into particular ways larger societal issues in the United States, such as the experience of living in a nuclear family, have been represented in our culture. That experience is ultimately more complex than the absence of a biological mother determines; however, the literary representation of the family minus its biological mother, especially in sports literature, reveals much about the practice and expectations of our sports culture.

The characters who are absent biological mothers may be considered, in Dale Bauer's terms, a "silenced zone," yet "even as a 'silenced zone,' the female voice competes and contests for authority" (713). As such a zone, the absent mothers' voices are filtered through developing characters and their relationships with the characters who function as their substitute mothers. How many families in baseball literature must function without their biological mothers? Westbrook's analysis of these family systems includes the following works:

- August Wilson's play *Fences*: Troy Maxson's absent mother (55) and Raynell Maxson's dead mother (60);

- W. P. Kinsella's *The Iowa Baseball Confederacy*: Gideon Clarke's absent mother, Darlin' Maudie (132–33);
- Bernard Malamud's *The Natural*: Roy Hobbs's absent mother (247);
- Mark Harris's *The Southpaw*: Henry Wiggen's dead mother (248);
- William Kennedy's *Ironweed*: the emotionally absent mother of Francis Phelan, Kathryn Phelan (248).

Westbrook's examination of these physically or emotionally absent mothers identifies the oedipal struggle as key to explaining the protagonists' troubled behavior. She writes, "The parade of maternal maladepts presented in literature serves an important function in the mythological enterprise of father-son atonement" (247). Morris also notes this process in Robert Coover's *The Universal Baseball Association, Inc., J. Henry Waugh, Prop.*: "Men are fused together through violent atonement. Once one male has proved himself through inflicting sudden and hideous violence on another, an equation of sexual disinterest has replaced one of potentially unhealthy interest, and the father and son (who underlie all such encounters...) can be united in a loving final tableau" (61). In these Freudian interpretations of the father and son conflict, Westbrook and Morris argue that the mother is represented negatively or absented so that male reconciliation can occur. Westbrook believes that the mother is portrayed unattractively for the son "to obtain the father's blessing, to become *at one* with him, and in the process, to depict and yet avoid the psychic dangers embodied in the mother" (247; emphasis hers). To restore the patriarchal alliance between fathers and sons threatened by oedipal conflict, mothers must be made sexually unattractive. If mothers were to remain attractive, fathers and sons would continue within the oedipal struggle instead of joining forces to restore male dominance of family systems. Or, as Morris suggests, in male reconciliation, "the female in the equation has been solved for and erased" (61).

Although the grotesque characterization of or absence of biological mothers may assist certain protagonists in reconciling with their fathers, such an interpretation overlooks the positive roles of the substitute mothers in baseball literature. For example, maternal qualities

Three. Absent Mothers and Mothering Men

appear in several substitute mothers, thereby recalling the characters' absent biological mothers. In this way, the "subs" give voice to the previously silenced biological mothers. Specifically, the actions and words of the substitute mothers reveal how a maternal presence may guide young ballplayers' character development. To illustrate the need for this maternal presence, the following list emphasizes the large number of absent biological mothers who are either dead or who never receive speaking roles:

- Paul Olsen's mother, Ilse, in Gertrude Schweitzer's "We Go Together";
- Roy Hobbs's mother, Memo Paris's mother, Iris Lemon's mother, and Pop Fisher's wife and his mother in *The Natural*;
- Roy Tucker's mother in John Tunis's *The Kid from Tomkinsville*;
- Bob and Spike Russell's mother in John Tunis's *Keystone Kids*;
- Henry Wiggen's mother and Holly Webster Wiggen's mother in the Mark Harris series of novels;
- Linda Sunshine's mother in Barbara Gregorich's *She's On First*;
- Irini Doyle's mother in Karen Joy Fowler's *The Sweetheart Season*.

The words and actions of these motherless characters speak the effects of their biological mothers' absences and their need for substitute mothers.

Although I focus on the maternal aspects of the ballplayers' substitute mothers, it should be noted that caregivers may also exhibit paternal qualities. While maternal care is generally defined as unselfish and consistent attention that emphasizes unconditional acceptance, these qualities contrast with what Swigart terms "paternal love [that] in our culture suggests a more distant, detached relationship, formed later and associated with one who guides, teaches, and encourages performance and achievement" (25). The paternal qualities of the caregivers in baseball literature reinforce certain expectations, particularly success on the baseball field, that the maternal qualities do not.

In Harris's *The Southpaw*, the substitute mother and coach Mike Mulrooney continues to support Henry Wiggen's pitching despite a poor performance in spring training (96). A father figure, according to

Swigart's definition of paternal love, may have been disappointed in Henry's mediocre showing, but Mulrooney, who functions as a substitute mother, is not. Although paternal qualities of the substitutes offer another dimension of characterization in baseball literature, I emphasize instead the maternal aspects of the caregivers as a way to establish a feminine presence previously overlooked in these works.

The Subs Take the Field

Substitute mothering for these characters is usually performed by members of the characters' extended biological family and/or by male mentors, such as coaches, who play vital roles in the maturation process of players. In the narratives, the subs care for young protagonists in supportive and nurturing ways, either directly or through example. In addition, their relationships may become mutually beneficial. Like biological parents, the substitute mothers take pride in the protagonists' accomplishments while the young players receive protection and guidance that help them flourish. Examples of these substitute mothers in baseball literature include:

- Mr. Olsen for Paul Olsen in "We Go Together";
- Sam Simpson and Pop Fisher for Roy Hobbs, and Pop Fisher for Memo Paris in *The Natural*;
- Grandmother Tucker and Dave Leonard for Roy Tucker in *The Kid from Tomkinsville*;
- Grouchy Devine for Bob and Spike Russell in *The Keystone Kids*;
- Pop Wiggen, Aaron Webster, Mike Mulrooney, and Berwyn "Red" Phillips Traphagen for Henry Wiggen and Aaron Webster for Holly Webster Wiggen;
- Al Mowerinski for Linda Sunshine in *She's On First*.

These substitute mothers often work together as multiple caregivers for one character. In the most basic of substitute mothering plots, a father is forced into a maternal role when his wife dies. In Schweitzer's "We Go Together," written for a young audience, the newly-widowed

Three. Absent Mothers and Mothering Men

father, Mr. Olsen, uses baseball as a way to spend time with his son, Paul. Before Paul leaves for a little-league game, he seeks support and comfort from his father: "Here goes to try that inside curve, Dad. Wish me luck." "That's the one we practiced Sunday? Yah, I wish you luck" (220). The father finds he is not completely comfortable with sole responsibility for his son, but they do know how to play baseball together. The absent mother, Ilse, weighs heavily on the father's mind throughout the story, and he experiences "a sudden sharp longing" for her (223). Schweitzer not only emphasizes baseball as a father-son activity, but she also acknowledges the father's maternal side through his care of Paul and their developing relationship.

Protagonists may also emulate their substitute mothers' qualities and thus achieve more complex character development than possible without a maternal presence. For example, the sustained presence of Henry Wiggen's substitute mothers allows him greater development of his nurturing qualities than Roy Hobbs, with the inconsistent presence of his substitute mothers, is able to achieve. In this way, Henry Wiggen's and Roy Hobbs's absent biological mothers are reified in substitute maternal figures who embody the qualities of nurturing caregivers. Substitute mothers give long-term physical, emotional, and psychological support to protagonists in baseball literature, often young characters whose development hinges on their supervision. So significant are their contributions that characters who do not have such support become painfully aware of the fact. In Fowler's *The Sweetheart Season*, Irini Doyle wonders why no one in her small community wants to help her as she struggles from the effects of her missing biological mother and her biological father's alcoholism: "Sometimes she thought she didn't know how to be close to people and that was because she'd had no mother to teach her. She'd grown up defending herself from pity over her motherlessness and so what she learned instead of intimacy was self-defense" (79). The absence of her biological mother and the lack of substitute mothers are the most painful experiences Irini Doyle suffers, perhaps even more than her father's constant drinking (196).

As in Fowler's work, two narrative paradigms identified by Morris also reveal the exigency of maternal qualities for character development, especially when the baseball novel works as a *bildungsroman,* the story of "the development of a young person, usually from adolescence to maturity" (Holman and Harmon 53). Morris notes that "the baseball novel is often ... a collision of two *bildungsroman* plots, stories about a young man's [or woman's] moral and spiritual development" (16). For Morris, the two plots are joining a baseball team and becoming a member of a new culture, whether it is an urban environment, for Roy Hobbs, or a new country, for Shirley Temple Wong in Bette Bao Lord's *In the Year of the Boar and Jackie Robinson* (1986). These *bildungsroman* plots can also be considered in the following two parts: the characters' early family drama, as determined by the absence or presence of biological mothers, and the characters' later development, often resulting in the protagonists' ability to form relationships, particularly romantic relationships, with other characters. Malamud's *The Natural* and Tunis's *The Kid from Tomkinsville* and *The Keystone Kids* provide paradigms for the examination of both the early family and later relationship *bildungsroman* plots.

Absent and Substitute Motherhood in The Natural

The early family dramas of *The Natural* are characterized by absent biological mothers, which leads to severe psychological distress, especially for Roy Hobbs. As a result, he is unable to form stable relationships with members of the opposite sex. Throughout the novel, Roy fixates on the memory of his mother, experiences disastrous romances, and suffers psychological disturbances due to her absence. Consequently, Roy's adult character development is grossly stunted and delayed until his repeated mistakes lead him to reevaluate his behavior at the novel's end.

Despite the amount of nurturing substitute mothers provide, the characters in baseball literature often face challenges that test severely their every ounce of energy. Those struggles represent a tension not easily resolved. While the valorization of a maternal presence in substitute mothers offers one resolution to this tension, such an approach minimizes the pain and inner turmoil many characters face

Three. Absent Mothers and Mothering Men

in the absence of their biological mothers. After all, a substitute never truly replaces the psychological imperative of an absent biological mother. Nowhere is this pain better represented than in Roy Hobbs. His story, perhaps the most fully developed example in baseball literature of the effects of an absent biological mother and the limitations of male substitutes, resonates with the results of a stalled oedipal process.

Malamud's novel clearly depicts the paradigm in which a character's biological mothers is absent, and, although the substitute mothers offer extensive caregiving, the repercussions of the absence usually constitute the core of the plot and evolve throughout the course of the narrative through failed romances. The facts of Roy Hobbs's story emerge *in medias res*, pieced-together from fragments that are randomly presented. Roy, an aging minor-league player searching for his big break, lost his biological mother around the age of seven, when he was sent to live with his grandmother (168). As is generally the case with absent mothers in baseball literature, she may have died, although the cause of her death is not specifically identified.[8]

While Roy's mother lived, she was probably the primary caregiver for him. Evidence of such responsibility occurs in the many works of baseball literature in which biological mothers are present and spend most of their time at home tending children, as in August Wilson's *Fences*, Mark Harris's novels, and Ring Lardner's *You Know Me Al*. It is crucial to Roy's characterization to know that his mother is absent because his perception of the world and his inability to function in it hinge on his lack of maternal guidance. In his biological mother's absence, Roy's substitute mothers offer him a maternal presence, emotional nurturing often found in scouts and coaches.

On the surface, scout Sam Simpson and coach Pop Fisher may appear to be father figures for Roy, as Candelaria and Westbrook have suggested. Candelaria describes both Simpson and Fisher as "surrogate fathers" and notes the presence of other father figures in Malamud's subsequent works (71). Westbrook calls Simpson Roy's "alcoholic mentor and father surrogate" who is ultimately responsible for his own death because he initiates the contest between Roy and the batter

Whammer (195). While certain evidence points toward the paternal qualities of Simpson and Fisher, their less overt maternal qualities have been overlooked.

Sam Simpson, who travels with Roy to Chicago by train for his first major-league tryout as a pitcher, also plays catcher for Roy during an impromptu pitching demonstration. Catchers, particularly if they are experienced players, are often substitute mothers, providing support for young pitchers both on and off the field. The scout's caretaking of Roy appears early in their train trip when "soft-voiced" Sam sacrifices his comfort for that of Roy, allowing the youngster to have a berth in the sleeper car (6). Later, their train makes an unexpected stop, and Sam plays catcher for Roy during his duel with all-star batter Whambolt, nicknamed "the Whammer." When Sam squats behind the plate, he assumes a birthing position, legs spread, introducing his new-found pitching star to the world.

As is sometimes the case in difficult deliveries, Sam does not survive the ordeal. In essence, Sam dies in childbirth when a lethal blow to the chest, a result of Roy's fastball, finishes Sam and his role as a maternal figure. Westbrook writes that such action is "father murder" (216) and that *The Natural* "approaches the order of irony of *Oedipus Rex*" (183); however, she does not recognize Sam's maternal qualities. Even as he approaches death, Sam sacrifices himself for Roy, gently calling him "kiddo" and reminding him to "make me happy" (31), displaying his maternal, unconditional acceptance of a child he will never see play ball again. Sam will later be replaced by Pop Fisher, a seemingly ineffectual coach who ultimately supports the aging Roy and helps him become a big-league star.

When Pop Fisher first appears in *The Natural*, he is "playing wet nurse" to the New York Knights (37) and looking like a "lost banana in the overgrown baseball suit he wore" (39), both images emphasizing his maternal rather than paternal qualities. In addition, his fingers are bandaged due to athlete's foot (37). Because Pop's hands represent illness, Westbrook identifies him as the Fisher King, whose malady indicates the imminent collapse of his people, in this case his team, who need Roy to return the team to health and greatness (189). The

Three. Absent Mothers and Mothering Men

bandages may also symbolize Pop's attempts at nurturing and healing roles instead of a coach's usual agonistic ones.

Pop, in addition to being a Fisher King, is maternal figure, leading a family of childish players. In a normal oedipal scenario, Roy would have to struggle against Pop, who often calls Roy "son" (41, 50), for the affections of a mother. However, Pop's withered appearance and status as a widower — Ma Fisher has died (37) — do not make him a virile threat to Roy's romantic interests. Although Pop's niece, Memo, becomes an object of Roy's desire, Pop provides no stage for Roy to play out at least symbolically his stalled oedipal process, halted by his biological mother's absence.

With Roy's ability to bond successfully with another person damaged, he embarks on a series of failed affairs. In fact, Roy tellingly compares his first love interest, the malevolent Harriet Bird, whose brutal shooting of Roy ends his pitching career, to his own mother (27). Not only is Harriet identified as a mother, but also Earl R. Wasserman identifies Roy's subsequent love interests, Memo Paris and Iris Lemon, as Roy's substitute mothers (446, 449). Instead of developing mature relationships with Memo and Iris, Roy uses their attention to feed his own ego, attempting to gain the attention he did not receive from his mother during the essential preoedipal and oedipal stages of his development. Moreover, Wasserman identifies Harriet and Memo as representations of the Jungian "Terrible Mother," signifying Roy's inability to reconcile his absent mother as both a positive and negative force in his life, the woman who gave him life but then left him alone. Instead, he sees Harriet and Memo only as "terrible seductive mothers, ... as whores" (Wasserman 454).

Until he meets Iris Lemon, Roy undergoes the psychological devastation Chodorow associates with the stalled preodipal/oedipal son: he suffers from a preoccupation with Memo and mild neuroses. He cannot stop thinking about Memo; over and over again, as her mnemonic name implies, she occupies his waking and sleeping thoughts. His inability to function in daily life is further diminished by his cravings for food and by disturbing dreams, both significant emblems of psychological stress for Freud. Although Roy does not experience a complete psychotic break with reality, he undergoes treatment in "a small maternity hospital" for his overeating (174), signifying both his infantilism and his need of a biological mother.

Roy is not the only character whose life is compromised by an absent mother. Memo Paris also suffers from the effects of an absent mother, although Pop Fisher, her uncle, unsuccessfully attempts to become her substitute mother. Memo's father left the family when she was "little" and later her mother dies, but no exact time references are given for the occurrences (108). Like Roy, Memo searches for her parents, but she seems to be more fixated on her absent father than on her mother, one of the characteristics of a stalled electra complex (Chodorow 115). Memo, apparently, never had the opportunity to resolve her feelings for her father because he abandoned the family. Such irresponsibility causes Memo tremendous psychological turmoil and results in her attraction to the immature practical joker of the team, Bump Baily, who tricks her into sleeping with Roy for Bump's own titillation (56).

Her attachment to the childish Bump intensifies with his death. She remembers, as her name clearly indicates, the abandonment of her father through Bump's untimely departure. With the loss of Bump, her father figure, she cries and howls inconsolably, rejecting the stumbling maternal qualities of the attentive, hand-wringing Pop Fisher. Instead, Memo later seeks a substitute father in the shady gambler Gus Sands, who, she tells Roy, is "just like a Daddy to me" (107). The untrustworthy and sinister Sands becomes a living memory of both her absent father and the dead Bump Baily. Thus, the effects of absent and substitute parents appear in Memo's life through several personal failures: she cannot develop a loving relationship with Roy, will not become a mature, caring partner for him, and does not recognize that Gus Sands is a terrible substitute father. Memo is as much a victim of an absent mother as Roy is. However, Memo ultimately sinks under her poor decision to stand by Sands's shifting weight while Roy receives better support from his substitute mother, Pop.

Interestingly, Pop Fisher also has an absent mother, his dead wife, nicknamed "Ma." During her life, Ma's greatest gift to him was his part-

Three. Absent Mothers and Mothering Men

ownership of his team, made possible by the financing of one of Ma's "rich relatives" (54). The presence of the team is a continual reminder of her, painfully corrupted by the loss of his majority of the shares to the other owner, Judge Goodwill Banner (54). Pop's and Memo's absent and/or substitute mothers reinforce the motif of an unfulfilled maternal presence throughout *The Natural* and adds to our understanding of the underlying psychology motivating their actions, attitudes, and reactions to others.

Often underappreciated, Pop Fisher offers care and support to Memo and Roy, who, despite the substitute mothering given them, struggle with their own relational incompetencies. This struggle can only be overcome, when, in Iris Lemon's terms, they learn from their mistakes and move on. She says, "We have two lives, Roy, the life we learn with and the life we live after that. Suffering is what brings us toward happiness" (143). Memo ultimately rejects Pop's nurturing example and refuses to acknowledge the shortcomings of Bump Baily and to cultivate mature relationships on her own. Without such self-awareness, she remains defined as a victim of abandoning parents, incapable of growing up. On the other hand, Roy slowly begins to understand his past mistakes with Harriet, Memo, and even Iris and to leave the haunting memories of his biological mother behind him.

In the face of such heartache, growth becomes possible for Roy only when he commits himself to Iris and their unborn child. In terms of the *bildungsroman*, Roy ultimately overcomes the tragedy of his family drama and forms a significant bond with Iris, creating a new family. Although his character development was backslidingly slow throughout *The Natural*, at the very end Roy's character finally begins to reach the threshold of the complexities necessary to be a loving husband to Iris and father to their child. Iris's role in his character formation is so significant that she becomes a "baseball goddess," a special designation that will be discussed along with the other women who assist in the transformation of a baseball hero from a self-centered player to a committed family member.

The "Kids" and Their Substitute Mothers

In John R. Tunis's young adult novels, the protagonists often do not have biological mothers, but the consequences for them are far less severe than for Roy Hobbs because of the sustained maternal presence of substitute mothers. For Roy Tucker of *The Kid from Tomkinsville* and the Russell brothers, Spike and Bob, of *The Keystone Kids*, the consistent support of substitute mothers prevents psychological upheaval in their lives. The subs' long-term, positive influence provides stability for the young characters' emotional development. At most, they miss their biological mothers, but the tragedy of their early family drama does not extend into their adult lives.

In this variation of the stalled oedipal motif in baseball literature, the player retains his close relationship with his substitute mother but never develops a psychological crisis from failed romantic relationships. The absence of romance from Tunis's novels may also be due to his young male audience, perhaps more interested in reading about baseball than finding love. Nevertheless, the first absent mother in baseball literature haunts the protagonist through his memories of her in *The Kid from Tomkinsville*.[9] Tunis's novel chronicles the first two years of nineteen-year-old pitching sensation Roy Tucker's career with the Brooklyn Dodgers. Hailing from the small town of Waterbury, Connecticut, Tucker is nicknamed "the Kid" by the press and veteran players.

Early in the narrative, Tucker's tragic family situation is revealed: his mother died two years before, but the time of his father's death is unclear (23). No specific information is given about the causes of either death. While ignoring these circumstances, Tunis gives Tucker's grandmother much attention, showing that Tucker is a loving grandson who is fond of her. Such a familial attachment is safe for Tucker as a developing player because it reveals his emotional bonds yet prevents romantic entanglements from distracting him.

Tucker lives with his grandmother on the family's farm but is forced to leave her for spring training. They are mutually affectionate; he gives her his signing money for a new roof for barn that was damaged

Three. Absent Mothers and Mothering Men

in a fall storm (144), and she lends him the money to get to training camp (22). He sends a portion of his paycheck to her every week (23) and writes home practically every day (48). Tucker remains in contact with her, often longing for her company and the reassuring comforts of home when crises develop with his playing and on the road (186).

In fact, the grandmother has a keen perception of baseball, perhaps developed through her intense care of Tucker, and their relationship benefits his career. Tunis writes, "Grandma knew baseball," as she closely studies his letters and the local papers and listens carefully to all of his games on her radio (152). During the games, she brews strong tea, almost medicinal in its restorative quality. The tea helps her stay awake during the long games, but she sometimes daydreams. In her resting mind's eye, she sees her grandson in the backyard, playing baseball in the country she has always known:

> Grandma stood listening, her gaze on the back road and the distant hills, hills she had seen as a child and as a woman, a sight so accustomed that from the window and over the sink she actually saw nothing. What she saw was a wide green field dotted with men and a boy standing alone in the middle, his hands on his hips. He was in trouble. What the trouble was she couldn't tell, yet something was wrong. (154)

Tucker and his grandmother have an almost psychic connection. She instinctively knows when he is ill or hurt, and he misses home and her care when he is suffering. He longs for the substitute mothering she projects to him when he is away.

This connection becomes most apparent in several games when the point of view suddenly changes from him to his grandmother and the radio provides play-by-play coverage of the action for her. Once, as Tucker gives up so many runs that he is pulled from a game, she thinks, "Roy was tired. He should have had a good rest, a week at home with good cooking, not the hotel stuff he had to eat" (157). During another decisive game, one that will name the winner of the national league pennant, her connection to Tucker is symbolized by a violent storm, much like the one that blew the roof off the barn. The game reaches its climax as Tucker catches the game-winning out in right field and then crashes violently into the outfield fence. Simultaneously, lightening strikes near the Tucker farm and shuts off the electrical power. The melodramatic situation requires that the radio be silent or the pain that Tucker suffers will overwhelm his grandmother (276). He is carried away on a stretcher as rain begins to fall on the Polo Grounds, the rain drops connecting him to the solitary old woman sitting in the storm-induced darkness in Tomkinsville.

Water, such as the rainstorms at the baseball field and at the grandmother's farm, plays an integral part in the imagery of Tucker's transformation from a hayseed pitcher to a seasoned and season-saving outfielder and slugger. Traditionally associated with birth symbolism, water appears at every significant change in Tucker's life. In an evolution similar to that of Babe Ruth and Roy Hobbs (from pitcher to hitter), Tucker starts his big-league journey when he is discovered pitching in Waterbury (69). In his first literary birth, he becomes a major-league pitcher in a "water" town. He then travels to a second "water" town, Clearwater, Florida, home to the spring training facilities of Tunis's Brooklyn Dodgers.[10] The appearance of the word "water" in each town's name explicitly and perhaps excessively anticipates a rebirth for the young player.

For example, in Clearwater he is reborn a slugger, Tucker's true identity as a major-league player. At one point there, yet another birthing image appears when he slips and falls in a locker room shower, his arm a victim to the roughhousing of celebrating players (149). The scene clearly reveals Tucker's rebirth as a hitter: "Someone reached in[to the shower] and hauled him up and out. Dripping wet, in a hush, and a deep silence" (149–50). As if describing the delivery of an infant, Tunis shows the new Tucker, minus injured pitching arm, now a slugger.

The novel's final birthing image, a deluge, occurs on the last day of the season. As his grandmother listens to her radio, Tucker solidifies his essential role on the team:

> Rain descended. It poured down against the windows, beat on the roof which Roy had covered with the first money he had earned from

Three. Absent Mothers and Mothering Men

baseball. In the Connecticut hills, round Tomkinsville, the storm struck furiously, and Grandma sat silently in the dark. While in the murky dusk of the Polo Grounds a boy writhed in agony on the green turf of deep right center. (276)

Now a hero for making the catch and holding onto it despite crashing into the wall, Tucker is reborn into the life of a career ballplayer, his position assured for the following season when he recovers. The next installment of Tucker's story, *World Series* (1941), reveals his play in the fall classic, but for now, rain falls on the Polo Grounds, Brooklyn celebrates, and his grandmother waits patiently in Tomkinsville for light to be restored to her, both in the form of electricity and in the sunshine that Tucker's return home will bring.

While Tucker knows that he has the support and love of his grandmother at home, several times in the narrative he needs the immediate nurturing of a substitute mother. Dave Leonard, older catcher and future manager of the Dodgers and substitute mother to Tucker, provides crucial emotional support for the young pitcher. In his review of Tunis's work, Adam Hammer mistakenly identifies the popularity of Tunis as "what appealed to kids": the power of youth and the fact that "old folks" are "washed up" (149). These sentiments may explain Tucker's dislike of Dodger owner Jack MacManus, but Hammer ignores Tucker's fondness for other "old folks," such as catcher Leonard and Grandma. The older catcher/younger pitcher theme is further developed in the film *Bull Durham* (1988) as aging catcher "Crash" Davis takes charge of young pitcher "Nuke" Laloosh. And, in an ironic reversal of the theme, pitcher Henry Wiggen cares for ailing catcher Bruce Pearson in *Bang the Drum Slowly* (1956).

The Kid from Tomkinsville opens with Leonard's leaving his wife and children, part of the process necessary in adopting a new family and charge, the Dodgers and Tucker. The initial scene between Tucker and Leonard is sensitively rendered, a mentor gently instructing his student on the finer points of pitching. When Leonard approaches him, Tucker assumes the worst, fearing that he may be subject to harsh criticism. Instead, Leonard is a kind, gentle teacher:

> "Show me how you hold that ball." The Kid showed him. "All right. That's fine if it's comfortable and you're used to it. But just try it this way a few times. You'll soon find out you get lots more stuff this way." He held the ball with his two forefingers over the top seam. "Try this now, and see how it goes."
> Yes, to his surprise he had more stuff. His control was better. The catcher grinned approvingly. (33)

Leonard suggests rather than demands the young pitcher try a new delivery. In the same maternal posture in which *The Natural*'s Sam Simpson later delivers the new pitching sensation Roy Hobbs to the public, Leonard squats to receive the newly improved pitches of the soon-to-be star Roy Tucker.

As a counterpart to "the kid" Tucker in the story and on the field, his battery-mate Leonard is called the "old kid" (13). Leonard intuitively senses Tucker's worth, saving him from an early release after Tucker does poorly in exhibition ball at training camp (74). Tucker's improvement in another exhibition game soon verifies Leonard's wisdom (77–78). Although the team values his trustworthy advice and experienced play, a ball club also needs youth to win, and Leonard is old. Juxtaposed against Tucker's rise to fame is Leonard's uncertain future. He does not know if he will remain on the team, and his family, dependent upon his income, shares his anxiety.

The issue of Leonard's future reaches a climax just before Tucker's first big-league start. Before the game, Leonard is given his release (107). Thinking quickly and indicating his increasing level of maturity, Tucker demands that the aging catcher be allowed to stay for the game (108). Rightfully giving Leonard the credit for his pitching ability, Tucker remembers that Leonard's help allowed him to survive training camp. Now Tucker provides the same support for Leonard's career. In a similar situation, pitcher Henry Wiggen demands that his catcher, Bruce Pearson, be allowed to stay with him for the season in *Bang the Drum Slowly* (68). By providing such unconditional support for each other, the ballplayers in Tunis's and Harris's novels fulfill their dreams of playing baseball.

Three. *Absent Mothers and Mothering Men*

Mothering More "Kids"

Another Tunis novel in which the absent mother motif appears but is not fully developed in terms of romances for the ballplayers is *The Keystone Kids*. Spike and Bob Russell are the "Keystone Kids," a nickname earned because as players and brothers they form the shortstop-second base combination usually responsible for the execution of a baseball team's key defensive move, the double play. By putting two outs on the scoreboard, the Russell boys are a "keystone" to the Brooklyn Dodgers' chances of success.

In Tunis fashion, the brothers are also orphans (13). The narrative later reveals that their father died when they were young and that their mother then raised them for a short period of time (199). Their mother must have died when they were still small children because they never played baseball until after her death, and most children begin playing the game at approximately ages five or six. No cause for her death is ever offered, yet her memory remains vivid to her sons.

Early in the novel, Spike and Bob recall their mother, whom they affectionately refer to as "Old Lady," setting up a pattern of mother memories Spike later shares with a fellow player (9). Because they cannot return to their mother and her home during the off season, Spike and Bob live in the same boarding house, Mrs. Hampton's on McGavock Street, they lived in before they joined the Dodgers (74). The Nashville boarding house becomes a substitute home for the Russell boys because it is later revealed that their mother owned a similar boarding house in Charlotte (199). Without memories of a home or a grandmother like Tucker has, Spike and Bob have fond memories of their current home, the Nashville house, and its delicious stew (21). They cling to comforting thoughts of the house when they arrive in New York and promptly become lost in Grand Central Station (21). Thus, Mrs. Hampton's house almost becomes a substitute mother for the Russells, a source of shelter, nourishment, and consolation.

In addition to Mrs. Hampton's house, Spike and Bob have another substitute mother, the coach of the team they play for en route to the Dodgers. Grouchy Devine, sympathetic coach of the Tennessee Volunteers, helps Bob and Spike adjust to the minor leagues as they prepare to become major-league stars. Reporters name the coach "Grouchy" because of his reluctance to speak to them. However, the nickname does not reflect his personality. In fact, the supportive Grouchy has several of the maternal qualities Spike later emulates in his role as a manager for the Dodgers: Grouchy neither chastises players in front of their peers nor yells at players who make mistakes. Instead, he graciously instructs the wayward player in private, helping him not to repeat his mistakes. Grouchy, therefore, is not the stereotypical macho ex-ballplayer turned coach, as we shall see in Dodger manager Ginger Crane, whose ultra-masculine qualities make him a demanding father figure rather than a guiding substitute mother.[11] Grouchy's gentle, maternal tutelage allows the Russell brothers to grow into major-league quality ballplayers, capable of handling the positions of shortstop and second base for the Dodgers.

Before Spike Russell becomes the Dodgers' manager, the brothers suffer the behavior of the current manager, Ginger Crane, who, without maternal characteristics, proves to be a poor coach and deficient role model. Upon their becoming Dodgers, Bob and Spike immediately notice the difference between the quality of their minor-league and major-league coaches. Crane yells at players, criticizes them in front of their peers and the press, and offers brutal treatment to officials, which often causes him to be thrown out of games.[12] Without their manager on the field, the players relax, but their defensive strategies suffer from lack of leadership. Thus, in addition to being a demanding father figure, Crane also becomes, in Wasserman's terms, a "terrible mother," one who hurts the team because it cannot function to its full potential either with or without him.

After many months of destructive behavior, Crane is finally fired, and the young Spike Russell takes his place. Spike emulates his former coach and substitute mother, Grouchy Devine, saying little to reporters and speaking softly to his players. Spike's role as a coach and substitute mother for the Dodgers receives its first major challenge when racism nearly destroys the team. Spike takes an active yet supportive role in combating the ignorance of his players, a role made possible

Three. Absent Mothers and Mothering Men

through the example of coach Devine and Spike's memories of his own absent mother.

Spike's mother memories appear at a key moment in the text when Jocko Klein, the rookie catcher who is suffering from the racially motivated hatred of his teammates, tells Spike about his family background. To gain the rookie's trust, Spike listens, then describes his own struggles as a rookie and the support of Dave Leonard who had urged Spike to stay in training camp (197). Once an outsider himself, Spike employs Dave Leonard's example of maternal care to comfort Jocko.

With kindness, Spike talks to Jocko about fighting the anti–Semitism around him. Jocko reveals that his father died "a long while ago," and his mother raised him, just as the Russell boys' mother did for them (199). Also, Jocko's mother ran a boarding house for butchers in Kansas City, recalling the boarding house that Spike and Bob's mother ran for railway men in Charlotte (199) and the boarding house in Nashville. These similarities offer the men a meaningful connection, which allows Spike to empathize with Jocko. Spike also determines that he will no longer permit the team's intolerable mistreatment of the young man. During their conversation, Jocko says, "You know how 'tis, if you don't remember your pa and your ma brings you up. You're closer to her, sort of" (199). Jocko and his mother, who keeps a large scrapbook of him, are close. He feels pride when he talks about her, and she thinks he's "the greatest ball player on earth," he reports (199).

In an alternate reading of this same scene, Timothy Morris argues that Spike's question to Jocko, "You don't ever think of yer ma as a Jew?" shows Jocko's need to deny her ethnicity if he is to join the American/Dodger team. In other words, Jocko must forget his mother and their family's Jewish ancestry, effectively "erasing the conditions of history" and his mother so that he can become an American and a Dodger (Morris 29). Thus, the team will no longer despise Jocko if he is no longer a Jew. However, this reading overlooks the strength and comfort Jocko finds in his mother, the first person who explains his Jewish heritage to him.

Spike listens attentively as Jocko reveals that as a young child he was once called a "kike," and he thinks he's jokingly being called a "kite"

(177). He tells his mother because he doesn't understand the joke. He quotes his mother's explanation to Spike: "'Son, ... you've got to know sometime; you might as well know right now. This is what we're up against, all of us, what we've been up against, what we've had to fight since the start of things" (178). She tells Jocko about the more than two thousand years of persecution Jews have faced. In fact, the Klein family history almost becomes the history of Israel itself, a wandering people in search of a home. The Klein family traveled from Morocco to Paris, then Bavaria, then Hanseatic States, Vienna, and finally to the United States, where Jocko was born (226–27). Jocko, a "wandering Jew," has found a home with substitute mother Spike and the baseball team family, who themselves represent a mix of racial, ethnic, and religious backgrounds.

This optimistic reading of Jocko's plight may be historically determined by Tunis's reaction to the injustices of the Nazi Germans during World War II. *The Keystone Kids* was published in 1943, two years after the United States entered the war following the Japanese bombing of Pearl Harbor. By this time, the stories of Nazi atrocities had slowly begun to filter across the Atlantic, and Tunis had a sympathetic ear. His Jocko Klein perhaps symbolized Tunis's hope that other displaced persons could live in this country, a place of comfort that, while not exactly home, was a good substitute for it.

As a result of Tunis's hopes, Jocko's story at times borders on overwhelming sentimentality, which is ultimately balanced by accounts of Jocko's mental and physical abuse. His own teammates, as well as players from the other teams, do their best to destroy him, often calling him "Buglenose" and attacking him at the plate and on the base paths. Tunis infuses these scenes, though brutal, with the underlying sense of hope that Jocko will survive. Only the expert maternal care of player-manager Spike Russell, as learned from Dave Leonard and Grouchy Devine, saves Jocko from the team and the team from disaster. The sport of baseball, in the form of these moral mothers/teachers, provides Jocko with mentors who possess both personal and professional ethics. Spike, as a part of this lineage of quality coaches, helps the team see that hurting a good player like Jocko only hurts the team. As a team,

Three. Absent Mothers and Mothering Men

they are equals, participating in a sport in which they must help each other to succeed.

Although they triumph in baseball, Spike and Bob Russell and Jocko Klein, like Roy Tucker, never extend their winning streaks into romantic relationships. These plots do not reveal if the feeling they all share, being "closer to her [their mothers]" than their fathers, harms or delays such developments. However, a clue exists to such possibilities as Spike mentally reviews his team. He remembers the changes he has seen in them over the course of the baseball season: "He knew them, knew them all, knew them even better than their parents, better than their wives and children would ever know them" (223). For Tunis, then, the team is the ultimate family, with Spike as their mother, giving birth to a new fraternal order after long months of pain. Racism is turned into professional support for the Jewish kid Jocko through the labor pains of Spike.

In fact, the end of the narrative finds the Dodgers celebrating their rise from sixth place to third place and their defeat of the league-leading St. Louis Cardinals. The change in their behavior is termed a "rebirth": "Though they didn't realize it, that's what the Dodgers were celebrating in the lockers — the re-birth of their team" (237). The party takes place in the lockers, with their ever-present showers steaming up the room. For Tunis, the birthing image and water appear yet again.

The Wind Up

As illustrated in *The Natural*, *World Series*, and *The Keystone Kids*, the "universal maleness" in baseball fiction has effectively muted women characters as maternal role models in the lives of Roy Hobbs, Roy Tucker, and Spike and Bob Russell. The absence of prolonged, meaningful interaction with women slows, even stops, the development of complex characterizations for these ballplayers. In fact, Hobbs, Tucker, and the Russell brothers retain their individual egos throughout most of the novels. They are all highly masculinized depictions of the twentieth-century American sports hero, idolized yet often isolated and removed from the experiences of everyday life, including successful romances. Hobbs is mostly anguished and confused, Tucker is inexperienced and lonely, and Bob and Spike struggle to sharpen their playing skills while remaining fiercely loyal to the team and to each other.

Despite this limited growth in their character development, these protagonists, through their early family dramas and their later adult relationships, provide ways to examine the vital roles of the substitute mothers in baseball literature. The presence of the substitute mothers shows that regardless of the predominance of men in the world of sports fiction, meaningful examples of maternal nurturance can and do provide support and instruction to young ballplayers. Without it, they suffer greatly from their emotional isolation and insular achievements. In addition, Hobbs, Tucker, and the Russell brothers serve as foils to the more complex characters in more recent baseball literature, who benefit from greater substitute mothering and are therefore better able to sustain successful romantic relationships. These characters, Henry Wiggen and Linda Sunshine, offer a more complex *bildungsroman* than their literary predecessors did, allowing us to see the full resolution of their early family dramas in the flowering of personal romances.

FOUR

Substitute Mothering in *The Southpaw* and *She's on First*

Baseball heroes achieve success because their substitute mothers or "subs" support them. The subs enter the field of play when young players are extremely vulnerable, suffering the loss or abandonment of their biological mothers. Thus, the ballplayers' early family dramas, part one of the two-part *bildungsroman*, are not effectively resolved before they are thrust into life's later developmental stages. As the characters seek resolution to their family dramas, the subs serve them as role models and caregivers. With such help, young players may enter adulthood and perhaps attempt to establish their own families. This success is possible because substitute mothers' goals for maturing athletes are often arguably the same as those of biological mothers, "to protect, nurture, and train" them for adult life (Ruddick 34).

When characters resolve their family dramas in the appropriate stage of life, they mature, especially as they face complex situations off the field of play. Narratives that explore the world outside the ball park often generate characters with greater depth than those limited to the baseball diamond. For example, the standard plots of young adult baseball literature limit character development because they focus on preparing for and winning the "Big Game," whether it is against a sand-lot nemesis or for a pennant or World Series title (Morris 155). In fact, in six of John R. Tunis's eight young-adult novels about baseball, the plot culminates in a pennant win or a World Series trophy for the Dodgers (155). The "Big Game" plot convention extends to adult novels as well, but in those works the characters and teams spend more time outside of such highly competitive situations than their young-adult counterparts do.

This crucial fact about baseball fiction forms an essential part of the Mark Harris tetralogy. In *The Southpaw*, Henry Wiggen is a rookie reader and first-time novelist. As he reads more complex baseball fiction, he complains about the lack of games presented in adult baseball fiction: "[Ring] Lardner did not seem to me to amount to much, half his stories containing women in them and the other half less about baseball *then* what was going on in the hotels and trains. He never seemed to care how the games come out" (Harris 34; emphasis mine).[1] Ironically, as Henry's words start to look more like standard written English, less action takes place in ball parks. Thus, his complaints about Lardner's stories, with their women, hotels, and trains, would later serve as a fitting summary of Henry's (and Mark Harris's) own work, which encompasses baseball as well as many other topics (Morris 104).

Tunis's novels, on the other hand, rarely stray from the ball park setting. In his fictional world, baseball is often depicted as a zero-sum game, meaning one team must lose and one team must win. This necessary conclusion comforts the readers of baseball novels who expect the home team to always win. The outcome presented by one winner and one loser offers a minimalist structure in many narratives, such as Eric Rolfe Greenberg's fictionalized Christy Mathewson describes in *The Celebrant*:

> It's a game of intricate simplicity.... Baseball is all clean lines and clear decisions. Wouldn't life be far easier if it consisted of a series of definitive calls: safe or out, fair or foul, strike or ball. Oh, for a life like that, where every day produces a clear winner and an equally clear loser, and back to it the next day with the slate wiped clean and the teams starting out equal. (84–87)

Mathewson understands that the complexities of life cannot be adequately represented through a child's game. His point is that life is not like baseball although the unreality of the game appeals to him. A game approaching a truer representation of life would probably look more

Four. Substitute Mothering in *The Southpaw* and *She's on First*

like the messy, endlessly tied ball game in W. P. Kinsella's *Iowa Baseball Confederacy* (1986), which lasts forty days and nights, through terrible rain storms and fly balls that refuse to drop from the sky. Characters like Henry Wiggen and games such as Kinsella's do not fit the "clean lines and clear decisions" of baseball.

In terms of Mathewson's observation, the simplicity of baseball as a zero-sum, winner-takes-all game is also deceptive. According to the Official Baseball Rules 4.12b, "Any regulation game called due to weather with the score tied ... is a tie game" (qtd. in Morris 147). Although tie games are rare, they do occur, and strange plays have led umpires to declare draws. Deprived of a clear winner or loser, baseball player and fans may express tremendous outrage. For example, the events at the end of a 1908 game between the New York Giants and the Chicago Cubs are still unclear (Seymour, *Golden* 149–50). At the bottom of the ninth inning, a young ballplayer, New York's Fred Merkle, was on first base, and his teammate, Moose McCormick, represented the winning run on third. After Al Bridwell hit safely to center to win the ball game for New York, Merkle failed to touch second base.

The historical circumstances of "Merkle's boner" make the young player a tragically misunderstood figure. At that time, the Giants usually headed for the club house after the final out to avoid the rush of fans from the bleachers. Merkle was simply following standard procedure when, after the winning run was hit, he ran for the club house instead of second base. However, sensing he could prevent the Giants from winning, the Cub second baseman, Johnny Evers, called for the ball to force Merkle out at second. Evers and Giants coach Joe McGinnity then struggled over the ball. Umpire Hank O'Day called Merkle out, but the game could not be continued because of darkness. No one could discern a winner and loser, and the game was ruled a draw, adding great complexity to the simple outcome the crowd and Merkle expected. As a result of this draw, Chicago and New York played a season-ending tie-breaker for the pennant. The Cubs won the game, making the "Merkle boner" and its outcome the "single most debated, most written-about play in baseball history" (Seymour 149). It took six years for

Umpire O'Day to name the reason he called Merkle out, McGinnity's interference.

The intricacies and surprises of the Merkle game and its aftermath as represented in Greenberg's *The Celebrant* foreshadow the narrative's depiction of the 1919 Black Sox scandal, perhaps the most ironic series of games in baseball history. A "small-time gambler," Billy Maharg, reported that "the White Sox deliberately lost the first and second games of the 1919 Series for a bribe" (Seymour, *Golden* 301). The resulting "Black Sox" scandal caused the appointment of a full-time baseball commissioner whose first act was to expel permanently the eight players from organized baseball. The city of Chicago dismissed its charges against the players, but their actions have never been fully exonerated. Many have defended the players because of their poor salaries and low level of education, most notably Eliot Asinof's novelized treatment of the events, *Eight Men Out* (1963), and its movie version of the same name (1988). The eight are still excluded from Cooperstown's National Baseball Hall of Fame, despite "Shoeless" Joe Jackson's almost flawless performance in the series and amazing career statistics. As Morris describes it, in "Black Sox novels [like Kinsella's *Shoeless Joe* and Greenberg's *The Celebrant*] they [the Sox] lose the World Series, but then they were trying to lose that World Series, so I suppose, in a twisted way, they win the World Series" (155; italics his). The Merkle game and the 1919 World Series offer glimpses into how a seemingly straightforward game can go awry when its "clean lines and clear decisions" blur.

Pushing the boundary between comforting stories of a simple game and more complicated narratives are Mark Harris's *The Southpaw* and Barbara Gregorich's *She's On First*. The protagonists of these novels emerge from early family dramas faced with the loss of their biological mothers. As a result, Henry Wiggen and Linda Sunshine often face crises other than the "Big Game," and the novels are textured with conflicts that produce opportunities for their greater development than their fictional predecessors, Roy Hobbs, Roy Tucker, and the Russell brothers. Malamud's Hobbs, and Tunis's Tucker and the Russell brothers remain virtually unchanged. While Hobbs struggles with several

Four. Substitute Mothering in The Southpaw *and* She's on First

failed personal relationships, Tunis's novels omit any romantic involvement for players. For Tunis, women were simply left home, as was Dave Leonard's wife in *The Kid from Tomkinsville*, or never depicted, though Tucker must have had a relationship with a woman at some point because in *Schoolboy Johnson* (1958) he inexplicably appears with his grown daughter, Maxine (Morris 63, 79). Without ongoing character development, Tucker and the Russells, like Hobbs, remain one-dimensional. Malamud does, however, enable the reader of *The Natural* to become aware of the psychological complexities missing from Hobbs. In this way, his character is richer than Tucker and the Russells in its possibility for development, but none of them become fully realized adult characters.

Although Henry Wiggen and Linda Sunshine share the loss of biological mothers with Malamud's and Tunis's characters, they depart from the absent mother paradigms by pursing fulfilling roles outside of ball playing. These challenges lead to greater psychological stability when augmented by the complex rendering of their substitute mothers. Most notably, Henry and Linda struggle with and succeed in romantic relationships, adding dimensions to their characters not possible if they were focused solely on the "Big Game." The character development present in *The Southpaw* and throughout *She's On First* demonstrates the crucial role substitute mothers play in making fully realized characters possible in baseball fiction. Subs help Henry and Linda effectively address the tragedies of their early family dramas, characterized by their absent biological mothers, and triumphantly become mature adults.

Substitute Mothering in The Southpaw

Henry Wiggen emulates the qualities of his numerous substitute mothers, and the continuity of their influence allows him to become thoughtful and introspective, contributing to his success at romance. While Roy Hobbs's subs either disappear quickly, like Sam Simpson, or are relatively ineffectual, like Pop Fisher, Henry benefits from the extended presence of four substitute mothers: his father, known as Pop;

Aaron Webster, who is Holly Webster's uncle; an understanding minor-league coach, Mike Mulrooney; and a sympathetic catcher, "Red" Traphagen, who gives Henry his full support on and off the field. They, along with Holly Webster, assist Henry in his gradual transition from an egocentric bush-leaguer to a professional ballplayer, a sensitive husband, and eventually a father. The gifts he receives from his substitute mothers — caretaking, pacifism, and empathy — plant the seeds of sensitivity and compassion that later grow during his courtship with Holly.

In his early writing, Henry is ambivalent about his absent mother: "Concerning my mother I can tell you practically nothing, for she died when I was 2" (17). His middle name, "Whittier," reminds him of her "because she was a fan of a poet by that name" (17). Henry's mother died after his crucial preoedipal phase, so he probably experienced some degree of significant bonding with her even if he does not remember it. However, after a brief paragraph describing her absence, Henry quickly moves to the true subject of his book's first chapter, his father.

The loving detail with which Henry describes his father, Pop, far overshadows his ambivalence toward his mother, evidence of the superb substitute mothering Pop provides. A maternal presence envelops Pop: he is a "caretaker" at the observatory next door, run by his friend Aaron Webster (17). Pop also drives the local school bus, and he is "crazy about kids" (17). Evidently, his ability to be a caretaker extends to his son, for Henry dedicates the first chapter of his first book to his father: "This chapter is Pop's, for it seems the least I can do is give him number 1..." (15).

As father and son, Pop and Henry engage in the usual game of catch; however, their relationship soon develops as Pop plays catcher to Henry's pitcher. Thus, Pop as catcher assumes the birthing posture reminiscent of *The Natural*'s Sam Simpson and *The Kid from Tomkinsville*'s Dave Leonard. In the catcher's position, a father in the traditional father-son catch assumes the maternal overtones of labor and "delivery," a word often associated with a pitch. Pop struggles through the labor pains of creating a ballplayer, his son. Both Henry and his father are left-handed, another example of their connectedness, and, as Henry explains, left-handed catchers are a rarity (15). As he

Four. Substitute Mothering in The Southpaw *and* She's on First

matures, Henry recognizes that his father has gone to great lengths to support him: "[H]e would catch me with a left-handed catcher's mitt made on order through a connection of Mr. Gregory N. Oswald, baseball coach at Perkinsville High..." (26). Thus, Pop becomes a substitute mother to Henry in addition to being his biological father, and throughout Henry's life, Pop is a steady maternal presence that subtly guides his son.

In conjunction with Pop, Aaron Webster also provides substitute mothering for the young Henry. Next-door neighbor and observatory scientist, friend to Pop and uncle to Holly Webster (Henry's future wife), Aaron's steady gaze and reassuring words rest comfortably around him. Even Pop seeks Aaron's advice on childrearing, particularly Henry's status as a "lefty." Because Pop believes left-handed children and adults suffer disadvantages in life, he tries to make Henry righthanded (15). Henry thinks he was approximately four years old when his father failed at the project: "But nothing he could do could change me, and finally what he done he took me to Aaron, for Pop has the greatest faith in whatever Aaron says, and Aaron said there wasn't nothing wrong with being lefthanded and some of the best people were lefthanded and all" (15). Such trust in Aaron Webster reveals the wisdom of Pop and the sensitive mothering both men exhibit toward Henry.

Aaron's influence can also be seen in Henry's pacifist tendencies, which are very maternal in nature. He remembers that his choice not to fight other boys would "bother Pop a lot, but Aaron said to Pop, 'Why should it bother you? Is it not better for a fellow to go down in his Coward Crouch [Henry's defensive posture] and live to fight another day?'" (37). In addition, before Henry leaves for his first spring training, Aaron is only person in his hometown to say goodbye to him that morning. He offers sound parental advice, telling the young ballplayer to be aware that his true friends will stand by him even when he does not play well (74).

Pop and Aaron are true friends to Henry, choosing to be a part of every aspect of his life as his adoptive mothers. In fact, Pop and Aaron settle in together, much like parents, once Henry and Holly marry: "So Pop is actually moved out of the house now, and over with Aaron, and

Holly is moved in over here. I kid Aaron and tell him that I got the best of the swap by far.... Those are the folks and also the end of the chapter" (18). Because Henry uses "folks" to describe Pop and Aaron's living arrangement, there is the sense that they are Henry and Holly's parents, united in their substitute mothering of the young couple. As substitute mothers, Pop and Aaron share mutual interests. In a letter to Henry, Aaron writes that he now understands the language of baseball "(thanks to your father)" (279). Such an acknowledgement of one man's gift to another reveals the depth of Aaron and Pop's friendship.

In addition to his folks, Henry's always jovial coach of the minor-league Queen City Cowboys, Mike Mulrooney, provides substitute mothering for the young pitcher. During his first spring training, Henry pitches poorly, but Mike offers him kind words: "Well, Hank, maybe this is just not your day. Why do you not go back and get under a nice warm shower?" (96). Mike also provides a supportive touch to him, placing a hand on his shoulder, as he agonizes over his poor performances (98). In such a maternal fashion, Mike takes the place of Pop and Aaron in continuing to develop the young player into an ace pitcher. Not surprisingly, Mammoth owner, Lester T. Moors, Jr., advises Henry to consider Mike such a parental figure during Henry's first salary negotiations. Moors says, "You have got to start considering Mr. Mulrooney in place of your pop, for he is in charge of you now" (101).

As Henry matures in Queen City, he watches Mike earn the respect and trust of his players, never yelling at them (108). Instead, Mike teaches each player to the best of his ability and even has a reputation for his maternal qualities. Speaking of another player's potential, Henry writes, "Lindon needs to be mothered like a baby, and there was nobody but Mike Mulrooney willing to give him the time" (104). Finally, in the tradition of Aaron Webster, Mike gives him parting advice as he leaves to join the major leagues (119–120); however, as a mother who sends children out into the world, Mike does not forget him, one of his favorite "ex-boys" (275).

When Henry leaves the Cowboys to join the big-league New York Mammoths, he is supported on the mound by seasoned catcher Red

Four. Substitute Mothering in The Southpaw *and* She's on First

Traphagen. Although Henry finds him a bit cynical, Red gives the lonely rookie pitching advice and friendship when other teammates refer to him simply as a "punk." As a catcher, Red joins Pop in the maternal posture of accepting the delivery of Henry's pitches (127). Red also takes the extra time to care for the young pitcher, who "had the regular blues, lonesome as the moon and not a soul to talk to" when he arrives for his second spring training in Aqua Clara (137). Sensitive to his isolation, Red initiates a conversation with him and establishes a relationship for which the lonely young man is grateful (138).

Later, when another team arrives in Aqua Clara for a spring training game, Red defends Henry, who forgets which opposing batter cannot hit a low curve ball (164). Red promises Mammoth manager Dutch Schnell to watch out for Henry rather than chastise him for his forgetfulness. Like Pop, Red supports Henry unconditionally. Red tells him before the beginning of his first major-league opener to "Throw anything you want the first pitch and after that listen to your redheaded papa" (204).

All these substitute mothers nurture the growth of certain qualities in Henry's personality: caretaking, pacifism, and empathy. Thus, he learns early in life to start thinking of others ahead of himself. For example, when Mammoth catcher Bruce Pearson arrives in training camp wildly drunk, Henry risks personal safety to calm him by placing him in a shower (141). Although Bruce will only respond to Mike's touch, the episode presents Henry's initial caring for Bruce, which blossoms fully in *Bang the Drum Slowly*. His empathy for others becomes further apparent when, after almost pitching a no-hitter, his thoughts remain with his friends who were cut from the team (229). Henry's early pacifism resurfaces when he is invited to tour with a baseball team that plays for the soldiers in Korea. Talking to newspaper reporter Krazy Kress, Henry does not understand the purpose of such a tour: "And it seemed to me that if I was too much of a coward to go and fight in the war against Korea myself I had no business going over and playing ball for them and encouraging them to be fighting it" (240). Such qualities of caring for and thinking of others start Henry toward his path of becoming an acceptable spouse for Holly Webster.

Harris's thoughtful portrayal of Holly represents a change in the representation of women characters in baseball fiction that began in the middle of the twentieth century. Holly is careful in her criticism of Henry and deeply loves him and their family. By 1987, Barbara Gregorich contributed a fully developed woman protagonist, Linda Sunshine, to baseball fiction. She is part of the growing list of fictionalized first-woman-in-organized-baseball players. Unlike earlier novels, however, Gregorich's *She's On First* treats the subject with great intelligence and dignity.[2] Her contribution to this subgenre may be fully illuminated against a brief survey of literature about the first girl then first women ballplayers. This literature, by both men and women, reflects society's growing acceptance of women playing baseball, which preceded Gregorich's novel.

Children's Literature by Women

An early example of a children's story which includes a girls' team and a woman baseball fan is "Double Play" by Thelma Knoles (1947). The team plays softball, not baseball, and the girl players admire Gail Clarke, a newspaper editor. One of the girls reports to her team, "She's wonderful. Can you imagine — she's a baseball fan. She's never played herself, but she goes to all the games and knows almost as much about the plays as Coach Thompson himself" (36). As an early prototype of the professional career woman and fan, Gail's character will be developed by Jennifer Paige (Janet Leigh), newspaper "household hints" columnist turned sportswriter in the 1951 movie *Angels in the Outfield*. Gail combines her love of the game with the newspaper business, and at the end of the story, she helps one of the players earn a position as a copy editor on her paper.

According to Andy McCue, the inclusion of girl players on fictional baseball teams in children's literature parallels the actual inclusion of girls on traditionally all-male little league teams, which occurred in the mid 1960s. By 1972 Isabella Taves wrote *Not Bad for a Girl*, possibly the first work of children's literature about girls playing regular little-league baseball. Taves explores the reaction of adults to the integration of girls on their sons' baseball teams, and the adults behave badly. The opposition to girls on little-league teams, as found in *Not Bad for a Girl*, becomes a theme of children's baseball literature.

Nancy Willard's first book, *The Highest Hit* (1978), is notable for its baseball-playing mother and her close relationship with her daughter. Perhaps a glimpse into Willard's future *Things Invisible to See* (1985) and its ballplayer mothers, *The Highest Hit* "refers to a hit Kate's mom makes in a neighborhood game after Kate gives her baseball lessons for her birthday" (McCue 118). Although Kate does not play baseball, the inclusion of a mother-daughter baseball lesson in which the daughter is the teacher was a new development in children's literature and remains extremely rare.

By the late 1980s and early 1990s, children's books written by women that feature co-ed baseball started making regular appearances on bookstores shelves. Jamie Suzanne's *Sweet Valley Twins: Standing Out* (1989), Lucy Ellis's *The Girls Strike Back: The Making of the Pink Parrots* (1990) and *All That Jazz* (1990), and Mary Haynes's *The Great Pretenders* (1990) are a few of the more interesting ones. In these works the girls are still trying to break the gender barrier of boys' baseball. Without a real life role model like Ila Borders, the idea that girls are still "pretenders" to baseball is understandable.

Children's Literature by Men

In children's literature by men, girls do not play baseball until the 1970s. Before that time, they had roles that placed them near but not on the diamond. For example, in Al Perkins's *Don and Donna Go to Bat* (1966) "he's the star. She becomes the equipment manager despite proving she can play" (McCue 89). While the girls waited for their turn to play, women characters coached boys' little-league teams. Matt Christopher's *The Year Mom Won the Pennant* (1968) shows a woman successfully influencing baseball when a mother's coaching skills help a team of little-league boys win games. By 1977 Christopher's *The Diamond Champs* includes girls as players.

In the 1970s the girls move to playing positions on the field, as in

Bill Carol's *Single to Center* (1974), which McCue summarizes as involving "a boy who must cope with sitting on the bench while his sister plays" (8). Books of the 1970s and 1980s which include girls playing alongside boys are Alfred Slote's *Matt Gragan's Boy* (1975), Richard Woodley's *The Bad News Bears* (1976), *The Bad News Bears in Breaking Training* (1977) and *The Bad News Bears Go to Japan* (1978), Matt Christopher's *Wild Pitch* (1980), Silky Sullivan's *Henry and Melinda* (1982), and Jeffery Kelly's *The Basement Baseball Club* (1987). During the second half of the twentieth century, these authors decreased the significance of girls playing on boys' teams and increased the importance of accepting good players, regardless of gender. In Sullivan's and Kelly's works, the boy players concentrate on winning ball games rather than excluding girls from their teams. The movement of girls from off the field to regular players is later found in literature by women.

Early Adult Literature by Women

Women writers of adult novels also looked to baseball as a theme for their work, with their protagonists at first admiring ballplayers rather than playing the sport themselves. Beginning in 1950, Lucy Kennedy's *The Sunlit Field* appeared, its title similar to Heywood Broun's *The Sunfield* (1923). Kennedy develops a romance between an Irish girl, Po, and a baseball player in 1860 Brooklyn in the lengthy novel (333 pages). Po never participates in a game of baseball, but she admires the sport and its players. McCue finds the work notable because this "may be the first baseball novel written by a woman for an adult audience" (59). While Po's appreciation of the sport develops out of her attachment to a ballplayer instead of on its own merits, Kennedy's novel heralds the approach of more complex baseball novels by women, which do not appear until almost thirty years after her venture into the genre.

During a short period of time in the 1980s, four novels by women about women professionals who are interested in baseball appeared. They are romance novels, characterized by the main characters' goal — the discovery of a suitable mate. The protagonists are happy in their professions and use baseball as a means of finding a man. Vella Munn's

Four. Substitute Mothering in The Southpaw and She's on First

Summer Season (1983), Natalie Stone's *Double Play* (1983), Sheila Paulos's *Wild Roses* (1983), and Anna Hudson's *Fun and Games* (1987) include secure women who are in search of romantic companions. In Paulos's *Wild Roses*, for example, journalist Nickie Alexander covers the local Seattle baseball team and falls in love with pitcher Craig Boone. After a few misunderstandings, the two decide to pursue their relationship despite the fact that as a sports writer Nickie must cover Craig's team. Nickie's character never really develops because she already possesses the qualities vital to an affair according to the formula of romance novels: strong communication skills, a good sense of humor, and high self-esteem. On the other hand, Craig must learn to talk about his feelings and to control his temper. Nickie, as a professional journalist, asks him both personal work-related questions and responds thoughtfully to his answers. She never doubts her ability to do her job, though she recognizes she may not be completely objective as she covers Craig's pitching. Paulos, along with Munn, Stone, and Hudson, depict static characters who enjoy the game of baseball but do not play it or suffer any ongoing personality crises.

The next step for women novelists was to portray the first woman professional on a formerly all male team. In Marilyn Sachs's *Fleet-footed Florence* (1981), Florence is the daughter of a major-league ballplayer, and she inherits his natural abilities on the diamond as well as his confidence. Her speed around the base paths earns her her nickname, and she holds a secure role on the team (McCue 94). Sachs's work is relatively free of the titillation that surrounds stories of the first-woman-ballplayer, especially in novels by men.

The First Woman Ballplayer, According to Men

Ray Puechner's *A Grand Slam* (1973) and Paul Rothweiler's *The Sensuous Southpaw* (1976) portray the first woman ballplayer as a sexual conquest for her teammates, a strategy designed to sell books rather than give the topic a serious novelistic treatment. However, a short review of their work shows how much progress women's novels on the same subject, especially Gregorich's *She's on First*, have made.

Peuchner's *A Grand Slam*, written forty years after the Nunnally Johnson's delightfully innocent story of the bouquet grabbing "Miss Gulp," is the first novel to explore this topic. Peter Bjarkman traces the development of the first-woman-to-play-professional-baseball theme, beginning with Peuchner's novel. Bjarkman calls his work "a less than mildly amusing sports novel about a gorgeous, tough-talking second baseperson on an obscure minor-league team. Swinging sex all too quickly pads out the sparse narrative action for Peuchner, and dramatic boredom descends rapidly into intellectual banality" (82). Bjarkman also reports that the overemphasis on the female baseball player's anatomy rather than her playing ability harms the novel (82).

Paul Rothweiler's *The Sensuous Southpaw* was written a few years later but without any change to the sexual overtones. As the title implies, Rothweiler gives us a respectable nod to Mark Harris's work but then focuses on the first woman ballplayer's possible sexual encounters. Bjarkman calls the work an "uneven and frivolous tale about Jeri 'Red' Walker, knuckle-balling ace of the minor league Portland Beavers. The team nickname itself should be sufficient to alert readers to Rothweiler's lust for the cheap literary joke" (82). *The Sensuous Southpaw*, like *Grand Slam*, allows a woman to play professional baseball, but a serious depiction of a woman on the field was yet to be written.

With time, men's plots focused on their fictional teams winning games rather than scoring off the field of play. Several works from the late 1970s and through the 1980s treat the first woman ballplayer with fewer sexual innuendoes and greater sensitivity: Merritt Clifton's *A Baseball Classic* (1978), David Ritz's *The Man Who Brought the Dodgers Back to Brooklyn* (1981), Ralph Michael's *The Girl on First Base* (1981), Garrison Keillor's "What Did We Do Wrong?" (1982), Donald Hay's *The Dixie Association* (1984), Mel Cebulash's *Ruth Marini: World Series Star* (1985), and Michael Bowen's *Can't Miss* (1987). These narratives, published almost one a year from 1978 to 1987, portray women as professional athletes. Their playing ability is more important to the stories than their status as sexual objects.

In Keillor's "What Did We Do Wrong?" Annie Szemanski is a fictional first woman major-league baseball player who is less than

Four. Substitute Mothering in The Southpaw and She's on First

accommodating to her admirers. Keillor's play on our usual expectations of a baseball "Annie"—an adorably dedicated and sweet fan of the game—makes the short story interesting and humorous. While her team "treated her like dirt," she responds in kind by telling the press that as the first woman in major-league baseball she feels "'like a pig in mud,' or words to that effect, and then turned and released a squirt of tobacco juice from the wad of rum-soaked plug in her right cheek" (316–17). This Annie spits, fights, curses, gets thrown out of a game, yells obscenities at the fans, and spews vile words at reporters, prompting a woman sportswriter to title her column "First woman attributes boos to sexual inadequacy in stands" (319).

Annie's attitude causes discontent among her fans, especially the men. They find themselves searching for a way to understand her as a woman ballplayer. In an amusing reversal of roles, the men agree that "she was great and it was wonderful that she had opened up baseball to women, and then they changed the subject to gardening, books, music, aesthetics, anything but baseball. They looked like men who had been stood up" (320). Annie doesn't care that her fans are upset: "She said she wasn't there to be liked, she was there to play ball" (320). The fans try to reconcile themselves to her by holding up signs that read "What did we do wrong?" and "If you would like to discuss this in a nonconfrontational, mutually respectful way, meet us after the game at gate C" (321). Annie resents their attention, and she quits the team rather than make a public apology for making a rude gesture at the stands after being called an unkind name. In this way, "the woman of their dreams, the love of their lives" leaves baseball forever (325). Keillor's clever inversion of a baseball Annie shows that perhaps a woman who is true to herself and to the game will not be what we expect.

Cebulash's *Ruth Marini: World Series Star* is the earliest example of a novel in which the first woman professional baseball player is a worthy member of her team because of her playing skills. She plays for the Los Angeles Dodgers as a rookie starting pitcher. Cebulash uses real geographical locations and professional team names, but his players, except when he refers to the historical Brooklyn Dodgers, are all fictional. Cebulash uses a third-person omniscient narrator to describe the time frame and Ruth's situation: "She missed baseball. It had been four weeks since Ruth, pitching as a Los Angeles Dodger, had fractured her leg during the All-Star game" (5). Ruth's identity as a ballplayer is established immediately, and no one, including fans, players, coaches, and management, ever doubts her role as an effective pitcher. She wins eleven games before the All-Star break and loses only two.

The leg fracture is a setback, but Ruth recovers to pitch during the end of the regular season, the playoffs, and finally in the seventh game of the World Series against the dreaded Yankees, thus winning the championship for the Dodgers. Along the way she dates Roger in California and maintains a long-distance relationship with Mike in New Jersey. Cebulash never uses sex to keep her story interesting. Instead, Ruth's life as a pitcher is as believable as Cebulash's detailed play-by-play commentary. The only crisis Ruth faces besides her injury is the conflict between her romantic interests. She must choose between two men.

Ruth is never forced to make that decision because Roger loses touch with her when she moves to Houston and Mike remains faithful. In fact, he sees her pitch in New York, and the ending of the novel implies that the two will continue their relationship: "The Dodgers were the World Champions! Laughing and crying at the same time, Ruth tried to spot Mike in the crowd, but there was too much commotion. She knew she'd be seeing him later. The season, Ruth's first, was over" (144). The Ruth Marini story does not fit the previous sexploitations of the first woman ballplayer. Cebulash allows Ruth to experience both romance and professional baseball without allowing her love interests to become the focus of the story. During the entirety of her story, Ruth knows she is a ballplayer, and her teammates accept her as such. Winning the World Series, the respect of her team, and the heart of her boyfriend, Ruth Marini is a fairly well developed character when compared with her predecessors. Ruth has moved from watching baseball to playing baseball without the motivation of finding a spouse

As a part of this setting, women soon became the main characters, creating a stronger link between them and the sport than was previously possible. Recent women characters in baseball fiction are serious fans of the game who played the sport as children and who also take up glove and bat as adults. As characters they develop by participating in the game they enjoy, which helps them overcome adversity and realize greater complexity and independence than the earlier portrayals of women admiring ballplayers.

Substitute Mothering on First

As an example of literature that reflects societal trends, Gregorich's work is criticized by Deeanne Westbrook for lacking the mythic qualities that infuse other baseball novels, such as *The Natural* (304). While Malamud's work can be appreciated as an example of mythopoeia, in which an artist consciously recalls ancient myth through contemporary media (Candelaria 64), the realism and issues of sexual inequality shape *She's on First*, aligning it with realistic narratives such as Ring Lardner's brilliant *You Know Me Al* and the Mark Harris series of novels. Because both techniques are capable of rendering intriguing and complex character studies, the realism of Gregorich's fiction neither detracts from its merit nor harms its representation of baseball. Comparing *She's on First* to *The Natural* is like comparing the clichéd though appropriate apples to oranges.

The protagonist of Gregorich's novel, Linda Sunshine, is a talented young baseball player who receives the support of adoptive parents and several substitute mothers. Although her biological mother is absent, Linda enjoys the stability of an adoptive mother and father, the Sunshines. They represent a family unit previously unexplored in baseball literature. Linda's adoptive family minimizes the effects of her biological mother's absence, and she develops into a young woman capable of sustaining relationships at many levels.

Throughout the novel, controversies surround her love life, mostly involving nosey reporters who refuse to respect her privacy. However, she is free from the neurotic infantilism and food fetishes that plagued other fictional baseball stars, such as Roy Hobbs. Instead, Linda faces a conflict between her career and her boyfriend, in this case a reporter whose kindness and sincerity distinguish him from the other journalists who cover her team. This conflict represents not only a choice between her career and the possibility of raising a family, a choice that often confronts women her same age, but also a conflict between being a loyal team member and allowing intimacy with a member of the press. In addition, she undergoes a revelation about her parentage, which produces in her a delayed oedipal/electral process, causing her to question her romantic relationship and her identity as a baseball player.

As a child, Linda inherited natural athletic talent, but the source of her talent remains a mystery throughout most of the novel. Her adoptive parents provide support for her growth as an athlete, allowing her to play little-league baseball on an (almost) all-boys team.[3] Linda's substitute parents give their daughter a stable arena to resolve her Electra conflicts. The Sunshines give her the continuity and psychological stability needed to avoid the inner conflicts other characters face. As a player and adult, Linda avoids the neuroses and immaturity symptomatic of the stalled psychological development afflicting her orphaned male counterparts in baseball literature. For her, however, the early family drama that was first resolved in her adoptive family resurfaces when she confronts her biological father and learns the story of her deceased biological mother.

Before Linda discovers her mother's story, she faces the extremely difficult process of joining organized baseball, an all-male world prior to her arrival. During her college baseball career, Al Mowerinski enters her life and prepares her for the major leagues. Al has professional and personal interests in Linda and become her substitute mother as she develops into a star shortstop. Al, the owner of a major-league team, defends and supports Linda throughout the novel, especially during the team's initial resistance to her. The journey to such a position takes her from the little leagues, through college, and onto the roster of the Chicago Eagles.

During little-league, Linda is unobtrusively observed by Al and Tim Curry, a scout for Al's organization, who inexplicably have time

Four. Substitute Mothering in The Southpaw *and* She's on First

to watch children play baseball. The scene is revealed in a flashback, occurring ten years prior to the start of the novel. Tim considers that the team's shortstop is the best player on the field. After the game, he asks the team's starters, "You like baseball?" (16). Much to his chagrin, he then discovers the shortstop is a girl, and he rudely tells her to forget about playing (17). Al promptly punches Tim for his impoliteness. This physical reaction is the first clue that Al has a deeper emotional attachment to Linda than simply anticipating her as a major-league prospect.

At Al's request, Tim begrudgingly scouts her again, this time in the final year of her successful college career. He reports that she is average shortstop material, but Al decides to schedule her for an interview. Her determination impresses him enough to offer her a contract, making her the first woman to play organized baseball. His eagerness to sign a reportedly "average" player to a key infield position again reveals his emotional investment in the young woman. He warns her that the fans, players, coaches, managers, and the press will mistreat her and that she must start in the minors. His gentle advice is maternal in quality and offers Linda much-needed protection and training for her future role as a member of his team. As a part of the Chicago Eagles franchise, which is much like an extended family to Al, she becomes almost like a daughter to him, hinting at a later plot development. He consistently provides guidance to her and assures her that the prejudice of the team and coaches will not prevent her from playing.

The first major test of their relationship occurs when Linda falls in love with a local newspaper reporter, Neal Vanderlin. He praises her athleticism in the *Chicago Sun Vindicator* and does not leak any inside information he learns from her. When Merle Isemonger, a starting pitcher with a sexist attitude and foul mouth, viciously attacks Linda, she defends herself, sending him to the hospital. Neal does not report the story.[4] Such protection fails to impress Al, who fears Neal is using Linda to further his career. Neal ultimately wins Al's approval by encouraging Linda to return to her teammates after she abandons them for her adoptive parents' home.

Sunshine leaves Chicago and the Eagles because of her shock over a tabloid newspaper's report that Al is actually her biological father.[5] His particular interest in her now makes sense. As a substitute mother, he was chiefly responsible for her recruitment and selection, though both Tim and the commissioner of baseball objected. In addition, he repeated overruled the decisions of his managers to bench Linda. Once she has the opportunity to play, she helps her team win, building her self-confidence and the team's confidence in her. The revelation that Al is her biological father, however, destroys this tenuous confidence, and she returns home to seek affirmation. She quits the Eagles and leaves town because she believes that having Al as a father is the only reason she plays.

During this electral crisis, Linda fails to recognize herself as a talented ballplayer who may have had a professional career without her father's help. She depends on her former substitute mothers, the Sunshines, for her self-confidence. She leaves the Eagles because she must overcome her disappointment in her father before she can return to him, his team, and Neal. This resolution is made increasingly difficult by the absence of her biological mother, Amanda Quitman.

The romance of Linda's biological parents, woven into the novel as a series of short flashbacks, explains her tremendous talent. In 1945, Amanda Quitman, a talented pitcher for the Hammond Chicks of the All-American Girls Professional Baseball League (AAGPBL), met and fell in love with Al during his early career as a centerfielder with the Chicago Eagles (184).[6] Although he proposed, Amanda refused because marriage would prohibit her play in the AAGPBL (188). The league stopped play in 1954, causing Amanda and Al great conflict. She demanded that he also stop playing baseball to preserve their relationship, but he refused. As her last name implies, she then left Al after she became pregnant. Without his knowledge, she decided to have her child at a home for unwed mothers. She again "quits," this time both Al and her daughter, when she died giving birth. Al learned of her fate through a private detective.

Without understanding her birth parents' tragic relationship, Linda cannot fully resolve the psychological anguish that such abandonment causes. Her adoptive parents provided care for her, food, shelter, and a setting for the initial resolution of the Electra complex. Yet

Four. Substitute Mothering in The Southpaw *and* She's on First

she belatedly faces a recurrence of the complex and the tragedy of her early family drama when she discovers that Al is her father. In this case, the *bildungsroman* plot suffers a tremendous setback, causing her to undergo her electral process not once, but twice: the first time with her adoptive parents and the second time with her biological father and absent biological mother.

The Electra complex differs from the Oedipus complex in several ways. Girls often have more difficulty resolving their feelings for their fathers than boys do with their mothers because "the oedipal situation is for a girl at least as much a mother-daughter concern as a father-daughter concern" (Chodorow 125). During this lengthy process, a girl is affectionate toward her father, maintains a certain level of affection for her mother, and then begins to see her mother as a rival for her father's attention (126–27). In contrast, a boy does not see his father as an object of affection; instead, his affection for his mother is intensified, sexualized during the Oedipus process as his father becomes a rival for his mother's affection (127).

Thus, as the boy needs both his mother's and father's presence for the resolution of the Oedipus process, the mother and father must also be present for a girl to resolve the Electra complex: "[A] girl develops important oedipal attachments to her mother *as well as* to her father. These attachments, and the way they are internalized, are built upon, and do not replace, her intense and exclusive preoedipal attachment to her mother and its internalized counterpart" (127; italics hers). As an orphan from birth, Linda does not have the benefit of a preoedipal attachment to her biological mother; furthermore, her biological mother's absence cannot be ignored as she tries to develop adult relationships with her biological father and her boyfriend. Her adoptive parents raised her to face the challenges of her current life, but she remains in conflict over her past, apparent as she returns to Chicago and the Eagles.

Her reunion with the team reconciles her in part to her father, but she does not see him before she plays. She is more comfortable without him, a distancing begun before her birth. She does, however, fully commit herself to her relationship with Neal once she and her father settle into an amicable working relationship, one that will take years to grow in intimacy. With a great amount of work, Linda begins resolving her early family drama while becoming an adult. Gregorich allows the novel to end with the hope that a close father-daughter relationship will develop, but, until then, Linda and Al remain distant, player and owner as well as father and daughter.

A number of substitute mothers, including Pop Wiggen, Aaron Webster, Mike Mulrooney, Red Traphagen, the Sunshines, and Al Mowerinski, establish a maternal presence in baseball literature by showing unconditional support for the young ballplayers entrusted to their care. Henry and Linda do not need to become successful professional ballplayers to earn the respect and love of their substitute mothers. Their affection is not based upon achievement, recalling the paternal mode of nurturance as defined by Jane Swigart. She writes that in our culture "paternal love ... suggests a more distant, detached relationship, formed later and associated with one who guides, teaches, and encourages performance and achievement" (25). These paternal qualities reinforce certain expectations, particularly success on the playing field, that the maternal qualities do not. Regardless of their performance as ballplayers, Henry and Linda have substitute mothers who help them resolve their early family dramas, part one of the *bildungsroman*, and begin pursuit of their adult lives, which is most often represented in baseball literature as a love interest, part two of the *bildungsroman*.

When men mother, baseball players receive added attention that may be the decisive factor in their becoming successful professionals as well as well-adapted adults. Henry Wiggen's substitute moms, Pop, Aaron, Mike, and Red, set the stage for his successful relationship with Holly Webster, allowing him the skills necessary for future emotional intimacy with her. Linda Sunshine's substitute mothers ensure that she will survive the revelation of her biological parents' identities and the tragedy they represent. Her character development is doubly tested by the simultaneous experience of reliving her early family drama and building her own family with Neal. The support of her substitute mothers allows her to face adult life successfully.

Four. Substitute Mothering in The Southpaw *and* She's on First

Despite the full attention of the subs, many protagonists in baseball literature still suffer without their biological mothers. Their torments can harm their character development, even if they are to some extent self-inflicted, as Roy Hobbs's are. Or characters may struggle through their early family dramas and have difficulty with relationships because they are victims of circumstances unknown to them, like Linda Sunshine. Nevertheless, while undergoing such crises, the young ballplayers rely on the support of their substitute mothers, making the journey from childhood to adulthood challenging yet survivable.

Balancing the absent and substitute mothers in baseball literature are the women characters who offer protagonists care and support as their biological mothers. August Wilson's Rose Maxson, a woman who exhibits the qualities of the Greek goddess Demeter, is perhaps the most representative mother in baseball literature because she is both a biological mother to her own children and a substitute mother to the children of others. She possesses extensive maternal qualities, which both rejoice in the raising of children and endure the enormous challenges of their care. Rose sets the standard for the other women characters with Demeter's qualities, such as Carlota and Consuelo, in Lamar Herrin's *The Rio Loja Ringmaster*.

FIVE

The Transformational Goddesses

Baseball, as defined by Earl R. Wasserman, is "the ritual whereby we express the psychological nature of American life and its moral predicament" (439–40). W. P. Kinsella writes in *What Baseball Means to Me* that "there is no time limit on a baseball game, and on a true baseball field the foul lines diverge forever, eventually taking in a good part of the universe. This makes for myth and for larger-than-life characters…" (126). The rituals surrounding baseball and its heroes are often a retelling of Greek myths with American ballplayers taking on the qualities of Greek gods. Wasserman's writing on the major figures in Arthurian and Greek myths gives limited attention to female characters. In addition, Cordelia Candelaria categorizes men in baseball literature according to the Greek myths of Apollo, Adonis, and Dionysus (20). Her taxonomy is useful, but to more fully represent "the psychological nature of American life" and the "myth" and "larger-than-life characters" found in baseball literature, a system categorizing the women characters as "goddesses" must be added.

The representation of women characters falls into the following three categories: the "simple goddesses," the "transformational goddesses," and the "compound goddesses." Each category reflects an increasing complexity of their characterization. First, the woman's or man's beauty may simply elicit the complimentary term "goddess" or "god" from their admirers. For example, when Marilyn Monroe is termed "the Goddess" in the dramatic monologue "The Goddess and the Yankee Clipper," it is simply because the speaker imagines that Joe DiMaggio is a great hitter "for no other reason than the most beautiful woman in the world loves a hitter" (Mueller 15). In these "simple goddess" roles, the women characters create romantic desire, or, in DiMaggio's case, superb batting averages. They may also be simplistically depicted as harmful to a player's career, as when the "most beautiful woman in the world" dies. The speaker of the monologue reports that "with her [Monroe] gone, I lost my incentive to hit" (24). Thus, these women often become objects of derision through their identification with destructive goddesses, such as Circe in Greek mythology and the witch Morgan in Arthurian legend.

The Simple Goddesses

As characters in baseball literature, the simple goddesses represent a shallow use of the term "goddess." In Celia Cohen's *Smokey O: A Romance* (1994), ballplayer Brenda Constance "Smokey" O' Neill describes sportswriter Claire Belle as "standing in the center [of the hotel lobby] like a sun goddess, her tawny hair shining in the muted light of the lamp globes" (94). Likewise, sports enthusiast William "Studs" Lonigan of James T. Farrell's Studs Lonigan trilogy sees his first love, Lucy Scanlan, as a "goddess" in *Young Lonigan* (1932). In a fascinating reversal of this situation, a woman admires a ballplayer who appears like a "god" to her in Heywood Broun's *The Sun Field*. Broun's Judith Winthrop describes outfielder "Tiny Tyler as "That man. You know — Apollo or whatever his name is" (37). Even men may admire an athlete, as in Greenberg's *The Celebrant*: "He [John McGraw] entered with ... a boy, a beautiful boy, a Mercury, a Mathewson drawn to smaller scale" (233). Those who perceive a person as a "god" or "goddess" merely objectify him or her, a prize to be pursued and won.

On the other hand, a simple goddess may be terribly destructive, like Circe, or a dangerous creature, like a siren. These women are profoundly harmful because, like Harriet Bird or Memo Paris in *The Natural*, they interfere with a ballplayer's career. As Circe turned men into stone, Roy Hobbs's desire for both Harriet and Memo paralyzes his

Five. The Transformational Goddesses

career by rendering him an ineffectual athlete. Harriet nearly ends Hobbs's career by shooting him; later, his unsuccessful romantic pursuit of Memo causes him to lose his concentration on the field. Further, in Lamar Herrin's *The Rio Loja Ringmaster*, professional ballplayer Dick Dixon foolishly attempts reconciliation with his unfaithful wife, Lorraine, who is termed a "siren" because she destroys their marriage: [W]ithout make-up now, without eye shadow and liner, with spiny stubbles for lashes, bland tablespoon depressions for sockets, and fish scales for eyes, with her face washed and puffed by the cold — looking exactly like the siren this deserted lake deserved, she said, 'It's time to talk'" (176). Once Lorraine has been termed a "siren," the outcome of her talk is evident. Her rejection of their marriage destroys his self-confidence, causing him to leave stardom and his professional career in the United States for Mexico, where he plays baseball as an unknown. Both Roy Hobbs and Dick Dixon suffer terrible consequences from their choice to be involved with tempting, destructive women.

Men who find themselves attracted to these ruinous women put their careers and even their mental and physical health at risk. Further, their behavior reveals more about their character than simply poor judgment in their private lives. Engaging in affairs with women who do not genuinely care for them reveals ballplayers' immaturity, for they focus solely on the women's outward appearance. The beauty and sensuality of the women often hide their destructive forces, recalling the Greek myth of the attractive yet deadly Siren. As the men soon discover, the women's appearance soon pales next to the damage they inflict.

The Transformational and Compound Goddesses

Women characters may, on the other hand, positively shape the lives they touch, as they do in the second and third categories. In the second category, women may possess the qualities of transformational goddesses, showing that men can change when they are given positive role models. The transformational goddesses represent a shift from the presentation of women as objects of beauty or destructive forces to women whose contributions to the development of other characters play a central role in the narratives. As transformational figures, they often inspire ballplayers as athletes and men by showing them how to value and express love for their homes, families, and children. In the third and final category, characters may become compound goddesses, who reflect more than one goddess type and who pursue personal goals by focusing on themselves.

Psychologist Jean Shinoda Bolen's *Goddesses in Everywoman: A New Psychology of Women* can be used as a critical framework for examining women characters in baseball literature as goddesses. Bolen's assigning goddess types to women's personalities expands Jung's work on the collective unconscious. The goddess designations are more flexible than Jung's archetypes, which are represented in the "simple-minded dichotomy of virgin/whore, mother/lover that afflicts women in patriarchies" (x). These dichotomies may be discerned in the simple goddesses, who are almost always beautiful, sometimes destructive, and often both. Instead, Bolen describes women's personalities as embracing several goddess types at once or taking on new goddess traits over the course of their lives.

Three of Bolen's goddesses, in her terms the "Demeter woman," the "Hera woman," and the "Hestia woman," provide a way of reading the roles of key women characters in baseball literature because their personalities and families parallel the mythical qualities and relationships of the Greek goddesses. These three types derive from Bolen's larger work in which she identifies three groups of goddesses: the "Virgin Goddesses," Artemis, Athena, and Hestia; the "Vulnerable Goddesses," Hera, Demeter, and Persephone; and the "Alchemical Goddess" Aphrodite (15–16). In Bolen's terms, calling a woman a "Demeter woman" means that she exhibits most clearly the personality of Demeter, "the maternal archetype, [who] represents maternal instincts fulfilled through pregnancy or providing physical, psychological, or spiritual nourishment to others" (171). Thus, a "Demeter woman" is a mother who enjoys feeding and supporting her family and those around her. Most representative of the mothering women in baseball literature is Rose Maxson of *Fences*. Joining her on the Demeter team are Consuelo

Five. The Transformational Goddesses

and Carlota, the mothers of *The Rio Loja Ringmaster*, who aid in transforming struggling ballplayer Dick Dixon from disheartened loner to responsible adult and father.[1] Women's maternal, caregiving behaviors reflect the qualities of Demeter and serve as a role model for men attempting to learn self-sacrifice for their families.

The other transformational goddesses are Hera and Hestia, who also possess qualities that enable men to become greater assets to their families. Holly Webster Wiggen in Harris's series of baseball novels possesses the features of Hera, who is, according to Bolen, attracted to a successful man she strives to improve. Iris Lemon in *The Natural* exhibits the qualities of Hestia, creating a home for the comfort of those she loves. Also a Hestia character, Annie Kinsella, of W. P. Kinsella's *Shoeless Joe*, keeps the home fires burning while her husband, Ray, searches across the country for the meaning behind their farm's baseball diamond and its phantom ballplayers.

Family Values Take the Field

In classical mythology, Demeter, Hera, and Hestia all value family stability in their lives and in the lives of the mortals who worship them. As these baseball "goddesses" play out their mythological roles, their ability to maintain their families through hardship has a profound impact on those closest to them. These women show others how to sacrifice themselves in a world where independence is too often overrated. Thus, the "goddesses" care for their families and homes and are productive catalysts for the transformations of the protagonists of baseball literature from self-centered immaturity to individuals who, despite defeats, will consistently contribute to the well-being of their loved ones.

In particular, the women characters who possess the features of Demeter offer unconditional support to their families and friends. Like the caring substitute mothers, these characters are additionally biological mothers who "protect, nurture, and train" their loved ones (Ruddick 34). Wilson' Rose Maxson expertly cultivates maternal qualities in her children by constantly providing them with food despite the behavior of her egocentric, rage-filled husband, Troy. Demeter women also appear in Herrin's *The Rio Loja Ringmaster* as Dick Dixon receives maternal support from his pregnant wife Consuelo and Carlota, Consuelo's mother. These women are all biological mothers who support their loved ones in ways that are predominantly maternal, recalling the qualities of Demeter.[2]

Rose Maxson as Demeter

The Demeter and Persephone myth is retold in a 1950s Pittsburgh setting in August Wilson's play *Fences*. The goddess Demeter's most important roles are as the mother of Persephone and as the preserver of the growing season, which could not have recurred had Persephone remained in the underworld with her abductor, Hades. His abduction of Persephone upsets Demeter so greatly that she "made it known that she would not set foot on Mt. Olympus or allow anything to grow, until Persephone was returned to her" (Bolen 170). During her search for Persephone, Demeter works as a nursemaid for a child named Demophoön, who is a source of consolation for the loss of Persephone. When the mother and daughter are eventually reunited, Demeter again permits vegetation to thrive on earth.

Mother of the Maxson family, Rose Maxson is a Demeter figure because her loyalty ultimately rests with her three children, only one of whom, Cory, is her biological son. According to Kim Pereira, Rose's "family means everything to her. It defines her very existence, and without it she would be lost" (49). Rose does not possess the same level of commitment to Troy, whose anger at not being allowed to play baseball in the white major leagues cripples him emotionally, causes him to victimize his family, and "stunts the development of his full potential as a father, husband, and friend" (Pereira 41). Troy's rage at the racism that destroyed his chance for a major league career surfaces when he must confront the daily frustrations of family life. He escalates normal family arguments into physical violence, exhibiting destructive behavior toward his loved ones. Formerly an accomplished player in the Negro leagues, Troy feels powerless against the racism he perceives as having ruined his life.

Five. The Transformational Goddesses

Instead of fighting against Troy's inner hostility, Rose models alternate, healthier attitudes about life for him by taking care of his children. Rose, in her giving capacities, refuses to become a victimizer like her husband. Her compassion becomes a cultural critique of racism, and the greatest expression of her compassion is through her role as a mother. Rose's motherhood is also her strongest connection to Demeter. As Bolen points out, "Part of Demeter's name, meter, seems to mean 'mother'.... She was worshipped as a mother goddess, specifically as the mother of the grain, and mother of the maiden Persephone" (168). In fact, both Demeter and Rose have only one biological child each, and the name of Rose's son, Cory, parallels another feature of the Demeter myth: one of Persephone's names is Kore.

As Demeter mothers at every opportunity, so does Rose. For example, her last child, the adopted daughter Raynell, parallels Demeter's adopted Demophoön, showing that Rose is a mother both by nature and by choice. Rose fills the role of mother for her society, her immediate family, her extended family, and several neighbors, just as the goddess Demeter provides nourishment for the population through her role as a harvest goddess.

Rose constantly mirrors this feature of Demeter by offering food to nearly all the characters in *Fences*. What Louise Westling observes about Eudora Welty's *Delta Wedding* applies to *Fences* as well: "One of the most important ways physical life is represented in texts is in scenes in which food is prepared by women and eaten in communal rituals" (29). Wilson stages these rituals prominently in many meal scenes, all involving Rose and her role as a Demeter woman, who enjoys feeding everyone near her (Bolen 173). In her important first appearance on stage, Rose is immediately associated with the kitchen, supper, and food, serving what Wilson calls "an integral part of the Friday night rituals" involving Troy and his friend Jim Bono (stage directions, 5). In Scene One of Act One, she offers supper to Bono, a dinner of chicken and collard greens she is preparing for Troy. She also asks Troy's son from a previous marriage, Lyons, if he would like to stay for the same meal. These actions translate into Rose's offering food to three different men when the audience first sees her. During the course of the play,

Rose constantly offers food to those around her: breakfast to Troy (21), a meat loaf sandwich to Cory (30), a sandwich to Gabriel and short ribs to Lyons (48), a ham sandwich for Gabriel (53), lima beans and cornbread to Troy (65), watermelon to Gabriel (67), cake to a church bake sale (81), dinner to Troy (82), breakfast to Cory (93), and eggs to Lyons (95).

Rose not only feeds people, but she also worries when she fears they are not eating well. When Troy's brother Gabriel comes to the house, she questions him about his eating habits because he has moved out of her home and into Miss Pearl's boarding house. Rose offers biscuits to him (26) and then expresses to Troy her concern for Gabriel's diet (27). Because Gabriel no longer lives under her roof, she cannot observe his eating habits. Such concern indicates her altruistic abilities — quite unlike Troy — to care for others purely, without self-interest. Rose has only one recourse: she emphasizes to Troy that someone needs to take care of Gabriel. Thus, Rose recalls Demeter's role as "the most nurturing of the goddesses," who is always thinking of how she can benefit others (Bolen 171).

In addition to these continual offerings of food and care, the most emotionally devastating scene for Rose and the dramatic climax of *Fences* occurs in the presence of food. Rose is about to feed Troy lunch when he gives her the news of his impending fatherhood, which crushes her and even makes her forget that food is on the table. In this inversion of the usual pregnancy announcement, Troy tells Rose that he has fathered another woman's child (65–72). The news shocks Rose, who learns that the other woman, Alberta, is now in labor. Rose has been so physically immersed in food and caring for others that she has forgotten to watch for potentially destructive forces surrounding her. Like the goddess Demeter, who found her only child suddenly and violently stolen from her, Rose is surprised that Troy could destroy their marriage. As she busily nurtured children and prepared food, Troy immaturely sought attention from another woman, a woman who at first had neither responsibilities nor children, making her an attractive escape for him.

Despite the hurt she endures from the revelation of the affair,

Five. The Transformational Goddesses

Rose refuses to allow harm to come to others. When Alberta dies while giving birth, Rose rescues Troy's motherless daughter, Raynell, from a life without a mother, a life Persephone faced in the underworld with Hades. Raynell needs to be saved from her loving but incompetent father. He is psychologically immature and physically unable to nurture her properly because of his emotional isolation and lack of experience with children.

As Demeter would respond to the needs of the child, Rose immediately chooses to become Raynell's mother. Annis Pratt valorizes this restoration-of-daughter-to-mother myth as an archetype in women's literature: "Jung identifies this woman/woman quest, in which mothers and daughters mutually empower each other, as the core of women's psychological maturation" (*Dancing* 63). Once Rose has adopted Raynell and turned Troy out of his house, she begins to nurture and raise Raynell as if she were her own.

Taking in the child of another woman is central to the role of Demeter as a mother. A Demeter woman will feather her empty nest with another's child if her grown biological children have left home (Bolen 173). Rose is now forty-three years old and without any dependent children of her own when she finds Troy holding the infant Raynell and waiting on her doorstep. According to the Greek myth, when Persephone returns to Demeter, vegetation returns to the world. In the same manner, a garden grows outside Rose's home in the final act of the play (90), symbolizing Rose's acceptance and nurturing of Raynell.

Through her investment in Raynell, Rose positively shapes the next generation of the Maxson clan and future African-American women as she becomes a role model for her family, husband, and community. In caring for her rival's child, Rose shows her estranged husband how to nurture others. Although he does not have consistent contact with his family after Rose throws him out of the house, he still delivers his paycheck to her so that she can feed their family (81).

In the last scene of the play, the family is preparing for Troy's funeral. A fresh plot of garden dirt with its hidden seeds appears on stage, resembling a grave and reminding us that the family patriarch will soon be buried. The garden also represents new life; Raynell and

Cory are growing into healthy adults, as evidenced by their singing "Old Blue," one of their father's favorite songs (99–100). This happy, life-affirming memory of their shared father uplifts the funerary mood of the final scene. The young members of the Maxson clan sing a moving tribute to the father they will, for better or worse, remember.

The setting of the final scene, a fenced-in garden, may be considered a *hortus conclusus*, the traditional site of love encounters in medieval literature, creating what Keith Byerman calls Rose's "home field" (99). The name "Rose" brings to mind the fourteenth century poem "The Romance of the Rose," with its *hortus conclusus* and central flower, the rose. Rose is associated with a flower as Troy "picked" (Bono's word) her from all his other baseball admirers to be his wife (62), and Gabriel brings her a rose, a symbol of his admiration for her, on two occasions (47, 66). Thus, the garden offers concluding and conclusive punctuation of the love in this family, love between siblings, mother and children, and ultimately the family and the memory of their father, who they must forgive despite his multiple dysfunctions.

The garden will also provide more food for the family, a legacy that Demeter made possible through her rescue of Persephone. Although *Fences* is set in a city, such connections are reminders that these characters, as literary creations, are mythological descendants of gods and goddesses and more immediately descendents of southern slaves with ties to Africa.[3] Rose's behavior is representative of African-American tradition as she takes care of everyone and makes them grow, tending her village as she would a garden. She gives a meal and a home to anyone who needs them, reflecting her history as a descendent of the slave women of the South: "During slavery, the destruction of families and forced separations engendered among black people a sense of community. Whoever needed a home received it as a matter of course" (Pereira 52).

The importance of food to the lives of Rose's ancestors and to the continuity of their community is played out on stage; food appears in every scene of the play. This feeding, nurturing legacy will continue because the garden in the final scene is specifically Raynell's garden: "Raynell, like Rose, is associated with the natural world of the garden"

(Kubitschek 188). As an African-American woman, Raynell will be responsible for providing food to make her people strong. Thus, the garden image is a metaphor for the survival of a family and a people as much as the fence is.

In *Fences*, however, one character does not survive to the end of the play. After the first three acts, the audience has little contact with Troy, none by the end of the play. He has removed himself from his family through his infidelity, and he must face the consequences of his actions. Rose refuses to allow him back into her home; she never trusts him again, but he does not completely disappear while he can be financially responsible for his family. His love, as broken and underdeveloped as it may be, continues in the only way that Rose will allow it, in the form of money. In this manner, Rose has helped him to achieve a level of concern for others, and ultimately the family will not forget his contribution.

The Ringmaster *Mothers*

Lamar Herrin's *The Rio Loja Ringmaster* offers another view of women's maternal qualities shaping a ballplayer, this time Dick Dixon of the fictional Cincinnati Brewmasters. As a pitcher, Dick is accustomed to being in control of a game, its pace, timing, and, to a great extent, its outcome. He typifies American baseball heroes and, as his first name implies, follows the tradition of "straight men in the process of reinforcing their straightness" (Morris 4). However, Dick's connection to the culture of Mexico provides him with an added dimension, where he becomes "a sensitive thinker (like Henry Wiggen) who associates himself with the sacred ringmaster of the classic Aztec ritual game *tlachtli*" (Candelaria 64). Dick describes this game in the opening of the novel:

> If you look for an indigenous Mexican ball game, not *fútbol* imported from Spain or *béisbol* from the States, all you'll find are the ruins of oblong Aztec courts and some sketchy information in the library. If you examine the ruins you'll discover narrow stone rings set on the walls on either side. In your books you'll read that the rarely attained

object of the game (the no-hitter) was to strike a small rubber ball with the hip or knee so that it passed through your designated ring. (9)

Dick becomes acquainted with *tlachtli* in Mexico, where he seeks refuge after his marriage and life fall apart.[4]

During the World Series, Dick loses the control he greatly values when he sees his wife, Lorraine, and her lover, Leo Grossman, in the stands together. The sight of them causes him to lose any faith he had in his marriage, which had been increasingly unhappy. After the game, Dick asks Lorraine for a divorce. He then returns to a small village in Mexico, where he had spent the last off-season separated from her and visiting a friend.

There he joins a local team in San Lorenzo and falls in love with the owner's daughter, Consuelo. After moving in with the owner's family to escape the *federales* and their purging of the region's Americans, he begins to recognize the concern his lover and her mother, Carlota, have for him. That bond intensifies when Consuelo becomes pregnant. Their child represents the reconciliation of cultures that Dick has achieved as an American ballplayer who lives in Mexico with a Mexican wife and family (Candelaria 79–80). He no longer suffers the facile affection of his American wife and friends. Instead, Dick's new family demonstrates maternal love through its Demeter women. They provide him with the strength to overcome the divorce of his unfaithful wife and to become a devoted husband and father.

After establishing Dick's situation with pregnant Consuelo, Herrin uses a series of long flashback sequences to explain the ballplayer's presence in Mexico (Candelaria 77). Herrin begins the flashback narrative with Dick's biological mother, who appears in stark contrast to Consuelo and Carlota. Susan Dixon's behavior as a shallow, "do-good Christian" and her relationship with Dick's alcoholic, neglectful father, Harry "Sarge," have devastating consequences for Dick's ability to form positive relationships with women (75). Sarge, himself a former professional third baseman, behaves brutishly toward his family, but Susan remains in the loveless marriage. Because of her inability to assist either

Five. The Transformational Goddesses

her husband or her son in becoming emotionally secure individuals, Susan, though a mother, does not possess the qualities of Demeter. Her role serves mainly as a sycophantic foil to the inebriated abusiveness of her husband.

In an especially poignant scene that reveals the childhood devastation Dick's family causes him, his father takes him to see the Cardinals play at St. Louis's Sportman's Park, where the young boy becomes lost. In a drunken stupor, Sarge passes out after the second game of a double-header. Dick runs onto the deserted field in an attempt to call for his father: "He tore out his lungs trying to shout. He discovered a new voice that was brambly it hurt so, a voice that would never hold a note but that ripped at his feelings like small animals and birds, until he'd used that voice up too. In the deepening shadows of Sportsman's Park he stood there, powerless to make a sign" (57). The lost son is eventually reunited with his father once an usher finds him. In an ironic reversal of parenting skills, Dick gently removes the ball game debris, "peanut shells and pieces of popcorn," from his father's body and forgives him: "He loved and forgave this now old man who'd peed in his pants" (58). Regardless of his ability to forgive his father, Dick suffers from his degeneracy, leaving him unable to express paternal compassion.

The powerlessness Dick experiences on the mound in St. Louis pursues him in his relationships with his parents and later into his own marriage. These emotional disabilities surface when he is faced with his own impending fatherhood. He finds himself struggling to commit to marriage with his pregnant lover. Dick's inability to offer her a home and family reflects both his situation as a foreigner in a hostile country as well as his damaged upbringing. In addition, he distrusts women because of a series of disastrous romantic affairs.

Before he meets Consuelo, Dick endures relationships with three women, Lorraine Kassner Dixon, Terry Myers, and Mercedes Morales Jiminez de Costas. Like a baserunner headed toward home plate, Dick stops briefly in each of these women's arms, but soon learns that they do not offer him the home he seeks, Consuelo, his home away from home in Mexico. In fact, on Dick's first trip south of the border, he feels as if "he's getting close to home" (90). He will find that home with Consuelo, but he is not quite there yet.

His three former loves, Lorraine, Terry, and Mercedes, are too solipsistic for him to form a mutually considerate relationship with — the kind he eventually develops with Consuelo. Lorraine is absorbed by her own sexual appetites and pursues affairs with Dick's closest friends, Lester King and Leo Grossman. Terry is an artist whose paintings consume her. Like the portrait she creates of a bloated half-woman, half-girl, Terry remains immature in her relationship with Dick and will not commit to him. She dies in a Mexico City hospital, swollen from hepatitis — a horrifying realization of her own painting and lifestyle. Mercedes, who is married to a San Lorenzo rancher, enjoys a longer courtship with him than his previous lovers, but he realizes that he will never be able to establish a home with her. She is a married woman, unable to divorce her Mexican husband according to her religious beliefs and social customs. Instead, their relationship is based on her sexual needs, ones that her husband will not fulfill. The solipsism he and his former lovers exhibit contrast sharply with Consuelo, who trusts him to meet her and her child's needs.

He first sees Consuelo as she is running errands for her family, evidence of her ability to help others, and he soon begins to understand and to appreciate her benevolence through their long courtship. He thinks, "Without me to give to, Consuelo would fall. She'd cave in.... Giving is how she replenishes her strength and learning how to receive is how I hold her up" (223). He responds to her generous nature by helping her, carrying her shopping bags daily through the village (272). After watching her make numerous purchases, he escorts her home, symbolic of the long journey he makes in discovering a home for himself. However, he is not invited inside until her father, Juan, discovers he plays baseball, and the local team Juan manages needs a good pitcher. With the opportunity to grow closer to Consuelo, Dick forgoes spring training in the United States to remain in San Lorenzo, a stunning decision coming from the winning pitcher of the previous season's World Series.

He comes to this decision as he realizes what makes a family. He

Five. The Transformational Goddesses

no longer desires to return to the North but has permanently crossed the border to establish the bonds that will reward him with greater achievements than a pitcher's won-loss record. Dick's dedication to this relationship is rewarded with the intimacy he and Consuelo develop. Later, after she becomes pregnant, her maternal qualities strengthen their ability to support each other. During a walk, he begins to understand how much they can give to one another as partners and parents. He thinks, "I'm out in the town; Consuelo clings to me, to me, for support.... If Consuelo weren't hanging on I wouldn't last a block. She steers, stabilizes" (171). Now a couple dependent on each other, he offers her strength while she guides him. The selfishness of his previous lovers has disappeared in the mutual dependency of his and Consuelo's love.

Without the permission of Consuelo's parents, Juan Antonio and Carlota, Dick would not have become close to her. Although Juan Antonio is in control on the ball field, Carlota manages the home and has sanctioned Dick's courtship of her daughter. In the beginning of the novel, Carlota's authority in the home is clear as plans are made for his stay with them. With such an arrangement, Juan Antonio will get his "yearly league championships" and "of course would do as he was told" (29). Carlota's authority is unchallenged, and Dick is initially confused by her acceptance of him in their home. As a divorced American, he thinks he is hardly the catch Carlota must have in mind for the most beautiful of her five daughters.

Carlota, "the steely family matriarch" (Candelaria 78), also has a softer side, when, as her Demeter qualities would require, she feeds Dick, her husband's team, and her family. Carlota first shows Dick how to court her innocent daughter, and he thinks of food as a metaphor for the process: "Chastity. In Carlota's hands it became table-rights to a feast.... Carlota taught him restraint with the hors d'oeuvres, decorum in his approach to the table, patience when he was the last to be served. His eating must be orchestrated, did he understand?" (274). From her he learns to be patient with Consuelo rather than making immediate demands upon her, which was the way he had treated Lorraine, Terry, and Mercedes. Although his "appetites were in a boil" (274), he soon understands from Carlota that discipline must temper his hunger.

Like Rose Maxson, Carlota opens her home and prepares food for others. She does so on one occasion because Juan Antonio has invited his ballplayers to a party designed to recruit Dick. Although she fears that the team will break her fine furniture, she tolerates their presence because she wants her husband's efforts to be successful (167). The food is plentiful, and Carlota's four other daughters, all Demeter women, serve the drunk players in a motherly fashion: "Rosalina and her sisters bring on the food — trays and plates and pots of enchiladas, tamales, beans, tortillas, rice dishes, chicken dishes, stuffed peppers — and go to work, spoon-feeding the snoring, stoking their gullets, and gradually nursing them up to an elbow where they can slop for themselves" (168). These women help the ballplayers to enjoy the food and ensure that he will be a part of their team and home.

After he takes up permanent residency, he eats his meals with the rest of the family. Carlota reveals to him how much he means to her as she brings him food. As Consuelo is recovering from childbirth, Carlota calls him to supper. He senses the aroma of food, reminding him of the loving women who have made him a member of their family and a father of his own family: "I step out into the garden, breathe the supper (chicken, squash, rice, tortillas, and for Consuelo, half a glass of wine)..." (289). They discuss the reality that an annulment is not possible for Dick's marriage to Lorraine, but Carlota has come to the conclusion that she should still bless his union with her daughter. She says, "From my heart, Ricardo, I don't care. I see you happy, I see you in love, and I see who you both are. I have a heart and sometimes it lets me see. Then I believe I am seeing what God wants me to see" (290). Significantly, the blessing of Carlota occurs in the family's garden during suppertime.

As in *Fences*, enclosed gardens play a substantial role in Herrin's work. Many of the novel's love scenes occur in a *hortus conclusus*, with its surrounding walls. Herrin opens the novel with an image of a *hortus conclusus*: "I know all about walls. Candide had a wall around his garden..." (1). Dick's walls represent the stultifying marriage he left in America, walls he most often remembers as the fences around the outfield in baseball stadiums (2). However, the walls of his current ball

Five. The Transformational Goddesses

field in Mexico are different, more dangerous than the padded wood fences in the United States:

> This one [wall] was made of cactus — straight stalks of organ cactus and patchy flat leaves of the prickly pear. It ran along in front of a cluster of adobe hovels and mesquite shrub, veered on a generous open angle out to a deep center field and stopped. But down the line, the right field line, it was close as that Coliseum screen had been in Los Angeles, and those cacti needles. (2)

In attempting to find his ways out of the walls of his previous home, he soon recognizes that all places have their walls, some protective and some more exclusionary.

The walls he has built around himself following his divorce must be torn down and then rebuilt around his new family as he comes to terms with his divorce from Lorraine. As he pitches in Mexico, he comes close to perfection, a no-hitter that is bungled by the approach of the *federales*: "In a crimson flash his life with Lorraine and the Brewmasters rushed by. Oh, yes, he wanted it out, all of it out! Make him a vessel fit to live again!.... The walls opened; he turned and ran" (267). The *Rio Loja* ball field's walls are dangerous because of the *federales* who would send him back to the United States, but he has adopted the friendly confines of his new family. With those comforting walls close by, he accepts them, no longer haunted with the past and faded dreams of a no-hitter. After the *federales* clear the field, he returns to Juan Antonio's home, with its central, enclosed garden. There is beauty and protection from Mexican officials in the garden, with bougainvillea, lime trees, an orange tree, marigolds, dahlias, and geraniums (20). Recalling the lushness of Eden, Dick finds his Eve there. In the garden, he and Consuelo will experience their new life together.

The gardens that appear throughout Herrin's work are both public and private, metaphors of Dick's life as a successful sports star and suffering husband. In recalling his childhood, he thinks of the world as a "righteously blossoming pleasure garden" before his loses his innocence along with his father at Sportsman's Park. During his first trip to Mexico, he initially stays in a small room "built like a lean-to into

Lester's back garden wall" (95). While he is attempting to seduce Mercedes, he waits for her in the "French Gardens, a park that included some playgrounds and the San Lorenzo waterworks, but also acres of secluded paths and tropical flora" (125). While courting Consuelo, she and Dick share their first kiss in the same garden: "Deep in the French Garden where this sort of thing occurred ... glass-covered Consuelo knocked off the glass and kissed the penitent as hungrily as she could" (274). Finally, much of the novel's action takes place in the "*Jardín*," which is a "little walled-in plaza with Afro-cropped trees —... a sanctuary, a kind of gringo preserve" (294–95). As he matures under the guidance of Consuelo and Carlota, he grows to appreciate the walls that surround him and his loved ones, especially the walled-in garden, the *hortus conclusus* of his home with Consuelo.

Together, the Demeter women Consuelo and Carlota show Dick, for the first time in his life, the inner workings of a family in which women are respected and provide support to their family members. In this matriarchal culture, he soon realizes that they will mother him as they mother other members of the family. He benefits from them because they show him how to concentrate his efforts on being a husband to Consuelo and a father to his son, born at the novel's conclusion. Both of those achievements become more special to him, he realizes, than any achievement on a ball field ever could.

Holly Webster Wiggen as Hera

Mark Harris's Henry Wiggen also learns that being a father to his four children is a skill only his wife Holly can help him achieve. When Harris places Holly Wiggen in his starting lineup of main characters in the Henry "Author" Wiggen series of novels, he presents a woman whose qualities are instrumental in the transformation of his protagonist from a bush-leaguer into a major-league star and published writer, and finally into a retired, responsible father. As a woman character with the attributes of Hera, Holly is attracted to a highly successful man, and her positive guidance of him is her most fulfilling project.

Holly appears in *The Southpaw* as a well-rounded character, a

Five. The Transformational Goddesses

woman with a life outside the sports arena and a connection to baseball through her devotion to her athletic future husband. She also has a balanced perspective of Henry's athletic life and his personal life, enabling her to express to Henry that he must become not only a quality pitcher but also a quality person. Thus, she molds Henry into a Hall-of-Fame pitcher and a published author: "Holly's influence upon Henry helps shape the three most important areas of his life — ball playing, personal values, and writing — and his attitudes toward them form the essence of his character" (Candelaria 86).

Before she marries Henry and becomes the mother of his children, Holly exhibits the qualities of Hera: "A Hera woman is attracted to a competent, successful man — a definition that usually depends on her social class and family" (Bolen 152). Holly admires Henry, who, as a successful pitcher, will become famous in not only his and Holly's hometown, Perkinsville, New York, but also throughout the world. However, he will return to his roots at the season's end to ask Holly to marry him. Before she decides to accept his proposal at the end of *The Southpaw*, she recognizes that more than his game needs polishing.

Zues, like Henry, has an "appealing, emotionally immature little-boy element that can touch the Hera woman when combined with the power she finds so attractive" (Bolen 153). Henry has a boyish side to him throughout the Harris series of novels, which makes him appealing even while he behaves unattractively. For example, early in his career he throws an illegal pitch, the spitball, and has a tendency to see himself as the center of all the attention on his team. Later, in *It Looked Like For Ever*, he refuses to retire when he can no longer physically maintain his role as a major-league pitcher.

In every stage of his career, Holly positively influences Henry. In his rookie year on the New York Mammoths, Holly Webster comes to the city as Henry's girlfriend to see him play. At first, she dutifully takes her place "waiting out under the El tracks where the wives and girl friends wait" (*The Southpaw* 303). She is upset with Henry because during an earlier game against Boston he threw a spitball, which has an erratic motion that could harm the batter. Henry had thought that his position and power would insulate him from the repercussions of throwing the spitter, including Holly's anger. Holly remains dedicated to him, but will not yet agree to marry him. After she refuses his proposal, Henry writes, "I begun to understand ... that time was running out with her and me and that I had best begin to show that I had more in my head then just baseball" (304). As his thoughts and grammatical mistakes ("then") prove, Henry must mature before he becomes worthy of Holly. She remains his girlfriend and hopeful of their future. She also senses there is promise in him; he is a struggling author and human being with a desire to become more accomplished at both.

Thus, even before her marriage, Holly displays Hera's qualities. According to Bolen, Hera women have an unconditional relationship with their men, a "for better or worse" commitment (144). Holly remains committed to Henry after the spitter incident though she is critical of his behavior. She calls him a "stupid goon" and tells him she will not tolerate his lack of ethics: "'I believe the best hand is the soft hand, the best heart is the soft heart, and the best man is the soft man. I want my soft Henry back, Henry the Coward Navigator.' And then she busted out crying all over the place" (*The Southpaw* 308). Henry accepts her criticism and never throws another spitter. He retains his pacifism throughout the Harris series, even to the point of opposing the presence of the United States in Korea. The comment, "Leave us forget Korea" (339), is immediately twisted by the reporter Krazy Kress into an insult of the armed forces, but the careful reader will realize that Henry is simply advocating pacifism, a role which Holly has helped him cultivate.

Once Henry returns to Perkinsville at the end of his rookie season, Holly finally decides to accept his fourth marriage proposal. Like Hera, who will support her man despite his shortcomings, Holly recognizes the strength of character in Henry, which she challenges him to improve, and decides she can make a life with him. She coaxes the fourth proposal out of him: "'Perhaps you will have better luck this time,' she said. 'You have sharpened your eye since February and April and September'" (349). Over the course of the baseball season and through Holly's initial refusals, Henry has had time to mature and gain a clearer vision of himself as a player, writer, and partner for Holly.

Five. The Transformational Goddesses

The intricacies which form Holly had not been developed in the women characters of any other previous work of baseball fiction. Holly is "a fully three-dimensional female character whose role in the sports hero's life builds not from cultural stereotypes of femininity but from human complexity and artistry" (Candelaria 87). Part of Holly's "complexity" and "artistry" is found in her role as a mother. She becomes pregnant in *Bang the Drum Slowly*, and by the time Henry comes to the end of his career in *It Looked Like For Ever*, the Wiggen brood stands at four girls: Michele, Rosemary, Millicent, and Hilary. Thus, part of Holly's cultivation of her marriage and family involves staying in Perkinsville while he travels. She never has a full-time job outside the home, but for the Hera woman, her job is her marriage (Bolen 151). While staying at home, Holly adopts writing as an avocation, but her writing also reflects her priority, her marriage.

Holly's book, *Baseball Wives*, was written after Henry's first book, and her maiden name Webster, like the dictionary, and her fondness of poetry show her close connection to words. The title of Holly's book literally defines her and those around her in terms of their marriages to ballplayers. The women near Henry first expose him to literature and its importance. In *The Southpaw*, his mother gave him the middle name "Whittier" (17), and Holly reads poetry to him (72). She also "was the first to speak" to him about his need to edit its chapter twelve (106).

Her identity is that of a baseball wife, and her friends are also baseball wives or women who are significant to the team. As a Hera woman, she feels most comfortable writing about the women who support Henry: "Holly wrote a very interesting chapter about [owner] Patricia [Moors] in her book in title *Baseball Wives* although Patricia was never any body's wife for long", and "Holly has wrote about Rosemary Traphagen in her book" (*Looked* 7, 202). Patricia Moors, co-owner of the New York Mammoths, almost functions as a mother for the team: "[I]n Aqua Clara in the spring of 1950 ... Patricia [was] wandering around like she was everybody's mother loaded with jewels to the armpits" (*The Southpaw* 334). As a Hera woman, Holly sees the wives or the team mother as appropriate subjects for a book; they are the "other half" of their ballplayer husbands (Bolen 151). Henry never

135

quotes from *Baseball Wives*; however, he quotes from fellow player Red Traphagen's book while he discusses Red's wife, Rosemary. Evidently, Holly does not complain that an excerpt from her book does not appear in *It Looked Like For Ever*. She perhaps does not mind the omission because she realizes it is Henry's work, and he and his troubled relationship with his daughter Hilary are its focus.

Henry's problem with Hilary stems from her screaming fits, and at first no one knows why the child is having tantrums. She screams uncontrollably if she does not have her way, and she becomes especially vocal when her father announces his retirement from baseball prior to her having seen him play (12–13). Hilary feels abandoned by her father because he has spent the majority of her life playing baseball. She also transfers these feelings of frustration onto her mother, alienating Holly through her screaming.

Holly purposely distances herself from this situation and Hilary's screams, giving Henry the opportunity to grow as a nurturing father. This distancing also reveals other tendencies of a Hera woman, whose focus on a man may lead her to feel estranged from her children (Bolen 156). Holly intentionally severs her bonds to Hilary to remedy her screaming and bring peace to the family. Holly must give Henry the opportunity to spend time with his child, time not available to him when he was out of town playing ball.

These opportunities occur throughout *It Looked Like For Ever*. The novel opens with the death of Mammoth manager Dutch Schnell, and Holly and Henry take Hilary to the funeral in St. Louis despite her behavioral problems. Hilary is thrilled by the chance to see a dead body, but she screams so persistently on the trip that Holly gives Henry a note: "I am handing you here with my temporary resignation as Hilary's mother. When the situation improves I will consider being recalled" (9). Thus, Holly again shapes Henry; her strike forces him to interact with his daughter.

On a later trip to Washington, D.C., their child screams so loudly in the airport that Holly resigns again: "She [Hilary] only continued screaming. Holly walked away very quickly in 1 direction and I walked away in the other and Hilary sat on our bags in front of the Hertz desk

Five. The Transformational Goddesses

screaming. Soon I returned, but Holly did not return. She went on to the hotel" (79). Holly's absence causes Henry to adopt a maternal role toward Hilary. He has not yet consistently nurtured Hilary due to his long-term involvement in baseball, and he wrongly thinks that his continuing to play will help her.

Holly allows Henry to grow with Hilary, confident that they can resolve their problems together. They visit a child psychiatrist, Dr. Schiff, for help, and she correctly tells him that his absences cause the child's screaming (31). As Hilary and Henry spend more time together, her screams fade. She has come to expect her father's presence at home rather than at the ball park, and she soon forgets her anguish over the end of his career. The entire family, including Henry, adjusts to his new life and forms more solid ties to replace the old elastic bonds that stretched over his baseball season absences.

Through the career of Henry Wiggen, the flower woman Holly sees him from the spring of his rookie year to the winter of retirement. She helps him survive his transformation from a young ballplayer to a retired pitcher and returned father. As a Hera woman, Holly has tolerated much, but she has also gained much from her loyalty to Henry. She raises four daughters, and they now will have the chance to get to know their father. She maintains their home and provides a sanctuary for Henry, now a returning, wounded, ego-bruised former pitcher.

Iris Lemon and Annie Kinsella as Hestia Women

In the same way that Holly Wiggen gives Henry a home for his retirement, Iris Lemon provides a resting place for the defeated Roy Hobbs in *The Natural*, and Annie Kinsella defends her home for her husband in *Shoeless Joe*, allowing Ray Kinsella a safe place to return after his cross-country journey. Malamud's Iris creates the setting for her future home with Roy while Kinsella's Annie protects her home from her opportunistic brother. Both Iris and Annie represent the homes and stability necessary to raise loving families.

Iris Lemon most clearly reflects the goddess Hestia. Although Hestia was a virgin goddess and Iris has a child and grandchild and becomes pregnant, her fertility and nurturing of Roy connect her with the home Hestia represents, a home that Roy lacks. According to Bolen, "Hestia's significance is found in rituals, symbolized by fire. In order for a house to become a home, Hestia's presence was required" (108). If the light of Hestia's fire is necessary to establish a home, then before Roy and Iris can create their own home together, they need to experience her presence.

Roy has never had a home. He grew up without a family and is a loner, living in hotel rooms and remaining aloof from personal attachments. Although Barbara Koenig Quart does not include *The Natural* in her discussion of Malamud's characters, she argues that his writings are "about nothing so much as learning a new relation to oneself through relation to others" (138). Her observation of Malamud's isolated characters and their need to strengthen their social bonds applies to *The Natural*: Roy's fear of relationships is the greatest challenge Iris must overcome.

Roy's seclusion sets the stage for his pattern of avoiding Iris. Roy, characteristic of Malamud's "deeply islolated men" (Quart 138), purposely stays away from her for most of the novel. When Roy and Iris are together, they have difficulty interacting. He struggles to understand his relationship with Iris, especially how he could be attracted to a grandmother, but finally accepts her love and their unborn child. With this acceptance of his role as father and grandfather, Roy changes from an isolated, immature ballplayer to a man with responsibilities and an immediate and extended family, with all the complexities such interactions will entail.

Thus, Iris represents the domestication of Roy. Without her, he would not have survived his failure as a ballplayer. By the end of the novel, he holds Iris, cradling her as a refuge from defeat. She is the stability he gains after he is betrayed by the woman he thought he loved, Memo Paris.[5] At first he denied his love of Iris and returned to Memo, "forfeiting the love of an honest woman for the treacherous embrace of a villainess" (Swados 24). Once Roy learns to seek the constancy of Iris rather than the deceit of Memo, whose appearance is a reminder of the handgun-wielding Harriet Bird, he finds a woman whose Hestia qualities can provide him with a home and a family.

Five. The Transformational Goddesses

Hestia's connection to hearth and home shows her significance as a goddess figure in *The Natural* because through Iris Roy begins to understand how to take responsibility for another individual. He previously focused selfishly on his own career or uncaring women, like Harriet Bird and Memo, who did not want to establish a home with him. Their destructive natures oppose the foundational strength of the home as represented by Hestia. Roy slowly learns the importance of having a home as he builds a fire for Iris during their first date. His actions parallel an ancient Greek marriage ceremony: "The bride's mother lit a torch at her own household fire and carried it before the newly married couple to their new house to light their first household fire. This act consecrated the new home" (Bolen 108). When Roy builds Iris a fire at the lake, he is symbolically establishing a home with her, though at first he refuses to accept responsibility for her. He will later realize his need for their home once everything he previously valued has been stripped from him as a result of his own bad choices. Without his career and baseball records, he recognizes home "as a sanctuary where people bonded together into the family" (Bolen 109).

Iris needs a place to call home as much as Roy does. She has also suffered: they both had difficult childhoods, and their adult lives have been full of misery. After experiencing painful events, Roy continues to make mistakes, but Iris as a Hestia woman has learned from hers. Hestia women possess wise spirits, full of the strength that can result from much adversity (Bolen 113). Iris as Hestia brings wisdom to Roy's life and continues to care for him, despite his initial rejection of her. In the mythical terms of the novel, Iris's adopts Roy as her life's project, and she will help him to live without baseball.

Iris first goes to the ball park after she has admired Roy in the newspapers. She stands in the crowd to support him, displaying the virtue of yet another virgin goddess, Aphrodite: "Iris assumes her Great Mother role as Aphrodite and unaccountably rises from a 'sea' of faces in the stands..." (Wasserman 455). In her unconditional support of Roy, Iris also becomes the "Great Mother of fertility" (Briganti 174). As Roy sees her, he looks past the ballplayer next to him and into a world of love, home, and family, where the sport of baseball has little meaning: "Roy's gaze went past him [the ballplayer], farther down the stands, to where a young black-haired woman, wearing a red dress, was sitting at an aisle in short left. He could clearly see the white flower she wore pinned on her bosom.... She interested him, in that red dress..." (130). Iris wears red and white, the colors of love and Aphrodite, whereas Harriet Bird was strictly associated only with white roses, a medieval symbol for death. Harriet wears a white rose on the train (8, 9), and there is a vase full of white roses in her hotel room (33). On the other hand, the flower Iris wears is freshly blooming, like the healthy breast to which it is pinned, and the appearance of Iris in the stands contrasts both Harriet's deadly whiteness and Memo's "sick" breast.

Iris continues to stand in the outfield seats, the only place where she could possibly make herself known to the man who thinks only of himself and baseball. When Roy has troubles batting, she stands again: "He caught the red dress and the white rose, turned away, then came quickly back for another take, drawn by the feeling that her smile was meant for him.... She seemed to be wanting to say something, and then it flashed on him the reason she was standing was to show her confidence in him" (133). Roy gives her actions a very self-centered purpose in his false epiphany, not realizing the true meaning of her behavior. He mistakenly thinks she is supporting him, but in her actions and apparel, we also see the flames of the future fire he builds for her at the lake. In the light of the Hestia woman's fire, we realize that Iris stands not only for him but also for herself, her home, and perhaps even their future child. Her image lingers in his mind and is reinforced by a newspaper photo of her at the ball park. Roy learns her name from photographer who took her picture and calls her for a date.

On the night before she has agreed to meet with Roy, Iris witnesses a storm and then goes outside to wander "in a field of daisies whose white stars lit up her bare feet" (135). Stars, as distant balls of fire, are an appropriate symbol for the Hestia woman's warmth, and they often appear in Iris's scenes with Roy. Another image of warmth, the sun's reflected rays in the form of moonlight, will later follow Roy

Five. The Transformational Goddesses

and Iris around the lake. Wherever she goes, Iris warms Roy and slowly allows him to feel the genuine affection that he needs.

When Roy first sees her on their date, he is disappointed in her brown dress. He makes a surface judgment about her because he thinks "she had lost something, in this soft brown dress, that she'd had in the red" (137). Although he misses the red dress, he is attracted to the smell of flowers that surrounds Iris, an image of fertility reinforced by the earthly color of her dress. The "lilac dust" and the "dress ... scented with lilac" gently encourage Roy to look deeper into Iris and eventually find her more attractive than superficial Memo.

The color red, which was initially attractive to Roy at the ballgame, frightens him when he gets closer to Iris. Red is the color of fire, representing the home of Hestia, and its associated responsibilities scare Roy. At first Roy does not want to establish a home with Iris, and thus they do not create a campfire at the lake even though they are cold (142). His previous negative experiences with women are also revealed through fire. He says, "I sure met some honeys in my time. They burned me good" (142).

During this conversation, Iris perceives the true struggle in Roy's spirit: the inability to resolve his lost past and live for the present. She says to him, "We have two lives, Roy, the life we learn with and the life we live with after that. Suffering is what brings us toward happiness" (143). Although Roy is still angry at having lost his first chance at baseball stardom to Harriet's bullet, Iris instinctively knows from her own losses how to let the past go. Iris looks beyond his appearance and into his suffering.

She then tries to initiate an intimate conversation with him by telling him about herself: "'I'm thirty-three,' she said, looking at the moonlit water" (144). He, however, is more interested in her current body than in her past life. When he decides to swim instead of listen, she responds: "She stepped out without a thing on and ran in the moonlight straight into the deep water, through the shallow part, and dived where it was deep" (144–45). After Iris has emerged from the womb-like water, she recalls the true meaning, a very maternal meaning, of her standing up for Roy: "She had really stood up because he

141

was a man whose life she wanted to share ... a man who had suffered. She thought distractedly of a home, children, and him coming home every night to supper. But he had already left her" (145–46).

He separates himself from her after their swim, and Iris realizes that to make her dream of hearth and home come true, they must light Hestia's flames. Convincing him to perform this ritual is easier after she has admitted her attraction to him by chasing him to the bottom of the lake: "As they dragged themselves out of the water, she said, 'Go make a fire, otherwise we will have nothing to dry ourselves with'" (146). Although Roy does not understand that such a fire symbolizes home and hearth for her, he willingly searches for firewood. For once, Roy is participating in an unselfish activity — covering her shoulders and searching for firewood.

In Malamud's detailed depiction of Roy's fire building, Roy and Iris are surrounded by flames, which start their home fire. Only in its fire does Iris feel comfortable and safe enough to express her love for Roy. He is already expressing his concern for her by taking the time and effort to build her a fire. The romantic light transforms her into the desirable woman in red he first saw in the stands as "it reddened her naked body" (147). Iris becomes like a flame, the red of the fire coloring her from head to toe.

Roy is reluctant to embrace the fire woman, and he wants the flames to disappear before he approaches her. Perhaps glimpsing her domesticating influence, Roy sits near her: "Watching her, he thought he would wait for the fire to die down, when she was warm and dry and felt not rushed" (147). He still does not approach her until the fire dies: "He watched the fire. The flames sank low. When they had just about been sucked into the ashes he crept toward her and took her in his arms" (147). After the flames are out, he is able to hold her.

Despite their night together, Roy returns to Memo, an act that will ultimately lead to his acceptance of a bribe and the demise of his baseball career. But Iris brings him hope of a life that does not include baseball and yet is happy. Roy had not previously considered such a life possible. In his final game, Iris again stands in the bleachers for him: "A dark-haired woman in a white dress had risen and was standing

Five. The Transformational Goddesses

alone amid the crowd. Christ, another one, Roy thought.... It [the ball Roy hits] caught the lady in the face, and ... she went soundlessly down" (204). But this is not another woman; this is Iris, and she has again sacrificed herself for her belief in Roy.

In the locker room, she says twice to him, "You must win," which confuses Roy (205). Iris had never before taken an interest in his career beyond watching him play. She, as a Hestia woman, has a different winning in mind. She says, "Darling, ... win for our boy ... I am pregnant" (205). With the realization that he is soon to be a father, Roy changes. His thoughts of sickly Memo disappear as he admits his love for Iris, home, and family: "Bending over, he kissed her mouth and tasted blood. He kissed her breasts, they smelled of roses. He kissed her hard belly, wild with love for her and the child" (206). His love for his new family will sustain him through the loss of baseball and his records.

The pain Roy experiences will heal, though it seems to consume him at the end of the novel. Echoing her previous comment to him about having two lives, Roy says to himself, "I never did learn anything out of my past, now I have to suffer again" (217). Thus, he discovers that he will learn from his current suffering and live another life after it, proving that for once he has gained something from experience. With Iris and their child, Roy will live in a home established by the care of Iris and founded by the fire he built for her at the lake.

Hestia Fights for the Family Farm

Annie, wife of Ray Kinsella in W. P. Kinsella's *Shoeless Joe*, possesses the qualities of Hestia because she maintains their home, making it a place of refuge for her family during their tremendous financial struggles. As a Hestia woman, Annie's work around the house is deeply fulfilling to her (Bolen 111). Hestia's flames were central to the personal and professional lives of the ancient Greeks, worshipped wherever they went (Bolen 107). By staying at home, which represents the place they live and their livelihood, Annie contributes to her family's well being and defends them from destructive forces. In addition, Annie tends the house while her husband travels. The image of Annie remaining behind at the farmhouse and preventing her brother Mark from buying it for a computerized farming conglomerate is significant for the novel because her work makes Ray's field of dreams possible. She allows him to spend a great deal of time away from home and still keep their farm. While Ray is on a quest directed by a mysterious voice that sends him messages, Annie's dedication to their property make his triumphant return possible and allows the ghosts of former ballplayers to continue their truncated careers in his cornfield ballpark.

Annie Kinsella and her daughter Karin love the farm and its land, as Ray does. Annie has a close association with the farmhouse, where she and Karin stay while Ray travels across the country. He calls home frequently, but she does not reveal to him the dire circumstances of their land. She does not want him to worry and calls upon the strength of her Hestia qualities to maintain his home until he can return and join the battle for it. Annie is a Hestia woman because she is constantly associated with warmth, symbolizing Hestia's fires. She also defends their home, the farmhouse that is overdue on its mortgage and about to be foreclosed, and she unconditionally supports her husband's plans, which often conflict with logic and appear to place her home and family in danger. With Annie's help, Ray eventually answers the questions and voice that plague him and saves the farm.

Ray's odyssey begins when a voice tells him, "If you build it, he will come," and he receives a vision of a baseball diamond in the corn of his Iowa farm (3–4). Deeanne Westbrook summarizes the mythological implications of this plot: "Like the classic tales of Odysseus or Sir Gawain, *Shoeless Joe*'s Ray Kinsella departs from home (farm-ball field), journeys far through time and space, encounters dangers, and returns to chase the usurpers from his house and field and bestow boons on his small society" (80). Like Odysseus, Ray leaves his home, and Annie faithfully waits for his return there. She does not, however, defend herself from suitors as Penelope did. Rather, she protects the family farm from becoming another small part of an automated super farm. Her dedication to her husband and the player/ghosts who practice on the field he built for them is clearly visible in her physical description.

Five. The Transformational Goddesses

Annie has red hair, "the color of cayenne pepper" (5) that is often "shimmering" (114), and she is closely associated with both the farm house and with heat, making her in essence a burning flame, thereby recalling Iris Lemon. In Kinsella's description of Annie, the fires of Hestia appear, much like they did in Iris. In fact, as Ray comes home from playing in his ball field, he "think[s] of the fierce warmth of the woman waiting for me in the house" (17). Annie's fiery nature comforts Ray as he travels, especially during a cold White Sox game: "Raindrops blow onto my scorecard, smudging the ink. I shiver and long for Annie's fierce warmth" (40). Additionally, the heat that Ray generates with his thoughts of Annie extends to form "the loving warmth of Iowa" (29), his adopted home state. With Annie keeping Hestia's fires alive while her husband is gone, the trip will be successful. Thus, Annie tends the home fire so that Ray can return safely to the ball park he has built.[6]

In the 1989 movie *Field of Dreams*, based on Kinsella's novel, Annie leaves the house for one important scene. She attends a meeting at local school and speaks against banning books. The scene does not appear in the novel and was probably added to give the feisty actress who plays Annie, Amy Madigan, more screen time and lines than Kinsella's novel would allow. It is significant that in the novel Annie remains at home, emphasizing her Hestia qualities.

Annie's close association with the farm does not end with the warmth she and it share. It was her idea to rent it, then buy it when Ray loathed his job as an insurance salesman (9). He is much happier on the farm, and although Ray's agricultural experience is limited, he develops a love for the land that he shares with his family. Annie is so perceptive of the land that she is the first person to notice when a ballplayer appears outside: "'There's someone on your lawn,' Annie says to me, staring out into the orange-tinted dusk" (10). Within the warmth of the sunset, Annie allows Ray to meet Shoeless Joe while she stays inside.

Annie understands the magic of her husband's baseball diamond and defends it from outside attacks. Maintaining the sanctity of her home becomes her priority as Mark and his business partner Bluestein attempt to buy their property and make it a part of an immense computerized farm. The impersonalized technology of their business contrasts sharply with the homemade bleachers and baseball diamond on the Kinsella property. When Ray calls Annie from the road, she downplays her brother's threatened takeover, trusting that Ray will be home soon: "I know you'll be back as soon as you can, love. Oh, Mark's been around again. He insists we should sell" (97). Both Annie and Ray know that their land cannot be sold, and Annie is even willing to fight her brother physically for it.

When Mark and Bluestein come to the farm with court orders for its possession, Annie resorts to violence in her defense of her home. Mark, a professor at the University of Iowa who studies the corn weevil (24), has become weevil-like in his dedication to the destruction of the Kinsella farm. As a ghostly ball game is interrupted, Annie fights her brother: "Like an irate manager, Annie kicks dirt all over Mark's shoes and the cuffs of his expensive suit. He grabs her and picks her up by the arm. Annie knees him" (202). Annie's willingness to fight, though she is greatly outweighed by her opponent, confirms her dedication to her family's farm. With the strength of Hestia, she refuses to give up her home and the family it shelters.

Annie's strong protection of her home, however, would seem to face its deepest challenge in her husband's behaviors. When he decides to build a baseball diamond on top of expensive farm land they need for crops, she thoroughly supports his decision. It is this unconditional support of Ray that shapes him most profoundly. He knows that he will be able to leave the farm and find her waiting when he returns. She tells him to do what he loves: "Oh, love, if it makes you happy you should do it" (5). Her strength of will ultimately makes it possible for him to keep the farm rather than sell it to the computerized conglomerate.

As a Hestia woman, Annie protects her home and inspires her husband to survive the challenges to its well being. In the final scene of the novel, Annie welcomes her husband back into their home, safe in the knowledge that it is theirs to keep. Together they have convinced Mark and Bluestein that there is something worth keeping in their corn although the ties on their business suits are probably so tight that they cut off the oxygen necessary for them to be privy to the full magic of the ghostly ball games. Annie's light, which glows with the flame of Hestia, shines from her red hair, to the farm house's porch, and out onto the cornfield diamond she helped preserve: "On the porch, we turn to look at the silent, satiny green of the field. I press the switch, and, like a candle going out, the scar of light disappears. Above the farm, a moon bright as butter silvers the night as Annie holds the door open for me" (224).

The Goddesses at Home

Thus, the transformational baseball goddesses have stakes in their interactions with their loved ones. Rose, Consuelo, Carlota, Holly, Iris, and Annie represent the advantages of providing families with stable homes and are therefore catalysts in the transformation of men from players selfishly pursuing their dreams (or being consumed by the memory of them) into men who genuinely care for others. For Troy Maxson, while not an active ballplayer, his frustration at having been denied the right to play in the white major leagues generates his anger at the world. He seeks release from his troubles in a mistress and is thrown out of his house, but he learns responsibility and charity from Rose and remains financially committed to his family. For Dick Dixon, his escape to Mexico brings him closer to others and helps him heal from a disastrous first marriage and the solipsism of a series of unfulfilling affairs. In the Mark Harris series of novels, Henry Wiggen's baseball odyssey begins in his hometown and ends in his own home, where he learns from Holly to care for his family, who demand more energy and dedication than he ever saw in spring training through the playoffs. Roy Hobbs gains a family though he loses his career and records. Finally, Annie Kinsella saves her farm and shows Ray the necessity of a stable home life. Together the transformational baseball goddesses offer a profound picture of the impact of women in baseball literature, setting the stage for the next set of goddesses who focus on self-improvement rather than transforming others.

Six

The Compound Goddesses

As we have seen, the transformational goddesses set examples for players during their growth from self-centered individuals to compassionate adults. Typically, this process involves their evolution from single-minded athletes pursuing a game to family men. While the transformational goddesses focus on the development of those they love, they become limited in opportunities for individual growth apart from their families. Demeter, Hera, or Hestia women provide clear benefits to their families and spouses, but their own personal development becomes secondary to those around them. The transformational goddesses are forever connected to their men, who may be viewed as their "works-in-progress" and who typically are the focus of literary analysis. Here women are again subordinated to heroic men, characters made successful by the women who support them.

Because such women focus their activities on others, they often appear as dedicated admirers.[1] From the grandstands, they gaze lovingly at their ballplayers. According to George F. Will, this admiration is most often seen in early baseball films: "In olden days, most baseball movies went like this. Boy meets baseball and falls in love. Then boy meets girl and inexplicably (one grand passion should suffice) falls in love yet again. The girl's role is to sit in the bleachers beneath a broad-brimmed hat and look anxious in his adversity and adoring in his inevitable triumph over it" (*Bunts* 100). Such a one-dimensional approach to women characters limits their roles to elated fans or supportive spouses. Like the transformational goddesses, the women characters of these early films focus on others and are not capable of representing the increasingly complex interactions between women and sport. Apparently, Will fails to recognize the future of such complexities as well.

As women characters move from the grandstands to the dugouts in baseball fiction, their roles, fortunately, become more compelling. However, women who become ballplayers instead of baseball fans and spouses are still regarded as anomalies, a feature of both young adult and adult fiction. For example, in his short story "Baseball in April," Gary Soto describes the consequences of boys' losing interest in their little-league team: "Jesse played until the league ended. Fewer and fewer of the players came to practice and the team *began using girls to fill in the gaps* [on the baseball field]" (27; emphasis added). As women increasingly fill the gaps in baseball fiction, they are no longer merely substitutes for men players but become fully developed characters, following and playing the sport as well as pursuing other professional and personal interests.

Baseball's Compound Goddesses

Nancy Willard's *Things Invisible to See*, Silvia Tennenbaum's *Rachel, The Rabbi's Wife*, and Karen Joy Fowler's *The Sweetheart Season* feature narratives which focus primarily on the personal development of women characters. Such a focus allows for the characters, Willard's Clare Bishop, Tennenbaum's Rachel Sonnshein, and Fowler's Irini Doyle to possess qualities more multifaceted than the attributes attached to a single goddess. In fact, Clare, Rachel, and Irini possess the features of more than one goddess type, making them compound goddesses who are empowered by their multiple goddess traits as they struggle to achieve personal and professional successes. Baseball plays an integral role in their personal development, allowing them an unconventional outlet for their emotional, physical, and artistic expressions.

Clare's, Rachel's, and Irini's features are most closely associated with the qualities of two classical Greek goddesses, Aphrodite, goddess of love and beauty, and Artemis, goddess of the hunt and the moon. According to Bolen, Aphrodite and Artemis exhibit independence,

Six. The Compound Goddesses

working toward their own self-interests and individual achievements. Aphrodite most often pursues her own interests, artistically and sexually, as she inspires women to explore their fertility (238). Similarly, Artemis is the "personification of an independent feminine spirit. The archetype she represents enables a woman to seek her own goals on terrain of her own choosing" (49). The word "terrain" recalls the significance of the setting in which Rachel, Clare, and Irini appear: the baseball field.

Moreover, the sport of baseball allows an Artemis woman, who exhibits tremendous physicality in her role as goddess of the hunt, a setting to test her competitive skills. Artermis's athleticism and competitiveness provide her greatest gratification (Bolen 46). Her competitive drive is also fulfilled in her relationships with men, which Bolen describes as "brotherly" (61). Thus, Artemis women enjoy the company of men they perceive as equals, both intellectually and physically, so that they may enjoy interacting with them in competitive situations (61).

As compound goddesses, Clare, Rachel, and Irini are a combination of Artemis and Aphrodite. Clare, an artist and student, recovers the mobility she lost in a baseball accident when she learns to pitch. Also an artist, Rachel suffers from low self-esteem, an unhappy marriage, and a stagnated career as a painter. Sharing her love of baseball with her son allows her to develop confidence and to revive her desire to paint, both of which give her hope in repairing her relationship with her estranged husband. Irini explores her creativity through cooking and her athleticism through baseball, though she is not always successful at her endeavors. Through the competition and spirit of baseball, Clare, Rachel, and Irini enjoy and play the sport and envision futures for themselves as professional women pursuing careers.

As ball players and artists, these compound goddesses represent the serious acknowledgement of the multiple roles women can play in sports literature. No longer in the shadow of their husbands, boyfriends, or heroes, they fulfill their own interests before they support others. Like Aphrodite and Artemis, their strengths inform their characters as they live their own lives, which may include but not be eclipsed by romance.

Bolen defines these kinds of women as "heroines" because they are "actively deciding" their lives' paths, making their own choices instead of allowing others to do so for them (281). Achieving such authority over their own lives, Clare, Rachel, and Irini overcome individual adversities and make crucial decisions as compound goddesses. The combination of Aphrodite and Artemis qualities found in them represents both the independence and complexity of their characters and the joy the find in baseball.

Now Pitching, Clare Bishop

As a compound goddess with the qualities of Aphrodite and Artemis, Clare Bishop practices her artistic skills, falls in love, and uses the sport of baseball to recover her physical health. After a baseball hits her on the head, Clare becomes paralyzed, losing the use of her legs. She overcomes her paralysis by learning the game of baseball as a means of mobility while her love interest, Ben Harkissian, is serving in World War II. His absence marks the general lack of male presence, particularly fathers and father figures, from much of the novel. A war-time setting may account to some degree for the absence of men characters. However, Willard's attention to women characters, a departure from previous works of baseball literature, increases the number of absent fathers, seven total: Ben and twin brother Willie Harkissian's father died in a car accident (4); a local high school baseball coach and father figure, Durkee, gets drafted early in the story, cutting baseball season short (10), and he later dies in action in the Philippines (135); Wanda Harkissian's father left her family because he was already married to another woman (21); Ben's first girlfriend, Marsha, lives with a stepfather because his mother has remarried (24); Clare's young cousin, Davy, has no father because he divorced Davy's mother after a six-month marriage (29); Clare's maternal grandfather is sent to live with other relatives in Grosse Pointe, Michigan, so that the Bishop family can care for his wife instead (40); and Clare's father, Hal, is drafted into the service and leaves for California (121).[2] In the absence of these characters, Clare's independent Aphrodite and Artemis qualities empower her

Six. The Compound Goddesses

to acquire the nascent baseball skills she uses in a winner-takes-all game against Death.

As a first novel, Willard's work received numerous positive reviews, but it has yet to receive significant scholarly attention. Despite the oversight of baseball literature critics, Willard's novel is remarkable for its serious depiction of women playing baseball. Through their participation in sport, Willard's women characters do more than simply "fill the gaps" left by the young male baseball players sent to war because Clare's compound goddess abilities lead the team to come from behind and tie a ball game. Because they bring to the field of play their own athleticism and confidence, Clare and her fellow players offer readers a new vision of women who overcome great hardship and determination to play baseball.

Willard uses magical realism to explore the lives of two families, the Bishops and the Harkissians, allowing the characters to accept fantastic situations as everyday events. The families' activities center on Clare and Ben and on their contact with supernatural forces. These forces inhabit Ann Arbor, Michigan, and settings on the other side of the world immediately before the start of and during World War II. The entire novel uses baseball as a background for Clare's developing her compound goddess qualities, particularly the generative qualities of Aphrodite.

As a compound goddess, Clare has the ability to love and to create artistically. Her almost instant attraction to Ben identifies her as possessing the features of Aphrodite, who, according to Bolen, is extremely passionate (241). Clare's choice of Ben as her love interest is significant to her as an Aphrodite woman. As Ben goes to boot camp, his role as a soldier identifies him with Ares, Greek god of war. According to Bolen, such a match "represent[s] the union of the two most uncontrollable passions — love and war, which, when in perfect balance, could produce Harmony" (235).

Clare initially meets Ben when she is hospitalized with a concussion. In an episode reminiscent of Roy Hobbs's hitting a baseball into the face of Iris Lemon, a baseball hit Clare in the head.[3] She, however, could not have possibly seen it coming because Ben hit the ball into the darkness while she walking in a neighboring park. The rest, as they say, is history when the guilt-stricken Ben decides to visit her. Although Ben does not confess his role in the accident, a lively romance ensures between them while she is still in the hospital. Once the war begins, Ben and most of his old ball team, the South Avenue Rovers, enlist, and Clare begins her physical therapy at home. She and Ben continue their love affair by correspondence while she starts pitching lessons with Ben's friend, Sol Lieberman, who believes baseball will help Clare regain her strength.

Before she begins her baseball life, Clare's character within the story is unformed. She is invisible. When Ben tries to find her in his school yearbook, he notices that "under the junior class picture for '41, her name was listed among the missing. She was also missing from the sophomore class picture in '40" (24). Although he finds her in the 1939 class picture, she "had her eyes closed at the wrong moment" (24). Foreshadowing Ben's MIA status in the war, Clare cannot yet see or be seen. Clare lacks this power because she has not yet encountered baseball until someone literally hits her on the head with one. This baseball is really aimed "with ... heavenly precision" (Kakutani 13).

Apart from her romance with Ben, Clare's Aphrodite traits are expressed through her creativity, specifically her ability to paint. In fact, Clare decides to study art at the University of Michigan when she recovers (62). Clare's artwork appears throughout the Bishop home: an angel, whose "body followed the contours of a large crack," on her grandmother's wall (42); "a riot of angels" inside a teacup (67), a pitcher, wooden bowl, and the kitchen cupboards (85); "a good portrait of [her aunt] Nell" (134); and a "little book of pictures" for her young cousin that she creates during her recovery (165). As an Aphrodite woman, Clare's interaction with her creations almost becomes another love relationship (Bolen 241). She continues her passion for painting throughout the novel, displaying her creativity apart from Ben.

Combined with her Aphrodite attributes, Clare possesses the qualities of Artemis, which demand physical activity and provide her with the impetus to throw a baseball even though she is paralyzed. Such

Six. The Compound Goddesses

activity improves her health and prepares her for her later role as a pitcher. Through baseball and her Artemis qualities, Clare evolves from a missing person, among "the invisible nation of the handicapped" (35), to the center of attention, the pitcher, in the South Avenue Rovers' game against Death. The game is the result of Ben's bargaining with Death after a storm washes away the remote Pacific Island on which he is stationed. After he floats in a life raft for several days, Death visits Ben to claim his life, but he doesn't want to die. Death bets him that his team (the Dead Knights) will beat Ben's team.[4] The stakes of the game are high — the lives of Ben and his teammates.

Death then arranges for Ben and his team to receive simultaneous furloughs from their various posts so that they may resume playing together. On game day, Ben's jealous twin Willie sabotages the team bus and causes the hospitalization of Ben's team. As the comatose Ben lies in a hospital bed, Clare must take his place as pitcher because she is listed as next-of-kin in the rules Death established for the game. In true nail-biting "big game" fashion, Clare regains her ability to walk just in time to join the female relatives of the injured soldiers as their leader and pitcher. Her teammates give her support on the mound, and Ben also miraculously recovers and returns from the hospital by the final inning of a three-inning game. They round the bases, but their story ends before they reach home plate, leaving us to assume that the women ballplayers and Ben have at least tied Death and that they could still win in extra innings.

Clare's movement from invisibility to visibility, from the wheelchair to the pitching mound, is reinforced by the novel's title, *Things Invisible to See*, originally a line from John Donne's 1633 poem "Song." The line "Things invisible to see" appears near the middle of the second stanza, the center of the poem. This stanza is concerned with human relationships, continuing a theme of overcoming impossibilities as developed earlier in the poem. The greatest impossibility, according to the speaker of the poem, is a faithful woman:

> If thou be'st born to strange sights,
> Things invisible to see,
> Ride ten thousand days and nights,
> Till age snow white hairs on thee,

> Thou, when thou retun'st, wilt tell me
> All strange wonders that befell thee,
> And swear
> Nowhere
> Lives a woman true, and fair.

The speaker easily finds the "Things invisible to see," things as miraculous as the occurrences in Willard's novel, but must search diligently for the faithful woman. Like the faithful woman, Clare lacks visibility early in the novel. However, as she practices her compound goddess traits, her visibility increases, especially on the baseball field.

Edmund Fuller's review of Willard's novel identifies her use of Donne's line as her title. To Fuller, the line has the significance of "suggesting infinite possibilities of vision" found in Willard's work (28). Further, Diane Cole writes that *Things Invisible to See* is "about different kinds of vision — psychic vision, poetic vision, some inner vision which allows us to look into another person's soul" (15). Clare also achieves an inner vision as she learns to look inside herself for the strength to save herself, Ben, her friends, and his team from Death.

Willard realizes all of these visions through the sport of baseball and in Clare's playing it. Wendy Lesser calls *Things Invisible to See* "a baseball story [which] rises to the level of myth" (470). Lesser's assessment that baseball can be myth emphasizes the presence of mythological qualities in Willard's characters. Myth and baseball infuse Willard's work, giving it "magic power" and "original vision" (Messenger, *Contemporary* 381).

Part of the powerful imagery Willard employs revolves around the motif of God's throwing a baseball. The pitching motif appears throughout the novel as a variation of the following passage: "He [God] tosses a white ball which breaks into a yellow ball which breaks into a red ball ..." (3). Just as God's role as a pitcher emphasis the power associated with the position in baseball, Clare's pitching emphasizes her goddess traits. Many examinations of the novel overlook Clare by focusing on the activities of the men characters, mainly the twins Ben and Willie and the character Death.

Deeanne Westbrook and a reviewer from the *English Journal* both

Six. The Compound Goddesses

greatly minimize the role of Clare in the novel. Westbrook points to Ben's winning home run as evidence that "whatever victory is achieved is won by the male protagonist, a man with two good legs and a bat" (75). She does not recount the scene prior to the homerun in which Clare and her goddess-like companion, the Ancestress, visit Ben's comatose spirit. There, with the help of her personal goddess, Clare heals him, allowing him to recover for the game (Willard 251). More significant than this oversight is the *English Journal* reviewer's outright mistake in writing that the men play a game of baseball against Death, but, in fact, they do not. The reviewer wrongly asserts, "What may be the most bizarre baseball story ever ends when Ben and his friends must field a team against the forces of Death, a team lead by such greats from the past as Lou Gehrig and Iron Man McGinnity" (86). Ben and his friends do not play against the dead baseball greats; the women characters do. Led by Clare's pitching, the women's team holds their opposition to just three runs in three innings, giving Ben time to arrive at the field and tie the game. Without Clare, the team would not have succeeded, and Ben would not have recovered in time to play. Ben's homerun is just the frosting on the cake that Clare so diligently baked to perfection.

Clare's part in their mutual success receives little to no attention in criticism of Willard's work. When Clare is mentioned, she is most often connected with the Ancestress, "her part-time guardian angel" (Eder 1). Thus, Clare is noted for her association with a goddess-type figure, but not for her ability to pitch or her love of baseball. Clare heals partly through the Ancestress but mostly through baseball, her Artemis qualities responding to its athleticism and her Aphrodite qualities acknowledged in her fondness for art and Ben. She becomes empowered as she progresses from the comfort of the Ancestress's company to the isolation of the pitcher's mound, where she ultimately controls a game of baseball.

Clare's recovery may also reflect the changes that occurred as the United States entered the war and women struggled to define their roles in it. When Clare is first confined to her bed, the U.S. was not yet at war, powerless to help its allies against Nazi invasions. Clare's immobility also represents the domesticity women were then forced to pursue in their exclusion from active military service. By the second half of the novel, several switches occur. The U.S. enters the war, and Clare's injury begins to heal with the help of Sol Lieberman and his pitching lessons. He sets up a mock baseball field in an orchard and places Clare in her recliner on the pitcher's mound.

The orchard recalls the green space of the baseball field, the *hortus conclusus* of Rose Maxson's garden in *Fences*, the many gardens of *The Rio Loja Ringmaster*, the corn field of *Shoeless Joe*, and Eden with its apple tree. Westbrook argues that by "evoking this ancient signifier [the garden] ... of sacred time and space, baseball itself is laden with significance; a myth in game form, baseball both interprets and demands to be interpreted" (99–100). In such outdoor terrain, mythical in quality, Clare as an Artemis woman begins to recover a limited mobility, discovering the empowerment that will later allow her to battle Death.

Clare's interest in baseball, unlike her literary forebears, is not a ploy to win the love of Ben. She already knows that Ben loves her; the romance bloomed off the diamond while Clare was immobile and he was on military assignment. Clare's motivation to recover her health is not what the nurse Ginny described during Clare's hospitalization: "to walk down the aisle" (58). In fact, when Clare and Ben first meet, Ben says to her, "You should get married.... A pretty girl like you" (62). Clare responds, "It takes five minutes to get married.... And then what? You can't just be married" (62). Through her comments to Ben, Clare displays courage and independence. She is no longer the invisible child who was passively struck by a baseball.

As Clare gains strength and visibility, the Ancestress no longer speaks to her, except when refusing to help her during the game (258). The pitching arm of Clare replaces the pitching arm of God in achieving success against Death and his teammates. Through the victory of the women's version of the South Avenue Rovers, Clare, as an Aphrodite and Artemis woman, achieves empowerment. Her love of Ben and her athleticism are fully expressed in one baseball game. Her pitches, full of the "stuff of being alive" (258), are impossible for even the legendary heroes of baseball's past to hit.

Six. The Compound Goddesses

The novel ends with Clare and Ben running around the bases toward home. The final line describes the characters as they approach home plate: "Clare starts running and Ben runs after her as they round the bases, past the living and the dead, heading at top speed for home" (263). The movement toward home, "baseball's finest diamond rhythm" (Messenger, *Contemporary* 382), also recalls the game that ends Herrin's *The Rio Loja Ringmaster*, with all the characters wildly careening around the infield. Like Willard's characters, the characters in Herrin's work are rounding the bases toward home as the novel ends. For both Willard and Herrin, the cyclical nature of life is realized in players' movements around a baseball diamond. Because life does not end for the characters after the end of the game, the narratives do not stop with a player crossing home plate. We are left to imagine them doing so and then continuing their lives.

Clare, as a compound goddess, will blossom as an artist and a love interest for Ben. Baseball will continue to generate great personal happiness for her. Once she has experienced the fulfillment as an Artemis and Aphrodite woman, Clare then extends her care and concern to others, particularly in becoming the winning pitcher of a baseball team. Empowered by the recovery of her mobility and her concern for Ben, Clare discovers her love for baseball and life.

Rachel Sonnshein, Athlete and Artist

Like Clare Bishop, Rachel Sonnshein of Silvia Tennenbaum's *Rachel, The Rabbi's Wife* passionately pursues baseball and art. A first novel that received many positive reviews but little scholarly attention, Tennenbaum's work chronicles Rachel's marital struggles in Gateshead, Long Island, during the late 1970s. Although the novel is textually rich and significant in women's sport literature, its plot is relatively unknown. Only Eric Solomon's article "'The Bullpen of her Mind': Women's Baseball Fiction and Silvia Tennenbaum's *Rachel, The Rabbi's Wife*" gives it a scholarly review. The following plot summary should give those who are not yet familiar with the novel a better understanding of Tennenbaum's achievement.

Rachel (a rabbetzin, the title of a rabbi's wife) and her husband, Seymour (a rabbi), live in a hostile environment because their conservative Jewish community disagrees with their 1960s liberal idealism. Rachel also suffers low self-esteem because of her husband's infidelity; however, she finds comfort in her art and in her son, Aaron, who shares her appreciation of baseball. He and Rachel have a close relationship and a mutual admiration for the New York Mets baseball team. Their temple (Shaare Tefilah) slowly rejects the Sonnshein's leadership as rabbetzin and rabbi, due in part to Rachel's nonconformist appearance. While she behaves appropriately, her artistic temperament and flowing, African robes do not meet the community's usual expectations of a Jewish middle-class wife and mother. Protecting herself from the community's rejection and her husband's extramarital involvements, she becomes immersed in her art.

Almost as significant to her as her art, Rachel loves baseball and shares her fondness of the sport with her teenage son Aaron. During the particularly stressful time following the temple elections, Rachel attends a Mets game with Aaron and visits New York City with her best friend, Sally, to view Modern Art exhibits. At Shea Stadium, Rachel and Aaron relish a game between the Pirates and the Mets, where she proclaims to him that baseball is a metaphor for her life. Mother and son enjoy each other's company; however, Seymour is outsider to their baseball-game bonding and to Rachel's enjoyment of the art exhibits.

After Rachel returns from New York, Seymour rents a beach-house for their summer vacation. At the seashore, Rachel dedicates herself to completing a series of family portraits begun at her mother's house during the Passover holidays. As Rachel's devotion to her art increases, Seymour's isolation grows. Because of his emotional distance from her and the lack of studio space in her home, Rachel decides to rent a room in town for a studio so that she can complete the family paintings.

Rachel's downtown studio becomes a refuge for her from the temple's congregation and Seymour's dejection. When she receives an offer to hold a show at a local university, she paints daily at her studio as an escape from Seymour's anxieties about his reelection, which he loses by a close margin. Seymour next accepts a position with a charitable

Six. The Compound Goddesses

organization in New York City, so the Sonnsheins leave Gateshead. As a result of their individual suffering and self-discoveries, the Sonnsheins remain married and live according to the idealism of their youth rather than the restrictive conservatism of the Gateshead temple.

Throughout the narrative's turmoil, Rachel clearly possesses the qualities of Aphrodite and Artemis, especially in her love of both her son and baseball. According to Bolen, an Aphrodite woman feels a significant bond with children, making them feel confident in themselves (252). While the conservative Gateshead temple expects its families to pass traditions from generation to generation through formal study of the Jewish language and by practicing the tenets of the Torah, Rachel and Aaron develop a special bond not found in orthodox religion. Rachel feels a particularly close attachment to her child though baseball.

The closeness of their relationship is most fully expressed when they attend baseball games together. Rachel easily identifies with the Aaron's appreciation of the sport because she played baseball when she was a girl. These were some of her childhood's most happy times, and she wants to share her love of the game with her son. Rachel communicates her affection for both Aaron and baseball at Shea Stadium. Their experience there reveals that the Jewish religion does not contain the Sonnsheins' generational identity. Instead, their love for baseball and each other is expressed over the course of the game.

Traditionally, the Torah is the entire Jewish experience for its followers, "the source of all knowledge, the word of God, ... the foundations of Jewish law, ethics, legend, ritual, theology, art, song ... the heart and soul of the Jewish people, the expression of divine will" (Frankel and Teutsch 178). Rachel and Aaron abandon the Torah; she refuses to attend temple services, and he never even sets foot in the temple during the novel. Together they identify with the baseball game, an identity that is not bound by Jewish tradition. By rejecting the traditional role of Jewish mother, Rachel "frees herself from a patriarchal Jewish rabbinical social situation in which she is an extension of her husband, ... forced by religion to stay in her place as a servant to the men who study the Torah" (Solomon 19). Instead, Rachel and Aaron empathize with one another without the help of established Jewish law, and she enriches their experience with her love of sport that began when she was very young.

Rachel's first memories in the novel are of the baseball she played as a girl. The scenes remind us that she was a ballplayer before she was a rabbetzin. Mistakenly identified as "an informed spectator" (Messenger, *Contemporary* 377), Rachel is more than a knowledgeable observer because her memories of playing baseball are defining moments in her physical and emotional development. Seen through a half-dream about a sandlot game with the neighborhood boys, Rachel's devotion to the sport and her insider status become apparent. Her memories of playing the game reveal her athleticism, a quality she possesses as an Artemis woman. Through the game she discovers her growing body and first observes the bodies of men.

Rachel's half-dream occurs in winter, representing her longing for youth and springtime and anticipating the renewal of the coming baseball season. Within the warmth of her bed, Rachel remembers a pleasanter time: "The pale gray light of a January morning contrasted sharply with the bright yellow ball field of Rachel's memory. A ray of terror entered her morning confusion. Rachel was tempted to cry out but forced her mind back to the image of herself at the plate, in full control, under a hot summer sun" (2). Although she can fully escape neither the cold of winter nor the worries of her adult life, she indulges in the memory of a girlhood baseball game because it provides an image of independence appealing to both her Aphrodite and Artemis sensibilities. Her connection to sport and the artistic overtones of her mental picture portray her as a compound goddess.

Another aspect of the half-dream that recalls her goddess nature is found in Rachel's growing awareness of her own body. Aphrodite women desire the attention of men (Bolen 256), and the young Rachel's teammates are all boys. This is her first adolescent contact with members of the opposite sex, an event she sees very clearly: "She rounded first, thinking she could stretch the hit into a double, but Jack Carroll, the red-headed second baseman, tagged her out. His worn soft glove touched her breast. Rachel remembered it exactly, even to the

Six. The Compound Goddesses

way the pleasure of that touch had plummeted to her crotch" (2). The half-dream shows that on the baseball field young Rachel verges on becoming a woman. Because she associates the game with awakening sexuality, she ties baseball to both her artistic and sexual awareness, both present in Aphrodite women.

The qualities of Artemis also surface in Rachel's half-dream as she recalls the athleticism of competition. Her competitive spirit is nurtured on the field as she plays against boys. Her attempt to stretch a single into a double indicates a strong desire to surpass her rivals. Despite being thrown out at second, Rachel's intensity as an athlete marks her as an Artemis woman, who has a tremendous ability to set goals and achieve them (Bolen 50).

Although the adult Rachel no longer plays baseball on a daily basis, she participates in the sport by eagerly anticipating spring training. Rather than observing the Jewish religious calendar, Rachel sees winter as one step closer to a new baseball schedule. She first looks for spring training news in the sports pages of the local paper, but the intensity of her anticipation is better revealed in a conversation with a friend, Truscott Boothby. He asks her how she is feeling, and she responds, "I'm waiting for spring training" (38), the start of which will undoubtedly improve her outlook on life.

Rachel enjoys Truscott's company as she once enjoyed playing baseball with boys. She and Truscott talk baseball, contrasting the current Mets with the teams of Rachel's youth. These kinds of conversations almost always find the participants indulging in sentimentality about past teams, but Rachel also finds herself reminiscing about the sensuality of the game: "She loved the game passionately, albeit in her own quixotic way, tied to summer and long childhood days under its sun. She had learned to know her body playing ball, to feel it acquire the only grace it possessed until she discovered the grace of copulation" (14). Despite their mutual attraction, fueled by baseball memories, Rachel declines Truscott's many passes. Their relationship reflects the brotherly affection that Artemis women find appealing in men (Bolen 61). Although they remain friends, her time with Truscott foreshadows her separation from Seymour.

Rachel also distances herself from her husband by expanding her relationship with her son, most clearly represented in their attendance at a Mets game. As her son, Aaron senses Rachel's connection to baseball better than the overwrought Seymour does. To Seymour, baseball is just a game, a distraction from his duties at the temple, but to Rachel baseball is a life-sustaining metaphor. Rachel's artistic temperament responds to the game's aesthetic qualities. Solomon notes that artists, particularly writers, find baseball appealing: "Baseball is America's shared history, our own youthful games, our country's rural past, and — especially for the quintessential urban Jewish writer — a green oasis in an asphalt city desert" (50). With the same artistic appreciation, Rachel synthesizes her view of the game into a work of art: "Rachel looked up and out beyond center field and saw Queens delicately drawn in the haze of the spring bleachers. From this distance the seats looked flat, like an element in a collage" (25). Because collage is one of Rachel's chosen media, she visualizes her surroundings as she would a work of art. As an Aphrodite woman, Rachel wants to share this creative experience with her son, who, as an adult, can love his mother both as a woman and as an artist.[5] Rachel and Aaron sense their physical and emotional connection to the sport as they communicate not as mother to child but as adult to adult.

At the game, the intimacy of their relationship appears as they sit close to one another and discuss each other's love life. In fact, Rachel hugs Aaron as they arrive at the stadium (145), and later in the game, "she leaned over to kiss him on his down-soft cheek. He did not shy away but instead put his arm around her shoulder and kissed her back" (153–54). Rachel notices he is comfortable kissing women, and she wonders if he has a girlfriend. Once they have discussed this personal topic, he, in turn, asks her about her relationship with his father. In a startlingly honest exchange, Aaron asks, "Do you think Dad's got a girlfriend?" (155). Rachel says that he probably does and reassures Aaron that he has not caused the situation. She tells her son that his father has had girlfriends before, but Seymour loves him. After Rachel unselfishly reaffirms Seymour's love for Aaron, the Mets take the lead in the bottom of the ninth inning to win the game. The Mets' victory reveals the

Six. The Compound Goddesses

hope Aaron senses in his father's love, and Rachel offers him that support unconditionally.

During the course of the novel, Rachel experiences her own sense of hope: she conceives the idea that baseball is a metaphor for the adult life that is unraveling around her. This epiphany occurs during the game she sees with Aaron: "it [baseball] had also become a metaphor in which the events of her life fitted and were recalled without threat" (149). If these events fit into the metaphor of baseball, then Rachel's life can only be understood in terms of the sport. For example, Rachel does not enjoy the company of large groups at temple functions; she would rather have the intimacy of baseball conversations with Truscott and Aaron. Rachel's commitment to the game is greater than her commitment to her religion. This situation does not reflect poorly upon her; rather, it reveals that for Rachel the congregation of her temple does not possess the same genuineness that a game of baseball does.

Rachel's rejection of those around her, the members of the temple and the behavior of her adulterous husband, for her honest appreciation of sport causes many critics to find her self-serving and self-absorbed: "The trouble with Silvia Tennenbaum is that even those of us who struggle toward freedom though art and despise the hypocrisy of bourgeois establishments cannot sympathize with Rachel's selfishness ... as a spoiled creature who loves being loved but loves no one better than herself" (Dworkin 37). The argument against Rachel is that she is too content with herself to understand the difficulties her husband faces as a rabbi. Such an analysis touches the surface of Rachel's character but disregards her honesty in her relationship with her husband and his beliefs. She rejects them because they and their hurtful behaviors are not genuine to her, not as real as a baseball game or as a work of art, and thus not worthy of her attention.

Critics are more sympathetic to Rachel when they focus on her interest in baseball rather than on her rejection of religion. So strong is Rachel's fascination with the sport that she has been connected to Alexander Portnoy, of Philip Roth's *Portnoy's Complaint* (1969). Tennenbaum and Roth are both Jewish intellectuals whose characters have an interest in baseball, but their childhood visions of themselves are not merely "camouflage or assimilation" (Ableman 22). More perceptively, Cordelia Candelaria describes Portnoy's "observations and recollections of boyhood baseball as a model of clarity and possibility" currently lacking in his adult life (59). Like Portnoy, Rachel's memories of baseball comfort her in the adult crises she faces. She is also an assimilated American Jew, and that identity is crucial to her struggles. As a result, she adapts the game to her own artistry and athleticism, making it a significant aspect of her Aphrodite and Artemis qualities.

Rachel feels less comfortable, however, when she attempts to play the game as a grown woman, perhaps accounting for some critics' overlooking her attachment to the game. Before the beginning of the summer, she stumbles upon a pick-up game played by some neighborhood boys. She "could not resist" coming close to the game (112). As Rachel watches, one of the outfielders throws a ball that gets past the catcher, and she retrieves it. She "bent casually (as though she were not a fortyish woman, carrying a pocket-book and wearing a well-cut flannel pant suit) and picked up the ball.... Rachel cocked her arm and threw to the pitcher" (112). As an Artemis woman, she believes this one motion will separate her in the minds of the players from non-athletic older women. Instead, they simply thank her, and the ball game resumes. Rachel feels that they did not recognize her natural talent. She thinks, "Didn't he see how good she was? Didn't he notice she didn't throw like a girl?" (112). Rachel, like the boys, fails to recognize that throwing like a girl is fine, especially if you are a girl. She takes solace from the ballplayers' failure to notice her by going home and discussing the Mets with Aaron.

Rachel brings to her son a history of appreciation for the sport which extends back into previous generations. In relating her own love of baseball, Doris Kearns Goodwin describes this shared history as "an invisible bond" between her sons and the grandfather they never met (28). Rachel's "bond" with Aaron exists through her telling him stories of the games she saw in her youth. Central to her baseball stories are her relationships with others, which Eric Solomon recognizes as the personal story of a woman analyzing and synthesizing her life:

Six. The Compound Goddesses

> Her expressed need, as in many feminist novels, is to become a person — once again.... It is fascinating to see how this baseball motif recurs in the novel, as image, as parallel, and, ultimately, in a wonderful day at the ball park, as a structural symbol for Rachel's breaking away to freedom, reinforcing mutual love with her son, and regaining individual identity. ("Bullpen" 23)

Communicating her most important ideas in the context of baseball, Rachel weaves Aaron a personal history when she describes Met player, Willie Stargell: "Reminds me of Johnny Mize.... Used to scare the shit out of me. I saw him once at Ebbets Field" (148). Rachel's mind shifts gently from one memory to the other, rejoicing in the relief that their presence provides. In this way, "the activity in the bullpen of her [Rachel's] mind was ... sporadic" (148), with details that await her like the relief pitchers in a bullpen — always available and fresh to continue working when she exhausts her current memory.

With the strength of her baseball memories and inspiration of her son, Rachel rejects the patriarchal Jewish role of rabbetzin embedded in Torah law and stagnated in a hypocritical congregation for a complex role as a compound goddess. Her creativity and athletic skill allow her to pursue her own interests as an artist and sports fan despite her husband's belief that women should not follow baseball. Exercising her Aphrodite/Artemis traits, Rachel, like Clare Bishop, becomes a multifaceted character who pursues her own interests apart from romance.

A Compound Goddess for the Future

The existence of self-determined compound goddesses like Clare and Rachel begs the question, what is next for the women characters of baseball literature? Irini Doyle of Fowler's *The Sweetheart Season* gives us a glimpse into the future because while she is basically a compound goddess and her story is set in the 1947, the richness of her characterization adds twists to the creativity of Aphrodite and the independence of Artemis. Not a traditional artist, Irini's medium is food, and her lackluster cooking skills often limit her to mixing ingredients for bread. This activity gives rise to the muscles in her throwing arm more often than acceptable dough. As the only child of an alcoholic father, she is forced into a sorrowful independence, mourning the loss of her mother who died giving birth to her. Because she does not exactly fit the mold presented by the compound goddesses Clare and Rachel, Irini's unique story presents a departure from them, perhaps revealing the next step of women in baseball literature.

Purposefully set in Jackie Robinson's 1947 in a small town in the upper Midwest, *The Sweetheart Season* features ballplayer Irini Doyle's adult daughter as narrator. The daughter recounts a year in her mother's life, a time before she had children and was young, single, and still living in her father's house. Her hometown was struggling to overcome its divisive past and forge a future for its single women seeking husbands following the loss of so many young men in World War II. Baseball at first appears to be the answer for Magrit's marriage woes as the town's biggest business, a breakfast cereal company named Margaret Mill, establishes a team of cooks from its Scientific Kitchen to advertise the company while playing against local teams. The women ballplayers hope to meet eligible bachelors on their travels, but only the team's chaperone succeeds in meeting a future spouse during a game. As a gifted player and motherless young woman, Irini discovers that she enjoys the game for its own sake. Her "involvement in baseball, although seemingly intended to bring about stable, heterosexual marriage, really allows them [the ballplayers] to explore their sexuality and innovative models for domestic life" (Collins 282). Irini discovers baseball is a comforting presence and challenging break from her struggles in the kitchen, where her attempts to place loaves of cheese bread in "motherly ovens" fail (205).

Irini learns baseball from her father, who teaches her valuable life lessons in addition to how to catch a pop-up: "The word 'pop-ups' was the key. If he had nothing awkward to discuss he'd say, 'Let's play catch'" (52). Their version of the father-son game of catch becomes a father-daughter pop-up practice, allowing him to talk about the birds and the bees in setting that is comfortable for him. These types of practice sessions and talks greatly benefit Irini's game: "It taught me great powers of concentration.... I was pretty resistant to the facts of life, but I did learn to keep my eye on the ball no matter what" (55).

Six. The Compound Goddesses

Irini becomes center fielder for the Sweetwheat Sweethearts with the arm she develops from her father's help and from mixing endless batches of bread. In center field she finds a place where she is comfortable. Her long-time friend, neighbor, and love interest Walter Collins becomes the team's coach, but she doesn't play to impress him. In fact, she spends most of the novel trying to figure out what he is thinking. When she can't, she takes solace in baseball. Irini's narrator daughter describes her game: "My mother could make the throw all the way to home. She was the only outfielder who could do this. Walter called her his grenade launcher" (110). The team becomes a family to Irini, one which the town previously failed to provide. Although Walter offers her friendship and coaching, she does not have a consistent substitute mother:

> And you might think, what with her father's drinking and her heathenism and her dinners of soda crackers and jam, that one of the other women in town would have stepped forward as a sort of mother substitute.... Probably more than one of the Magrit mothers would have liked to take her in hand, packed nutritious school lunches, hem her skirts at a proper length, so they touched the ground when she kneeled, teach her to pray. But Irini was not an easy, affectionate, or grateful sort of child. Instead, she was good at fending people off. (196)

Irini's unruly nature sets her apart from the kindness of Clare and the sensitivity of Rachel. She wears emotional armor because she feels that the people around her are judging her situation and her father. The armor dissolves when she faces the loss of baseball.

After a fairly dismal season that features losses to young boys and a terrible bus accident reminiscent of *Things Invisible To See*, the Sweetwheat Sweethearts face the end of summer. With the fall fast approaching and their chaperone now engaged and therefore off the team, Irini realizes that they have probably played their last game together. This realization has a great affect on Irini, one that she does not anticipate: "She retired to her bedroom, where she progressed from tears to great gulping sobs, crying in a way she hadn't cried since she was twelve. And it was all for baseball" (325). Her father senses her loss and tries to comfort her with a round of pop-ups, signifying that he has something significant to tell her. The loss of her baseball family will be mitigated by her father's announcement that he plans to wed, starting a new family for her.

Irini's father asks for her permission to remarry, a sign that perhaps he is beginning to recover from the alcoholic stupor that has consumed him since her mother died. In addition, he graciously offers to pay for her college education by selling their home and moving in with his new bride. It is a ticket out of small town life for Irini, an opportunity to become educated and begin a career. While she is initially stunned by his proposal, she soon warms to the idea of leaving Magrit and Walter behind, whose inconsistent attentions leave her undecided about whether to pursue him.

Surrounding Irini as well as the entire town of Magrit is the goddess-like figure of Maggie Collins, the fictional matriarch of the mill. As an apparition who surfaces at key moments in the text, Maggie has a firm hold on the Mill's owner, who is also Walter's father, Henry Collins. So strong is Henry's attachment to Maggie that he requires his employees put money in a blue pig anytime they make allusions to her fictional nature. Maggie ultimately becomes a metaphor for the way in which the people in Magrit choose to live their lives. She is at first spotted by Irini's neighbor Sissy Tarken, who claims that Maggie was wearing an apron and holding a knife near the waterfall outside of town. Although Sissy later recants the story, Irini finds Maggie's message to Sissy interesting: "She [Maggie] told me I would spend the rest of my life cooking and cleaning for some man.... She made it sound like something bad!" (249). Sissy, who often frets that no one will marry her, projects her deepest fears about becoming a wife on Maggie.

Tradition in the town dictates that an appearance by Maggie means the lucky girl who sees her will soon become engaged. While Sissy is delighted with this possibility, it takes another appearance by Maggie to reflect Irini's fears. Irini goes to the falls because she is worried that Walter is helping his aging father make a foolish swim across the river, another town tradition. As she rushes to them, she must pass behind the falls, where she sees Maggie:

Six. The Compound Goddesses

> There, hovering inside the water, she could just make out the liquid figure of a woman. She wore an apron tied in the back with a bow, like Maggie, but otherwise naked. Her breasts, behind the striped bib, were large and maternal. She gazed upward, her arms curved out beyond her breasts, the way you could catch a large ball, the way you would hold a small child. She wavered in the water, all motherly anticipation. (319)

Maggie's maternal presence soothes Irini, letting her know that her concern for Walter and his father makes her a good person, potentially a good mother. Just as baseball provides a source of comfort for Irini, so does the apparition of Maggie. The two, baseball and Maggie, could be conflated into what Vanalyne Green calls "Mother Baseball." Green writes, "No one mentions the obvious structural relationship between a baseball stadium and a womb: in design, a stadium is both a circle and a 'Y,' two notorious female symbols" (224). Irini, with the help of her "Mother Baseball," Maggie Collins, finds the men safe at the river. Through her vision, Irini soon understands that though she does not have a mother, not even a substitute mother, she will find the strength within herself to care for a family just as she so profoundly cares for her sport, Walter, and his father.

In the "Afterword" to the novel, Irini's daughter concludes, "My mother believed in baseball" (350). Irini's life lessons to her daughter are framed in tales of Jackie Robinson and the exclusion of black women from professional baseball: "The All American Girls' Baseball League has said it was because there was no black woman good enough. My mother never believed that. When she told me the story of Cassiopeia, the queen so beautiful she made the goddesses jealous, my mother made sure I knew she was from Africa" (350). Perhaps the greatest lesson Irini's daughter learns is that "we all get the goddesses we deserve" (352). While Sissy's goddess carried a knife and Irini's made her feel a mother's unconditional love, the more recent incarnations of Maggie reflect disturbing trends in home and family.

After Irini leaves town, Magrit witnesses Maggie with "the eight arms of Kali," grief stricken because Henry Collins, the only person who believed in her and defended her, abandoned her along with his company's ideals when he retired. Maggie then becomes a goddess that reveals the troubles surrounding society as well as individuals: "She ushered in the fifties as the fifty-foot woman, the unfortunate product of gamma rays and the bite of an irradiated ant. In the sixties she dressed as a guerrilla and carried a flamethrower. No one saw her at all in the eighties, but she struck with the precision and training of a ninja" (352). In the twenty-first century, Maggie perhaps goes fully undercover and remains there as we wait for the next terrorist attacks.

The Sweetheart Season includes "A Conversation with Karen Joy Fowler" at the end of the book. When asked what the narrator means by "We all get the goddesses we deserve," Fowler replied, "The World War II generation was hearty and sensible and hard-working so they get a hearty, sensible, hard-working goddess. But if my own generation chooses instead to emphasize victimization and entitlement and self-pity, then we can expect to see a different aspect. We'll find our goddess checked into the Betty Ford clinic." Fowler reminds us not to abandon ourselves, our own personal goddesses. While we may never have a war to believe in, we could trust in the innate goodness of our country and the people around us.

Fowler concludes *The Sweetheart Season* with Irini's daughter giving us a final warning about Maggie as a goddess:

> She is the mother of us all, the mother of birth and death, queen of the circle, with the circle just coming round again. But she is a bit disappointed in us; we are not the people are parents were. It doesn't mean she doesn't love us. She is preheating her ovens, sharpening her knives. She is waiting, waiting, waiting, waiting, and this woman is a professional, she knows *exactly* how to prepare you. (352)

As a goddess and a "Mother Baseball," Maggie evolves with her times and reminds us to look inward for strength when comfort is needed. Irini found that strength in baseball, allowing her to leave Magrit and attend college. She later meets Walter again, and they decide to marry. The baseball field allowed their relationship to grow, but the ballpark and their relationship were not the center of the story. Irini and her

Six. The Compound Goddesses

goddess show us the future of women's baseball literature, one we should greatly anticipate.

Home Once Again

Clare, Rachel, and Irini share the qualities of compound baseball goddesses. They exhibit independence in character development, separate from their love interests. These women shift the focus of baseball novels away from the shallow characterizations of women who pursue baseball players romantically to deeper expressions of emotional and intellectual appreciation of sport for its own merits. The compound goddesses allow for the representation of women who care passionately about themselves and others while they pursue their own personal development.

Clare, Rachel, and Irini receive assistance in balancing these competing interests, care of one's self and care for others, through the attributes of Aphrodite and Artemis. The qualities the compound goddesses exemplify — independence, artistry, compassion, and strength — allow them to be artists as well as athletes. They are no longer defined by the mates they have chosen; rather, they have defined themselves within the context of their interest in baseball.

As women characters who develop a love of baseball apart from their relationships with men, Clare, Rachel, and Irini are exciting anomalies in a literature dominated by male protagonists. The compound goddesses represent women's fledgling inclusion in generally male pursuits: the sport of baseball, its literature, and its criticism. The triumph of such participation proves that "baseball is ... radically open in temporal and spatial possibilities that hurl it beyond the inner diamond" (Messenger, *Contemporary* 386). As more and more women characters appear in the "inner diamond" of baseball literature, Clare, Rachel, and Irini remain significant for their groundbreaking roles.

As women characters in a traditionally male-dominated sport, they overcome difficulties when they use their own gifts in competition, rather than try to play baseball like men do (Messenger, *Contemporary* 191). The struggles of such characters also affect society's perceptions of real women (190). The relationship between women and power surfaces in other real-world arenas, such as politics, the workplace, and higher education. To address these power plays, Naomi R. Goldenberg calls for a "feminist theory of sport because the exclusion of women from male groups occupied with using sticks to chase balls ... parallels the exclusion from male groups doing more serious stuff elsewhere in culture" (275). Goldenberg, despite her admirable call for a "feminist theory of sport," fails to recognize that the literary representation of women's participation in sport is "serious stuff." Our literature reflects the greater power issues at work in society, its institutions, and its cultural practices. As women fans and athletes pursue sport in larger numbers, their commitment to once all-male sports such as baseball, will further their acceptance and the acceptance of other previously excluded persons on all diamonds of human experience.

Chapter Notes

Introduction

1. Ila Borders "was also the first woman ever to earn a baseball scholarship (Southern California College, 1993) and to win a men's college game: 12–1." In addition, she "won MVP honors three years out of the six during her junior high/high school years" and "dominated her Little League all-star team three years in a row" (Ardell 2).

2. Examples of revisionist histories that attempt to include women in previously unrecognized roles are Linda Grant De Pauw's *Founding Mothers: Women of America in the Revolutionary Era* (1975) and Cokie Roberts's *Founding Mothers: The Women Who Raised Our Nation* (2004).

3. For further discussion of the gate image in August Wilson's plays, see *May All Your Fences Have Gates: Essays on the Drama of August Wilson*, ed. Alan Nadel (Iowa City: University of Iowa Press, 1994).

4. For a complete understanding of the previous discussions of the roles of women and mythology in baseball literature, see Tristram Coffin Potter, *The Old Ball Game: Baseball in Folklore and Fiction*; Robert J. Higgs, *Laurel & Thorn: The Athlete in American Literature*; Eugene C. Murdock, *Mighty Casey: All-American*; Earl R. Wasserman, "*The Natural*: Malamud's World Ceres"; Peter C. Bjarkman, "Diamonds are a Gal's Worst Friend: Women in Baseball History and Fiction"; Cordelia Candelaria, *Seeking the Perfect Game: Baseball in American Literature*; Eric Solomon, "Jews, Baseball, and the American Novel"; and Deeanne Westbrook, *Ground Rules: Baseball & Myth*.

5. See Westbrook's *Ground Rules: Baseball & Myth*, 247–54. I offer my sincere thanks to Professor Westbrook for her contributions to this work.

6. For further discussion of "gender exclusivity," see Cordelia Candelaria's "literary nine," a summary of the motifs of baseball literature (13–15).

One

1. The critics most often associated with *l'écriture féminine* are Hélène Cixous, "The Laugh of the Medusa," *Feminisms: An Anthology of Literary Theory and Criticism*, ed. Robyn R. Warhol and Diane Price Herndl, rev. ed. (New Brunswick: Rutgers University Press, 1997) 347–62, and Luce Irigaray, *This Sex Which Is Not One*, 1977, trans. Catherine Porter (Ithaca: Cornell University Press, 1985). For an introduction to fem-

inist dialogics, see Dale Bauer, *Feminist Dialogics: A Theory of Failed Community* and "Gender in Bakhtin's Carnival," *Feminisms: An Anthology of Literary Theory and Criticism*, ed. Robyn R. Warhol and Diane Price Herndl, rev. ed. (New Brunswick: Rutgers University Press, 1997) 709-20.

2. See C. G. Jung, "Psychological Types," *Contributions to Analytical Psychology*, trans. H. G. and Cary F. Baynes (New York: Harcourt, 1928) 295-312.

3. Westbrook identifies other characters whose mothers left them or died: Henry "Author" Wiggen from Mark Harris's *The Southpaw* (Indianapolis: Bobbs-Morrill, 1953); Gideon Clarke from W. P. Kinsella's *The Iowa Baseball Confederacy* (New York: Houghton Mifflin, 1986); and Troy Maxson from August Wilson's *Fences* (New York: Plume, 1986). See Westbrook's *Ground Rules: Baseball & Myth*, 247-54. She omits Roy Tucker from John R. Tunis's *The Kid from Tomkinsville*, intro. Bruce Brooks, 1940 (New York: Harcourt, 1987).

4. Frye argues that "we may note that each period of Western culture has made conspicuous use of the Classical literature nearest to it in mode: romanticized versions of Homer in the Middle Ages; Virgilian epic, Platonic symposium, and Ovidian courtly love in the high mimetic; Roman satire in the low mimetic; the products of the latest possible period of Latin in the iron phase of Huysmans' *À Rebours*" (63).

5. See Ring Lardner, *You Know Me Al*, 1914 (New York: Scribner's, 1960) and "Women," *The Complete Baseball Stories of Ring Lardner*, ed. Matthew J. Brucoli (New York: Scribner's, 1992) 455-64; and Heywood Broun, *The Sun Field*, (New York: G. P. Putnam's Sons, 1923).

6. See Cordelia Candelaria, *Seeking the Perfect Game: Baseball in American Literature* (Greenwood, CT: Greenwood Press, 1989).

7. In the April 2004 issue of *National Geographic*, the article "Worldwide, It's a Hit" notes that "of the 827 players who opened the 2003 major league season, 28 percent came from foreign countries and Puerto Rico."

8. In Garrison Keillor's "What Did We Do Wrong?", Annie Szemanski's crude behavior upsets her adoring fans. See Keillor's "What Did We Do Wrong?", *We Are Still Married* (New York: Penguin, 1990) 316-325. For novels about the first woman ballplayer, see Michael Bowen, *Can't Miss* (New York: Harper & Row, 1987); Mel Cebulash, *Ruth Marini of the Dodgers* (Minneapolis: Lerner Publications Co., 1983); Barbara Gregorich, *She's On First* (Chicago: Contemporary Books, 1987); Ray Puechner, *A Grand Slam* (New York: Warner Books, 1973); Paul Rothweiler, *The Sensuous Southpaw* (New York: G. P. Putnam's Sons, 1976); Marilyn Sachs, *Fleet-Footed Florence* (Garden City, NY: Doubleday & Co., 1981).

Two

1. See Roger Kahn, *The Boys of Summer* (New York: Harper & Row, 1971); Lawrence S. Ritter, *The Glory of Their Times: The Story of the Early Days of Baseball Told by the Men Who Played It* (New York: Macmillan, 1966); Douglass Wallop, *Baseball: An Informal History* (New York: Norton, 1969); George F. Will, *Bunts: Curt Flood, Camden Yards, Pete Rose and Other Reflections on Baseball* (New York: Scribner, 1998) and *Men at Work: The Craft of Baseball* (New York: Macmillan, 1990).

2. See Barbara Gregorich, *Women at Play: The Story of Women in Baseball* (New

York: Harcourt, 1993); Gai Ingham Berlage, *Women in Baseball: The Forgotten History* (Westport, CT: Greenwood Press, 1994); and Susan E. Johnson, *When Women Played Hardball* (Seattle: Seal Press, 1994).

3. See, among others, Roger Kahn, Lawrence Ritter, Douglass Wallop, George F. Will, and Benjamin G. Rader. Benjamin G. Rader, *Baseball: A History of America's Game* (Urbana: University of Illinois Press, 1992).

4. Murdered by his brother, Osiris was brought back to life by his wife Isis, making him god of the underworld. "Osiris represented both the rebirth of the land through the Nile floods, and the rebirth of the body in the afterlife" (Murdoch 38).

5. Other sports discussed in Henderson's work include Polo, *La soule*, Tennis, Stoolball, Bridal Ball, Hurling, Knappan, Shinty, Racquets, Golf, Billiards, Lawn Tennis, Cricket, and Lacrosse (ix–x). Henderson also includes chapters on the development of indoor tennis, or racquets, in monastery cloisters and on the appearance of tennis in English literature (55; 59–69). To his discussion of English literature I would add the Wakefield Master's use of a tennis ball as the third shepherd's gift to the Christ child in *The Second Shepherd's Pageant*: "Hail! Put forth thy dall! / I bring thee but a ball: / Have and play thee withal, / And go to the tennis." Wakefield Master, *The Second Shepherd's Pageant, Everyman and Medieval Miracle Plays*, ed. A. C. Cawley (London: J. M. Dent & Sons, 1990) 108.

6. Trickster figures, such as the Coyote, the Spider, the Rabbit, and the Raven, appear often in Native American folklore. See Richard Erdoes and Alfonso Ortiz, eds., *American Indian Trickster Tales* (New York: Viking, 1998) and Paul Radin, *The Trickster: A Study in American Indian Mythology* (New York: Greenwood Press, 1956).

7. For further discussion of Memo's health and other women characters in *The Natural*, see Candelaria pp. 64–74.

8. The movie does, however, provide Lorri (Rachel Griffiths) with one memorable line that is not in the book: "Jimmy Morris, I'm a Texas woman, which means I don't need the help of a man to keep things running."

9. I am indebted to Professor Cordelia Candelaria for first suggesting the significance of flower symbolism to my study.

10. Dale Ritterbusch's poem "She Throws Like a Girl" brilliantly inverts expected shortcomings of a father-daughter catch. The poem proudly concludes, "And I think \ how my daughter throws like a girl —\ my girl — and with an arm like spring steel."

11. In his essay "The Interaction of Semiotic Constraints," Greimas devises the semiotic square as a useful way to visualize an individual's personal motivations or drives in a market economy. Algirdas Julien Greimas, "The Interaction of Semiotic Constraints," *On Meaning: Selected Writings in Semiotic Theory*, trans. Paul J. Perron and Frank H. Collins (Minneapolis: University of Minnesota Press, 1987).

12. These descriptions are derived from Jean Shinoda Bolen's *Goddesses in Everywoman: A New Psychology of Women* (San Francisco: Harper, 1984), as introduced in chapter one. Annie Savoy of the movie *Bull Durham* would make an amazing baseball goddess, combining the strength of Artemis, the intelligence of Athena, and the passion of Aphrodite. She deserves fuller explication than this work that is concerned with the literature of baseball can provide. *Bull Durham*, unfortunately, was not a book first.

Three

1. Timothy Morris, *Making the Team: The Cultural Work of Baseball Fiction* (Urbana: University of Illinois Press, 1997).
2. Richard Ruland and Malcolm Bradbury, *From Puritanism to Postmodernism: A History of American Literature* (New York: Routledge, 1991); James Fenimore Cooper, *The Pioneers* (New York: A. L. Burt, 1899); Washington Irving, *Bracebridge Hall, or the Humorists, the Writings of Washington Irving* (New York: G. P. Putnam's Sons, 1931); Herman Melville, *Moby Dick* (Cambridge: Houghton-Mifflin, 1956).
3. Mark Harris, personal interview, 10 July 1997.
4. Henry Fielding, *Tom Jones* (London: Wordsworth, 1992); Charles Dickens, *David Copperfield* (London: Wordsworth, 1994), *Oliver Twist* (London: Wordsworth, 1990), and *Great Expectations* (Philadelphia: Running Press, 1992). For further discussion of Thomas Hughes's *Tom Brown's School Days* and *Tom Brown at Oxford*, Gilbert Patten's "Frank Merriwell's Trip West," "Frank Merriwell's Sport's Afield," and *Dick Merriwell at Fardale*, and Owen Johnson's *Stover at Yale*, see Messenger's chapter, "The Boys' School Sports Story" (*Dreaming*, 155–79).
5. Jeanne Lampl-de Groot first brought the preoedipal phase to the attention of Freud. Jeanne Lampl-de Groot, "The Evolution of the Oedipus Complex in Women," 1927, *The Psychoanalytic Reader: An Anthology of Essential Papers with Critical Introductions*, ed. Robert Fliess (New York: International University Press, 1969) 180–94.
6. Men acting as substitute mothers have been observed in other genres of literature. In the Louise Erdrich novel *Love Medicine*, for example, Uncle Eli, a traditional Chippewa, takes on the role of adoptive parent for nine-year-old June: "He hunts, traps, and is linked to earth, the giver and sustainer of life, the mother of all. At this point, Eli takes over mothering or, more precisely, parenting June" (Wong 182).
7. In *Between Voice and Silence: Women and Girls, Race and Relationship* (1995), Jill McLean Taylor, Carol Gilligan, and Amy M. Sullivan discuss the need for young girls to vocalize their feelings and make connections with others are crucial to their psychological health; however, qualities often associated with a feminine ideal, selflessness and subservience, may render young women silent. Their study calls for a change in the perception that to be feminine means to be helpful and quiet.
8. The literary representation of sickly mothers has been explored fully by Diane Price Herndl. Sick women often become absent mothers when their illnesses are fatal and they leave their children behind (61–62). Diana Price Herndl, *Invalid Women: Figuring Feminine Illness in American Fiction and Culture, 1940–1940* (Raleigh: University of North Carolina Press, 1993).
9. Although Jack Keefe's mother is not mentioned in Ring Lardner's *You Know Me Al* and mothers are rare in children's pulp fiction published before Malamud's *The Natural*, Roy Tucker is the first character I have found whose absent mother is significant to a narrative through a character's memories of her and through the contributions of a substitute mother, in this case Roy's grandmother.
10. Interestingly, the New York Mammoths hold spring training in Aqua Clara ("Clear Water"), Florida, in the Mark Harris series of novels.
11. Faced with the team Mike Shropshire describes as "a new and different category of pain-in-the ass" (74) in *Seasons in Hell: With Billy Martin, Whitey Herzog and*

"The Worst Baseball Teams in History"—The 1973–75 Texas Rangers (1996), Texas Ranger manager Whitey Herzog takes a similar "paternal approach" with his players, resulting in disastrous seasons (72).

12. Also behaving badly in the original *Angels in the Outfield* (1951), coach Guffy McGovern (Paul Douglas) hears the voice of an angel who tells him, "Lay off swearing and fighting, and I'll win you some ball games." Once McGovern takes a more maternal approach with his players, they and the angels respond with a pennant-winning season.

Four

1. Harris intends the word "then" because the young Wiggen's early writing contains much errata.

2. For an interesting evaluation of the previous first-woman-in-organized-baseball novels, see Eric Solomon's article "'The Bullpen of Her Mind': Women's Baseball Fiction and Silvia Tennenbaum's *Rachel, The Rabbi's Wife*," *Arete* 3.1 (1985): 19–31.

3. The plight of girls who want to play baseball surfaces from time to time as they reach the age when they are expected to switch to softball. In 1997, a twelve-year-old catcher from Boca Raton, Florida, protested her baseball league's requirement that everyone wear a protective cup by coming to a game with one strapped to her ankle. After the umpire sent her to the outfield, she "got through the inning without injury to her cupless body, her ankle, or anyone else in the ball park, except those who suffered groin pulls from uncontrollable fits of laughter." Until young women are encouraged to play beyond little league, these episodes will unfortunately continue. Crepeau, Dick, "Sport and Society Broadcast," 29 May 1997, WUCF-FM, Orlando, Florida.

4. The name "Isemonger" recalls the name of an unpopular newspaper reporter in baseball history, James Isaminger. He published the story "Gamblers Promised White Sox $100,000 To Lose" in the Philadelphia paper *North American* and therefore broke the 1919 Black Sox Scandal (Seymour, *Golden* 301).

5. The scout Curry, having learned from Al that Linda is his daughter, tells the Chicago Eagles' manager, Lenny Black. When Al fires Lenny over his poor treatment of Linda, he releases the news to a tabloid.

6. Phil Wrigley and Branch Rickey formed the AAGPBL while many male professional ballplayers left the country to serve in World War II. Interestingly, Al Mowerinski also has an absent mother, who died when he was seventeen (182).

Five

1. The mothers in Nancy Willard's *Things Invisible to See* (1985) also aid their children by substituting for them as ballplayers in a winner-takes-all game against Death; however, this chapter focuses on adult romantic relationships.

2. Although Holly Wiggen in the Mark Harris series of novels is also a mother, she clearly possesses Hera's qualities, as they are described by Bolen. Mothers Iris Lemon of *The Natural* and Annie Kinsella in W. P. Kinsella's *Shoeless Joe* have Hestia's attributes.

3. In Eudora Welty's novel *Delta Wedding*, the Demeter figure also appears in the "pastoral comedy of plantation life which Welty intuitively linked to the myth of Demeter and Kore" (Westling 33).

4. The mythological implications of Dixon's association with an ancient Aztec game are curiously overlooked by Deeanne Westbrook in *Ground Rules: Baseball & Myth*. Herrin's work receives no mention in Westbrook's book, representing a larger absenting of non–Western and non–Greek mythologies in discussions of baseball literature.

5. Other critics have associated Memo with figures from mythology, such as Mnemosyne, the goddess of memory and the mother of the muses (Candelaria 69), Helen of Troy (Alter 80), and King Arthur's half sister and seducer, Morgan, and the Lady of the Lake (Wasserman 442).

6. Ray also mentions his daughter's warmth (33), Annie's warmth during their first hug after his return (153), her warm fingers as they watch a ball game on their land (211), and that "she is warm as sunshine" (223).

Six

1. One notable exception to the role of admirer in the characters examined in the previous chapter is August Wilson's Rose Maxson. Her scathing evaluation of her husband's infidelity and subsequent removal of him from her home reveals her intolerance of any behavior that harms her children (79). Additionally, Holly Webster is very critical of Henry Wiggen's behavior when he throws a spitter.

2. The effects of absent fatherhood in the novel, beyond opening the door for more participation by women characters, would be tangential to this study. However, two recent novels, both by Greg Garrett, are interesting in this respect. The main characters of both *Free Bird* (2000) and *Cycling* (2003) are men who suffer the effects of their fathers' absences.

3. Here I gratefully acknowledge Michael Oriard's personal observation to me that Clare's injury recalls the scene in *The Natural* (204).

4. The team name "Dead Knights" recalls the New York Knights of *The Natural*. In addition, players from beyond the grave appear in Kinsella's *Shoeless Joe*, Willard's *Things Invisible to See*, the 1951 movie *Angels in the Outfield*, and the 2004 movie *Angels in the Infield*.

5. The reviewer from *The West Coast Review of Books* writes that Rachel and Aaron's relationship "hints of incestuous lusts" (28). Although they discuss the details of Aaron's love life, I think the conversation reveals a healthy mother-son trust rather than lust.

Bibliography

Ableman, Paul. "Rabbetzin." *Spectator* 24 June 1978: 22.
Alter, Iska. "The Good Man's Dilemma: *The Natural, The Assistant,* and American Materialism." *Critical Essays on Bernard Malamud.* Ed. Joel Salzberg. Boston: Hall, 1987. 75–98.
Andreano, Ralph. *No Joy in Mudville: The Dilemma of Major League Baseball.* Cambridge: Schenkman, 1965.
Angels in the Infield. Dir. Robert King, 2004.
Angels in the Outfield. Dir. Clarence Brown, 1951.
Angels in the Outfield. Dir. William Dear, 1994.
Ardell, Jean Hastings. *Breaking into Baseball: Women in the National Pastime.* Carbondale: Southern Illinois University Press, 2005.
———. "History of Women's Baseball: Ila Borders Retires." www.baseballglory.com/History/Borders.
Armstrong, Nancy. "Some Call It Fiction." *Feminisms: An Anthology of Literary Theory and Criticism.* Ed. Robyn R. Warhol and Diane Price Herndl. Rev. ed. New Brunswick: Rutgers University Press, 1997. 913–30.
Ashby, Ruth, and Deborah Gore Ohm. *Herstory: Women Who Changed the World.* New York: Viking, 1995.
Asinof, Eliot. *Eight Men Out.* New York: Holt, Rinehart, and Winston, 1963.
Austen, Jane. *Northanger Abbey.* 1818. New York: Penguin, 1985.
Bakhtin, Mikhail. *The Dialogic Imagination: Four Essays.* Ed. Michael Holquist. Trans. Caryl Emerson and Michael Holquist. Austin: University of Texas Press, 1981.
———. "Discourse in the Novel." *The Dialogic Imagination: Four Essays.* Ed. Michael Holquist. Trans. Caryl Emerson and Michael Holquist. Austin: University of Texas Press, 1981. 261–83.
———. *Rabelais and His World.* Cambridge: University of Cambridge Press, 1968.
Bassin, Donna, Margaret Honey, and Meryle Mahrer Kaplan, eds. *Representations of Motherhood.* New Haven: Yale University Press, 1994.
Bauer, Dale. *Feminist Dialogics: A Theory of Failed Community.* Albany: State University of New York Press, 1988.
———. "Gender in Bakhtin's Carnival." *Feminisms: An Anthology of Literary*

Theory and Criticism. Ed. Robyn R. Warhol and Diane Price Herndl. Rev. ed. New Brunswick: Rutgers University Press, 1997. 708–20.

Baym, Nina. "The Madwoman and Her Languages: Why I Don't do Feminist Literary Theory." *Feminisms: An Anthology of Literary Theory and Criticism.* Ed. Robyn R. Warhol and Diane Price Herndl. Rev. ed. New Brunswick: Rutgers University Press, 1997. 279–92.

———. "Melodramas of Beset Manhood." *The New Feminist Criticism: Essays on Women, Literature, and Theory.* Ed. Elaine Showalter. New York: Pantheon, 1985. 63–80.

Belsey, Catherine. "Constructing the Subject." *Feminisms: An Anthology of Literary Theory and Criticism.* Ed. Robyn R. Warhol and Diane Price Herndl. Rev. ed. New Brunswick: Rutgers University Press, 1997. 657–73.

Berlage, Gai Ingham. *Women in Baseball: The Forgotten History.* Westport, CT: Greenwood Press, 1994.

Bjarkman, Peter C. "Diamonds are a Gal's Worst Friend: Women in Baseball History and Fiction." *The SABR Review of Books: A Forum of Baseball Literary Opinion.* Ed. Paul D. Adomites. Garrett Park, Maryland: The Society for American Baseball Research 4 (1989): 79–95.

———. "Introduction." *The Bingo Long Traveling All-Stars and Motor Kings.* New York: Harper and Row, 1973. xvii–xxx.

Bolen, Jean Shinoda. *Goddesses in Everywoman: A New Psychology of Women.* San Francisco: Harper, 1984.

Bourdieu, Pierre. *Sociology in Question.* Trans. Richard Nice. London: Sage, 1993.

Bowen, Michael. *Can't Miss.* New York: Harper & Row, 1987.

Brashler, William. *The Bingo Long Traveling All-Stars and Motor Kings.* New York: Harper and Row, 1973.

Briganti, Chiara. "Mirrors, Windows and Peeping Toms: Women as the Objects of Voyeurisitic Scrutiny in Bernard Malamud's *A New Life* and *Dubin's Lives*." Critical Essays on Bernard Malamud. Ed. Joel Salzberg. Boston: Hall, 1987. 174–86.

Brooks, Bruce. *What Hearts.* New York: HarperCollins, 1992.

Broun, Heywood. *The Sun Field.* New York: G. P. Putnam's Sons, 1923.

Bull Durham. Dir. Ron Shelton. Orion Pictures, 1988.

Byerman, Keith. "America's Passed Time: Baseball and Race in August Wilson's *Fences. Baseball/Literature/Culture: Essays, 1995–2001.* Ed. Peter Carino. Jefferson, NC: McFarland & Co., 2001. 94–100.

Caillois, Roger. *Man, Play, and Games.* 1958. Trans. Meyer Barash. New York: Free Press of Glencoe, 1986.

Campbell, Jane. *Mythic Black Fiction: The Transformation of History.* Knoxville: University of Tennessee Press, 1986.

Campbell, Joseph. *The Hero with a Thousand Faces.* 1949. 2nd ed. Princeton: Princeton University Press, 1972.

Candelaria, Cordelia. *Seeking the Perfect Game: Baseball in American Literature.* Greenwood, CT: Greenwood Press, 1989.

Carol, Bill. *Single to Center.* Austin: Steck-Vaughn, 1974.

Bibliography

Cebulash, Mel. *Ruth Marini of the Dodgers*. Minneapolis: Lerner Publications Co., 1983.
Christian, Barbara. *Black Feminist Criticism: Perspectives on Black Women Writers*. New York: Pergamon Press, 1985.
Christopher, Matt. *The Diamond Champs*. Boston: Little, Brown, and Co., 1968.
_____. *Wild Pitch*. Boston: Little, Brown, and Co., 1980.
_____. *The Year Mom Won the Pennant*. Boston: Little, Brown, and Co., 1968.
Chodorow, Nancy. *The Reproduction of Mothering: Pschoanalysis and the Sociology of Gender*. Berkeley: University of California Press, 1978.
Cixous, Hélène. "The Laugh of the Medusa." *Feminisms: An Anthology of Literary Theory and Criticism*. Ed. Robyn R. Warhol and Diane Price Herndl. Rev. ed. New Brunswick: Rutgers University Press, 1997. 347–62.
Clifton, Merritt. *A Baseball Classic*. Richford, VT: Samisdat, 1978.
Coffin, Tristram Potter. *The Old Ball Game: Baseball in Folklore and Fiction*. New York: Herder and Herder, 1971.
Cohen, Celia. *Smokey O: A Romance*. Tallahassee, FL: Naiad Press, 1994.
Cole, Diane. "The Pick of the Crop: Five First Novels." *Ms*. Apr. 1985: 15.
Collins, Tracy J. R. "Reflections on Teaching Sports Literature in the Academy." *Pedagogy* 3.2 (2000): 281–285.
Cooper, James Fenimore. *The Pioneers*. New York: A. L. Burt, 1899.
Coover, Robert. *The Universal Baseball Association, Inc., J. Henry Waugh, Prop*. New York: Plume, 1968.
Crepeau, Richard C. *Baseball: America's Diamond Mind*. Lincoln: University of Nebraska Press, 2000.
_____. "Sport and Society Broadcast." 29 May 1997. WUCF-FM. Orlando, Florida.
Dickens, Charles. *David Copperfield*. 1850. London: Wordsworth, 1994.
_____. *Great Expectations*. 1861. Philadelphia: Running Press, 1992.
_____. *Oliver Twist*. London: Wordsworth, 1990.
Dally, Ann. *Inventing Motherhood: The Consequences of an Ideal*. New York: Schocken, 1983.
Daly, Brenda O., and Maureen T. Reddy. "Introduction." *Narrating Mothers: Theorizing Maternal Subjectivities*. Ed. Brenda O. Daly and Maureen T. Reddy. Knoxville: University of Tennessee Press, 1991. 1–20.
Dawidoff, Nicholas, ed. *Baseball: A Literary Anthology*. New York: The Library of America, 2002.
De Pauw, Linda Grant. *Founding Mothers: Women of America in the Revolutionary Era*. Boston: Houghton Mifflin Company, 1975.
Donne, John. "Song." *Norton Anthology of English Literature*. 5th ed. New York: W. W. Norton and Co., 1986. 1064.
Dworkin, Susan. "Review of *Rachel, The Rabbi's Wife*." *Ms*. Jan. 1978: 37.
Eagleton, Terry. *Literary Theory: An Introduction*. Minneapolis: University of Minnesota Press, 1983.
Eder, Richard. "Review of *Things Invisible to See*." *Los Angeles Times: The Book Review* 20 Jan. 1985: 1.

Eight Men Out. Dir. John Sayles. 1988.
Ellis, Lucy. *The Girls Strike Back.* New York: Sports Illustrated for Kids, 1990.
———. *All That Jazz.* New York: Sports Illustrated for Kids, 1990.
Erdoes, Richard, and Alfonso Ortiz, eds. *American Indian Trickster Tales.* New York: Viking, 1998.
Farrell, James T. *Studs Lonigan: A Trilogy Containing* Young Lonigan, The Young Manhood of Studs Lonigan, Judgment Day. 1932, 1933, 1934. New York: Vanguard Press, 1978.
Ferber, Edna. "A Bush League Hero." *Buttered Side Down: Stories by Edna Ferber.* New York: Stokes, 1912. 58–77.
Field of Dreams. Dir. Phil Alden Robinson. Universal, 1989.
Fielding, Henry. *Tom Jones.* 1749. London: Wordsworth, 1992.
Fitzgerald, F. Scott. *The Great Gatsby.* 1925. New Haven: Chelsea House, 1986.
Fordham, Frieda. *An Introduction to Jung's Psychology.* 1953. New York: Penguin, 1966.
Fornoff, Susan. *Lady in the Locker Room: Uncovering the Oakland Athletics.* Champaign, IL: Sagamore Press, 1993.
Fowler, Karen Joy. *The Sweetheart Season.* New York: Ballantine, 1996.
Frankel, Ellen, and Betsy Platkin Teutsch. *The Encyclopedia of Jewish Symbols.* Northvale, NJ: Jason Aronson Inc., 1992. 178.
Freud, Anna, and Dorothy Burlingham. *Infants Without Families: The Case For and Against Residential Nurseries.* New York: International University Press, 1944.
Freud, Sigmund. "On Narcissism: An Introduction." 1914. *Freud on Women: A Reader.* Ed. Elisabeth Young-Bruehl. New York: Norton, 1990. 190–95.
Frye, Northrop. *Anatomy of Criticism: Four Essays.* Princeton: Princeton University Press, 1957.
Fuller, Edmund. "Fantastic Voyage." *The Wall Street Journal* 5 Feb. 1985: 28.
Gardner, Martin. *The Annotated* "Casey at the Bat." New York: Clarkson N. Potter, 1967.
Garrett, Greg. *Cycling.* New York: Kensington Books, 2003.
———. *Free Bird.* New York: Kensington Books, 2000.
Giamatti, A. Bartlett. *Take Time For Paradise: Americans and Their Game.* New York: Summit Books, 1989.
Gilman, Charlotte Perkins. *Herland.* 1st ed. New York: Pantheon, 1979.
Goldenberg, Naomi. "On Hockey Sticks and Hopscotch Patsies: Reflections of the Sexuality of Sport." *Limited Edition: Voices of Women, Voices of Feminism.* Ed. Geraldine Finn. Halifax: Fernwood Publishing, 1993. 256–65.
Graham, John Alexander. *Babe Ruth Caught in a Snowstorm.* Boston: Houghton Mifflin, 1973.
Graves, Robert. *The White Goddess: A Historical Grammar of Poetic Myth.* 1948. New York: Farrar, 1966.
Green, Vanalyne. "Mother Baseball." *Diamonds Are a Girl's Best Friend: Women Writers on Baseball.* Ed. Elinor Nauen. Boston: Faber, 1994. 224–28.
Greenberg, Eric Rolfe. *The Celebrant.* 1983. New York: Penguin, 1986.

Bibliography

Gregorich, Barbara. *She's On First.* New York: Contemporary Books, 1987.
_____. *Women at Play: The Story of Women in Baseball.* New York: Harcourt, 1993.
Greimas, Algirdas Julien. "The Interaction of Semiotic Constraints." *On Meaning: Selected Writings in Semiotic Theory.* Trans. Paul J. Perron and Frank H. Collins. Minneapolis: University of Minnesota Press, 1987.
Hammer, Adam. "Kidsport: The Works of John T. [sic] Tunis." *Journal of Popular Culture* 17:3 (1983): 146–49.
Harris, Mark. *Bang the Drum Slowly.* New York: Knopf, 1956.
_____. "Each Game was a Crusade." *Diamond: Baseball Writings of Mark Harris.* New York: Primus, 1994. 159–64.
_____. *It Looked Like For Ever.* New York: McGraw-Hill, 1979.
_____. Personal interview. 10 July 1997.
_____. *The Southpaw.* Indianapolis: Bobbs-Morrill, 1953.
_____. *A Ticket for a Seamstitch.* New York: Knopf, 1957.
Hawthorne, Nathaniel. *The Scarlet Letter: A Romance.* 1850. New York: Penguin, 1986.
Hayes, Donald. *The Dixie Association.* New York: Simon and Schuster, 1984.
Haynes, Mary. *The Great Pretenders.* New York: Bradbury Press, 1990.
Hemingway, Ernest. *The Sun Also Rises.* 1926. New York: Chelsea House, 1987.
Henderson, Robert W. *Ball, Bat and Bishop: The Origin of Ball Games.* New York: Rockport Press, 1947.
Herndl, Diane Price. *Invalid Women: Figuring Feminine Illness in American Fiction and Culture, 1840–1940.* Raleigh: University of North Carolina Press, 1993.
Herrin, Lamar. *The Rio Loja Ringmaster.* New York: Viking, 1977.
Higgs, Robert J. *Laurel & Thorn: The Athlete in American Literature.* Lexington, University Press of Kentucky, 1981.
Holman, C. Hugh, and William Harmon. *A Handbook to Literature.* 6th ed. New York: Macmillan Publishing Company, 1992.
Hudson, Anna. *Fun and Games.* New York: Dell Publishing, 1987.
Janeway, Elizabeth. *Man's World, Woman's Place: A Study in Social Mythology.* New York: Morrow, 1971.
Johnson, Nunnally. "Miss Gulp." *An American Omnibus.* Intro. Carl Van Doren. New York: Doubleday and Co., 1933. 47–51.
Johnson, Susan E. *When Women Played Hardball.* Seattle: Seal Press, 1994.
Jung, C. G. "Psychological Types." *Contributions to Analytic Psychology.* Trans. H. G. and Cary F. Baynes. New York: Harcourt, 1928. 295–312.
Kahn, Coppelia. "The Absent Mother in *King Lear.*" *Rewriting the Renaissance: The Discourses of Sexual Difference in Early Modern Europe.* Eds. Margaret W. Ferguson, Maureen Quilligan, and Nancy Vickers. Chicago: University of Chicago Press, 1986. 33–49.
Kahn, Roger. *The Boys of Summer.* New York: Harper & Row, 1971.
Kakutani, Michiko. "The Real and the Fantastic." *The New York Times* 12 Jan. 1985: 13.

Keillor, Garrison. "What Did We Do Wrong?" *We Are Still Married.* New York: Penguin, 1990. 316–325.
Kelly, Jeffery. *The Basement Baseball Club.* Boston: Houghton Mifflin, 1987.
Kennedy, Lucy. *The Sunlit Field.* New York: Crown, 1950.
Kennedy, William. *Ironweed.* New York: Viking, 1983.
Kinsella, W. P. Entry. *What Baseball Means to Me: A Celebration of Our National Pastime.* Ed. Curt Smith. New York: Warner Books, Inc., 2002.
_____. *The Iowa Baseball Confederacy.* New York: Houghton Mifflin, 1986.
_____. *Shoeless Joe.* Boston: Houghton Mifflin, 1982.
Knoles, Thelma. "Double Play." *Teenage Sports Stories.* Ed. Frank Owen. New York: Grosset Publishers, 1947.
Kolodny, Annette. "Dancing through the Minefield: Some Observations on the Theory, Practice, and Politics of a Feminist Literary Criticism." *Feminisms: An Anthology of Literary Theory and Criticism.* Ed. Robyn R. Warhol and Diane Price Herndl. Rev. ed. New Brunswick: Rutgers University Press, 1997. 171–90.
Kubitschek, Missy Dehn. "August Wilson's Gender Lesson." *May All Your Fences Have Gates: Essays on the Drama of August Wilson.* Ed. Alan Nadel. Iowa City: University of Iowa Press, 1994. 183–99.
Lampl-de Groot, Jeanne. "The Evolution of the Oedipus Complex in Women." 1927. *The Psychoanalytic Reader: An Anthology of Essential Papers with Critical Introductions.* Ed. Robert Fliess. New York: International University Press, 1969. 180–94.
Lardner, Ring. *You Know Me Al.* 1914. New York: Scribner's, 1960.
_____. "Women." *The Complete Baseball Stories of Ring Lardner.* Ed. Matthew J. Bruccoli. New York: Scribner's, 1992. 455–64.
A League of Their Own. Dir. Penny Marshall. 1992.
Leeming, David Adams. *Mythology: The Voyage of the Hero.* New York: HarperCollins, 1981.
Lesser, Wendy. "Bloated and Shrunken Worlds." *The Hudson Review* 38 (1985): 470.
Lord, Bette Bao. *In the Year of the Boar and Jackie Robinson.* New York: HarperTrophy, 1986.
Major League. Dir. David S. Ward. Morgan Creek Productions, 1989.
Major League II. Dir. David S. Ward. Warner Brothers, 1994.
Major League: Back to the Minors. Dir. John Warren. Warner Brothers, 1998.
Malamud, Bernard. *Dubin's Lives.* New York: Farrar, Straus and Giroux, 1979.
_____. *The Natural.* New York: Farrar, Straus and Giroux, 1952.
McCue, Andy. *Baseball by the Books: A History and Complete Bibliography of Baseball Fiction.* Dubuque, IA: William C. Brown Publishers, 1991.
McGimpsey, David. *Imagining Baseball: America's Pastime and Popular Culture.* Bloomington: Indiana University Press, 2000.
Mead, Margaret. "The Changing Cultural Patterns of Work and Leisure." Seminar on Manpower Policy and Program. U.S. Department of Labor. Washington, D.C.: Office of Manpower, Evaluation, and Research, 1967.

Melville, Herman. *Moby Dick*. 1851. Cambridge: Houghton-Mifflin, 1956.
Messenger, Christian K. *Sport and the Spirit of Play in American Fiction: Hawthorne to Faulkner*. New York: Columbia University Press, 1981.
_____. *Sport and the Spirit of Play in Contemporary American Fiction*. New York: Columbia University Press, 1990.
Michaels, Ralph. *The Girl on First Base*. New York: Nordon, 1981.
Miles, Rosalind. *The Women's History of the World*. Topsfield, MA: Salem House, 1988.
Morris, Jim, and Joel Engel. *The Oldest Rookie: The Incredible True Story of a Man Who Never Gave up on his Dream*. New York: Little, Brown, and Co., 2001.
_____. *The Rookie: The Incredible True Story of a Man Who Never Gave up on his Dream*. New York: Warner, 2002.
Morris, Tim. *Making the Team: The Cultural Work of Baseball Fiction*. Urbana: University of Illinois Press, 1997.
Motz, Lotte. *The Faces of the Goddess*. New York: Oxford University Press, 1997.
Mueller, Lavonne. "The Goddess and the Yankee Clipper." *Baseball Monologues*. Ed. Lavonne Mueller. Portsmouth, NH: Heinemann, 1996. 13–25.
Munn, Vella. *Summer Season*. New York: Harlequin Books, 1983.
Murdoch, David. *Tutankhamun: The Life and Death of a Pharoah*. New York: DK Publishing, 1998.
Murdock, Eugene C. *Mighty Casey: All American*. Westport, CT: Greenwood Press, 1984.
Nadel, Alan, ed. *May All Your Fences Have Gates: Essays on the Drama of August Wilson*. Iowa City: University of Iowa Press, 1994.
Norworth, Jack. "Take Me Out to the Ball Game." *Baseball: A Literary Anthology*. Ed. Nicholas Dawidoff. New York: The Library of America, 2002. 18–19.
Oriard, Michael. *Dreaming of Heroes: American Sports Fiction, 1868–1980*. Chicago: Nelson-Hall, 1982.
Paulos, Sheila. *Wild Roses*. New York: Dell Publishing, 1983.
Pereira, Kim. *August Wilson and the African-American Odyssey*. Urbana: University of Illinois Press, 1995.
Perkins, Al. *Don and Donna Go to Bat*. New York: Random House, 1966.
Peterson, Robert W. *Only the Ball Was White: A History of the Legendary Black Players and All-Black Professional Teams*. Englewood Cliffs: Prentice-Hall Publishers, 1970.
Pratt, Annis. *Archetypal Patterns in Women's Fiction*. Bloomington: Indiana University Press, 1981.
_____. *Dancing with Goddesses: Archetypes, Poetry, and Empowerment*. Bloomington: Indiana University Press, 1994.
The Pride of the Yankees. Dir. Sam Wood. RKO Pictures, 1942.
Puechner, Ray. *A Grand Slam*. New York: Warner Books, 1973.
Quart, Barbara Koenig. "Women in Bernard Malamud's Fiction." *Studies in Jewish American Literature* 3 (1983): 138–50.

Rader, Benjamin G. *Baseball: A History of America's Game*. Urbana: University of Illinois Press, 1992.
Radin, Paul. *The Trickster: A Study in American Indian Mythology*. New York: Greenwood Press, 1956.
"Review of *Rachel, The Rabbi's Wife*." *The West Coast Review of Books* 4 (1978): 28.
"Review of *Things Invisible to See*." *English Journal* 74 (1985): 86.
"Review of *Things Invisible to See*." *Publisher's Weekly* 2 Nov. 1984: 65.
Rich, Adrienne. *Of Woman Born: Motherhood as Experience and Institution*. New York: Norton, 1986.
Ritter, Lawrence S. *The Glory of Their Times: The Story of the Early Days of Baseball Told by the Men Who Played It*. New York: Macmillan, 1966.
Ritterbusch, Dale. "She Throws Like a Girl." *Aethlon* XV:1 (Fall 1997): 108.
Ritz, David. *The Man Who Brought the Dodgers Back to Brooklyn*. New York: Simon and Schuster, 1981.
Roberts, Cokie. *Founding Mothers: The Women Who Raised Our Nation*. New York: HarperCollins Publishers, 2004.
Robinson, Lillian S. "Treason Our Text: Feminist Challenges to the Literary Canon." *Feminisms: An Anthology of Literary Theory and Criticism*. Ed. Robyn R. Warhol and Diane Price Herndl. Rev. ed. New Brunswick: Rutgers University Press, 1997. 115–28.
Roof, Judith. "'This is Not For You': The Sexuality of Mothering." *Narrating Mothers: Theorizing Maternal Subjectivities*. Ed. Brenda O. Daly and Maureen T. Reddy. Knoxville: University of Tennessee Press, 1991. 157–73.
The Rookie. Dir. John Lee Hancock, 2002.
Rose, Mary Beth. "Where Are the Mothers in Shakespeare? Options for Gender Representation in the English Renaissance." *Shakespeare Quarterly* 42 (1991): 291–314.
Roth, Philip. *The Great American Novel*. New York: Holt, Rinehart, and Winston, 1973.
_____. *Portnoy's Complaint*. New York: Random House, 1969.
Rothweiler, Paul. *The Sensuous Southpaw*. New York: G. P. Putnam's Sons, 1976.
Ruddick, Sara. *Maternal Thinking: Toward a Politics of Peace*. Boston: Beacon Press, 1989.
_____. "Thinking Mothers/Conceiving Birth." *Representations of Motherhood*. Eds. Donna Bassin, Margaret Honey, and Meryle Mahrer Kaplan. New Haven: Yale University Press, 1994. 29–45.
Ruland, Richard, and Malcolm Bradbury. *From Puritanism to Postmodernism: A History of American Literature*. New York: Routledge, 1991.
Runyon, Damon. "Baseball Hattie." *Baseball Tales: Major League Writers on the National Pastime*. Ed. Lawrence S. Ritter. New York: Viking Press, 1993. 81–99.
Ruotolo, Lucio. "Bernard Malamud's Rediscovery of Women: The Impact of Virginia Woolf." *Twentieth Century Literature* 3 (1994): 329–41.
Sachs, Marilyn. *Fleet-Footed Florence*. Garden City, NY: Doubleday & Co., 1981.

Bibliography

The Sandlot. Dir. David Mickey Evans. 1993.
Schwartz, Richard Alan. "Postmodernist Baseball." *Modern Fiction Studies* 33:1 (1987): 135–50.
Schweitzer, Gertrude. "We Go Together." *Teen-age Baseball Stories.* Ed. Frank Owen. New York: Grosset Publishers, 1948.
Seymour, Harold. *Baseball: The Early Years.* New York: Oxford University Press, 1960.
———. *Baseball: The Golden Age.* New York: Oxford University Press, 1971.
———. *Baseball: The People's Game.* New York: Oxford University Press, 1990.
Shapiro, Ann-Louise, ed. *Feminists Revision History.* New Brunswick: Rutgers University Press, 1994.
Showalter, Elaine. *Sisters Choice: Tradition and Change in American Women's Writing.* Oxford: Clarendon Press, 1991.
Shropshire, Mike. *Seasons in Hell: With Billy Martin, Whitey Herzog and "The Worst Baseball Teams in History"—The 1973-75 Texas Rangers.* New York: Donald I. Fine Books, 1996.
Skolnik, Richard. *Baseball and the Pursuit of Innocence: A Fresh Look at the Old Ball Game.* College Station: Texas A&M University Press, 1994.
Slote, Alfred. *Matt Gragan's Boy.* Philadelphia: Lippincott, 1975.
Solomon, Eric. "'The Bullpen of Her Mind': Women's Baseball Fiction and Silvia Tennenbaum's *Rachel, The Rabbi's Wife.*" *Arete* 3:1 (1985): 19–31.
———. "Jews, Baseball, and the American Novel." *Arete* 1 (1984): 50–73.
Soto, Gary. "Baseball in April." *Baseball in April and Other Stories.* New York: Harcourt, 1990. 16–28.
Spacks, Patricia Meyer. *The Female Imagination.* New York: Knopf, 1975.
Spencer, Pam. "Review of *Things Invisible to See.*" *School Library Journal* 31 (1985): 115.
Spivey, Donald, ed. *Sport in America: New Historical Perspectives.* Westport, CT: Greenwood Press, 1985.
Stone, Natalie. *Double Play.* New York: Dell Publishing, 1983.
Sullivan, Silky. *Henry and Melinda.* Chicago: Children's Press, 1982.
Suzanne, Jamie. *Sweet Valley Twins: Standing Out.* New York: Bantam Books, 1989.
Swados, Harvey. "Baseball a la Wagner: The Nibelung in the Polo Grounds." *Critical Essays on Bernard Malamud.* Ed. Joel Salzberg. Boston: Hall, 1987. 23–25.
Swigart, Jane. *The Myth of the Bad Mother: The Emotional Realities of Mothering.* New York: Doubleday, 1991.
Taves, Isabella. *Not Bad for a Girl.* New York: Evans Press, 1972.
Taylor, Jill McLean, Carol Gilligan, and Amy M. Sullivan. *Between Voice and Silence: Women and Girls, Race and Relationship.* Cambridge: Harvard University Press, 1995.
Tennenbaum, Silvia. *Rachel, The Rabbi's Wife.* New York: William Morrow, 1978.
Thayer, Ernest L. "Casey at the Bat." 1888. *The Annotated "Casey at the Bat."* Ed. Martin Gardner. New York: Clarkson N. Potter, 1967.

Thoreau, Henry David. *Walden* and "Civil Disobedience." 1854 and 1849. New York: Penguin, 1980.
Tunis, John R. *The Keystone Kids*. 1943. Intro. Bruce Brooks. New York: Harcourt, 1987.
_____. *The Kid from Tomkinsville*. 1940. Intro. Bruce Brooks. New York: Harcourt, 1987.
_____. *Rookie of the Year*. 1944. Intro. Bruce Brooks. New York: Harcourt, 1990.
_____. *Schoolboy Johnson*. 1958. New York: Morrow, 1990.
_____. *World Series*. 1941. Intro. Bruce Brooks. New York: Harcourt, 1987.
Ward, Geoffrey C., and Ken Burns. *Baseball: An Illustrated History*. New York: Knopf, 1994.
Wakefield Master. *The Second Shepherd's Pageant. Everyman and Medieval Miracle Plays*. Ed. A. C. Cawley. London: J. M. Dent & Sons, 1990. 81–108.
Walker, Alice. "In Search of Our Mothers' Gardens." In Search of Our Mothers' Gardens. New York: Harcourt, 1983. 231–243.
Walker, Barbara G. *Amazon: A Novel*. New York: HarperCollins, 1992.
Wallop, Douglass. *Baseball: An Informal History*. New York: Norton, 1969.
Warhol, Robyn R., and Diane Price Herndl. "About Feminisms." *Feminisms: An Anthology of Literary Theory and Criticism*. Ed. Robyn R. Warhol and Diane Price Herndl. Rev. ed. New Brunswick: Rutgers University Press, 1997. ix–xvii.
Wasserman, Earl R. "*The Natural*: Malamud's World Ceres." *The Centennial Review* 9:4 (1965): 438–560.
Westbrook, Deeanne. *Ground Rules: Baseball & Myth*. Urbana: University of Illinois Press, 1996.
Westling, Loise. "Food, Landscape and the Feminine in *Delta Wedding*." *The Southern Quarterly* 30:2 (1992): 29–40.
Will, George F. *Bunts: Curt Flood, Camden Yards, Pete Rose and Other Reflections on Baseball*. New York: Scribner, 1998.
_____. *Men at Work: The Craft of Baseball*. New York: Macmillan, 1990.
Willard, Nancy. *The Highest Hit*. New York: Harcourt, 1978.
_____. *Things Invisible to See*. New York: Knopf, 1985.
Wilson, August. *Fences*. New York: Plume, 1986.
Wisse, Ruth R. "Suburban Kitsch." *Books in Review* 65 (1978): 78.
Wong, Hertha D. "Adoptive Mothers and Thrown-Away Children in the Novels of Louise Erdrich." *Narrating Mothers: Theorizing Maternal Subjectivities*. Ed. Brenda O. Daly and Maureen T. Reddy. Knoxville: University of Tennessee Press, 1991. 174–94.
Woodley, Richard. *The Bad News Bears*. New York: Dell, 1976.
_____. *The Bad News Bears in Breaking Training*. New York: Dell, 1977.
_____. *The Bad News Bears Go to Japan*. New York: Dell, 1978.
"Worldwide, It's a Hit." *National Geographic*. April 2004.

Index

absent fathers 64–66
absent mothers 10–11, 15, 41, 52, 56–90
Achilles 35
Adonis 50, 58, 115
Ajax 35
All-American Girls Professional Baseball League (AAGPBL) 5
Anatomy of Criticism 19
Andreano, Ralph 26, 32
Andrews, Jane 43
Angels in the Infield (2004) 4
Angels in the Outfield (1951) 4, 100
Angels in the Outfield (1994) 4, 100
Aphrodite 12, 21, 23, 47, 56, 118, 139–140, 150–173
Apollo 50, 115–116
Archetypal Patterns in Women's Fiction 20, 24
Ardell, Jean Hastings 3
Ares 153
Artemis 12, 21, 23, 56, 118, 150–173
Asinof, Eliot 94
Austen, Jane 31

Babe Ruth Caught in a Snowstorm 55
Baker, Jordan 39
Bakhtin, Mikhail 17–19
Bang the Drum Slowly 6, 52, 83–84, 99, 132–137
Baseball and the Pursuit of Innocence: A Fresh Look at the Old Ball Game 29
Baseball by the Books: A History and Complete Bibliography of Baseball Fiction 100–103

"Baseball Hattie" 42–43
"Baseball's Anthem for All Ages" 4
Bauer, Dale 16, 68–69
Belle, Albert 35
Berlage, Gai Ingham 5, 26–27, 30
bildungsroman 20, 74–90, 91–113
The Bingo Long Traveling All-Stars and Motor Kings 26, 50, 55
Bird, Harriet 40, 43, 47, 77, 116–117, 138–139, 140–141
Bishop, Clare 12, 45, 150–159, 173
Bjarkman, Peter C. 10, 26, 42–43, 45, 104
Black Sox Scandal 36, 53, 94
Bolen, Jean Shinoda 1, 23–24, 118–147, 150–173
Borders, Ila 5, 12, 27, 101
Bowen, Michael 104
Brashler, William 26, 50, 55
Breaking into Baseball: Women in the National Pastime 3
Brooks, Bruce 11, 52–54
Broun, Heywood 25, 43, 102, 116
Brown v. Board of Education, Topeka, KS 7
Bull Durham 83
Bunyan, Paul 35
"A Bush League Hero" 10, 44

Caillois, Roger 16
Campbell, Joseph 48
Candelaria, Cordelia 1–2, 10, 12, 25, 49, 50–51, 57, 75, 107, 115, 125–126, 129, 133, 135, 166

Index

Carol, Bill 102
Cartwright, Alexander 25
Casey, Katie 4, 6, 12
"Casey at the Bat" 37–38, 50
Cassiopeia 23, 171
Cebulash, Mel 104–106
The Celebrant 50, 92, 94, 116
Chodorow, Nancy 63–66, 77–78, 111
Christian, Barbara 21–22
Christopher, Matt 101–102
Circe 22, 47, 116
Clifton, Merritt 104
Cobb, Ty 36
Coffin, Tristram Potter 35–36
Cohen, Celia 65, 116
Collins, Maggie 170–173
compound goddesses 12, 115, 117–118, 150–174
Cooper, James Fenimore 39, 58
Cooperstown, NY 16
Coover, Robert 8, 70
Corcoran, Donna 4
Crepeau, Dick 10

Dally, Ann 68
Daly, Brenda O. 67–68
Dancing with Goddesses: Archetypes, Poetry, and Empowerment 21, 123
Daphne 20
Delta Wedding 121
Demeter 2, 11, 56, 113, 118–125, 149
Devine, Grouchy 72, 85–88
Diamonds Are a Girl's Best Friend: Women Writers on Baseball 6
DiMaggio, Joe 30, 116
Dionysus 50, 58, 115
Dixon, Consuelo 11, 45, 52, 54, 113, 118–120, 125–132, 147
Dixon, Dick 52, 117, 119, 120, 125–132, 147
Dixon, Harry "Sarge" 126–127
Dixon, Lorraine 125–132
Dixon, Susan 126–127
Donne, John 155–156
Doyle, Irini 11–12, 45, 71, 73, 150–152, 167–173

Dreaming of Heroes: American Sports Fiction, 1868–1980 3, 42, 48–49
Dubin's Lives 41
Duggan, Jimmy 3

Eagleton, Terry 20
Eight Men Out 94
Electra 108, 110–111
Ellis, Lucy 101
Everett, Laurel 4

The Faces of the Goddess 25
Fences 7–8, 45, 52, 75, 118–125, 158
Ferber, Edna 10, 44
Field of Dreams 53, 145
Fisher, Ma 71, 77–79
Fisher, Pop 71–72, 76–79, 95
Fitzgerald, F. Scott 39
Fornoff, Susan 4, 12
Fowler, Karen Joy 4, 11, 23–24, 71, 73, 150–152, 167–173
Frye, Northrop 19–20

Gehrig, Lou 30, 35, 45, 157
"The Goddess and the Yankee Clipper" 115–116
Goddesses in Everywoman: A New Psychology of Women 1, 23, 118–147, 150–173
Goldenberg, Naomi R. 174
Goodwin, Doris Kearns 166
Gordon-Levitt, Joseph 4
Graham, John Alexander 55
Graves, Robert 24
The Great American Novel 68
The Great Gatsby 39–40
Green, Vanalyne 171
Greenberg, Eric Rolfe 50, 92, 94, 116
Gregorich, Barbara 5, 11, 30, 71, 100, 103, 107–113
Greimas, Algirdas Julien 54–56
Ground Rules: Baseball & Myth 1, 10, 51–52
Gulp, Mildred 44

Haas, Moose 5
Hades 120, 123
Harris, Mark 6, 9, 11, 26, 50, 59,

70–71, 75, 92, 104, 107, 119, 132–137, 147
Hawthorne, Nathaniel 39
Hay, Donald 104
Haynes, Mary 101
Hemingway, Ernest 40
Henderson, Robert W. 16, 31, 33
Hera 2, 11–12, 56, 118–119, 132–137, 149
Herrin, Lamar 11, 45, 52, 113, 117, 120, 125–132
Hervy, Lady Mary 31
Hestia 2, 11–12, 56, 118–119, 137–143, 149
Higgs, Robert J. 1, 10, 50–51
Hobbs, Roy 11, 40–41, 43, 46–48, 50, 58–59, 61, 64, 66–67, 70–79, 82, 84, 89, 94–95, 107, 113, 137–143, 147, 153
Hopper, De Wolf 37
Hortus conclusus 124, 130–132, 158
Horus 24
Huck Finn 61
Hudson, Anna 103
Huizinga, Johan 16

Imagining Baseball: America's Pastime and Popular Culture 3, 53
In Search of Our Mothers' Gardens 21
In the Year of the Boar and Jackie Robinson 74
The Iowa Baseball Confederacy 70, 93
Irden, Hettie 8
Irvin, Brittney 4
Irvin, Will 33
Isis 24
Isolde 20
It Looked Like For Ever 6, 132–137

Jackson, "Shoeless" Joe 145
Jacobi, Jolande 15
Janeway, Elizabeth 8
Johnson, Nunnally 44, 104
Johnson, Susan E. 5, 30
Jung, C. G. 14–15, 118, 123

Kahn, Coppélia 62
Keefe, Florrie 43

Keefe, Jack 43
Keillor, Garrison 104–105
Keller, Ivy 10, 44–45
Kelly, Jeffery 102
Kennedy, Lucy 102
Keystone, Louis 50
The Keystone Kids 11, 66, 71–72, 80, 85–90
The Kid from Tomkinsville 11, 66, 71–72, 80–84, 95–96
King Lear 62
Kingman, Dave 5
Kinsella, Annie 12, 20, 45, 65, 119, 137, 143–147
Kinsella, Karin 144–147
Kinsella, Ray 65, 119, 137, 143–147
Kinsella, W. P. 12, 65, 70, 93, 115, 119, 143–137
Knoles, Thelma 100
Kolodny, Annette 14
"Kong the Rat" 5

Lady in the Locker Room: Uncovering the Oakland Athletics 5
Landis, Judge Kenesaw Mountain 36
Lardner, Ring 18, 25, 42–43, 75, 92, 107
Latona 23
Laurel & Thorn: The Athlete in American Literature 1, 50
A League of Their Own 3, 5
Leeming, David Adams 57–58
Lemon, Iris 12, 15, 40–41, 45–48, 51, 71, 77, 79, 119, 137–143, 145, 153
Leonard, Dave 72, 83–84, 96
Lord, Bette Bao 74

Major League 59
Making the Team: The Cultural Work of Baseball Fiction 57, 59
Malamud, Bernard 40–41, 64, 70, 95, 138
Man's World, Woman's Place: A Study in Social Mythology 8
Marini, Ruth 104–106
Mathewson, Christy 30, 50, 92–93, 116

INDEX

Maxson, Cory 121–125
Maxson, Gabriel 122–124
Maxson, Raynell 69, 118–125
Maxson, Rose 7–9, 11, 45–46, 52, 54, 113, 188–125, 130, 147, 158
Maxson, Troy 7–9, 52, 69, 120–125, 147
Mays, Willie 35
McCue, Andy 100–103
McGimpsey, David 3, 11, 53
McGwire, Mark 35
Mead, Margaret 16
Medea 20
Medusa 20–21
Messenger, Christian K. 24, 35, 38–40, 54–56, 156, 159, 162, 173
Michael, Ralph 104
The Mighty Casey 38
Minerva 23
"Miss Gulp" 44, 104
monomyth 48–49
Monroe, Marilyn 115–116
Morris, Jim 45
Morris, Lorri 45
Morris, Timothy 57, 59, 70, 73–74, 87, 91, 93–94, 125
"Mother Baseball" 171–172
Motz, Lotte 24–25
Mowerinski, Al 72, 107–113
Mueller, Lavonne 116
Mulrooney, Mike 71–72, 96–99, 112
Munn, Vella 102–103
Murdock, Eugene C. 10, 35, 37–38

The Natural 10–12, 15, 40–43, 46–48, 50, 58, 64, 66, 70, 71, 74–79, 84, 95–96, 107, 116–117, 119, 137–143
Nauen, Elinor 6
Northanger Abbey 31
Norworth, Jack 4

oedipal phase 63–65, 77–80, 108, 111
Oedipus 58, 76
The Oldest Rookie 45
Olsen, Ilse 71, 73
O'Neill, Brenda "Smokey" Constance 65, 116
Only the Ball Was White: A History of the Legendary Black Players and All-Black Professional Teams 26
Oriard, Michael 3, 10, 42–43, 45–46, 48–49, 51
Osiris 24, 33–34
Outerbridge, Mary E. 34

Paris, Memo 10, 15, 40–41, 47, 71–72, 77–79, 116–117, 138–139, 140–143
Paulos, Sheila 103
Pereira, Kim 120, 124
Perkins, Al 101
Persephone 20, 50, 118, 120, 123
Peterson, Robert W. 26
Potter, Tristram Coffin 10
Pratt, Annis 20–22, 24, 123
The Pride of the Yankees 45
Prynne, Hester 39
Puechner, Ray 103–104

Quart, Barbara Koenig 40–41, 138
Quitman, Amanda 107–113

Rabelais, François 17
Rabelais and His World 17
Rachel, the Rabbi's Wife 12, 45, 52, 150–152, 159–167
Rader, Benjamin G. 31
Reddy, Maureen T. 67–68
The Reproduction of Mothering: Psychoanalysis and the Sociology of Gender 63–66
Rich, Adrienne 67
The Rio Loja Ringmaster 11, 45, 52, 117–120, 125–132, 158–159
Ripkin, Cal, Jr. 37
Ritz, David 104
Robinson, Jackie 26–27, 30
Roof, Judith 62
The Rookie (film) 17, 45
The Rookie (Tunis) 43
Rose, Mary Beth 62
Roth, Philip 68, 165–66
Rothweiler, Paul 103–104
Rowling, J. K. 62
Ruddick, Sara 67–68, 91, 119

Index

Runyan, Damon 42–43
Ruotolo, Lucio 41
Russell, Bob 11, 66, 71–72, 80, 85–90, 94
Russell, Spike 11, 66, 71–72, 80, 85–90, 94
Ruth, George Herman "Babe" 11, 30, 35–36, 50, 61, 82
Ruth Marini: World Series Star 104–106
Ryan, Nolan 37

Sachs, Marilyn 103
Sacramento Bee 4–5
The Sandlot 3, 10, 53
Sands, Gus 78
The Scarlet Letter 39
Schweitzer, Gertrude 71–73
Seeking the Perfect Game: Baseball in American Literature 1, 49–51
Seymour, Harold 30, 93–94
Shakespeare, William 62
She's on First 11, 71–72, 91, 94, 100, 103, 107–113
Shoeless Joe 12, 20, 45, 65, 94, 119, 137, 143–147, 158
Showalter, Elaine 13–14, 39
simple goddesses 115–118
Simpson, Sam 72, 75–76, 84, 95–96
Skolnik, Richard 29
Slote, Alfred 102
Smithsonian 4
Smokey O: A Romance 65, 116
Solomon, Eric 10, 42–45, 159, 161, 164, 166–167
"Song" 155–156
Sonnshein, Rachel 12, 45, 49, 52, 54, 150–152, 159–167, 173
Sosa, Sammy 35
Soto, Gary 150
The Southpaw 6, 8, 46, 70–71, 91–100, 132–137
Spalding, A. G. 16
Sport and the Spirit of Play in American Fiction: Hawthorne to Faulkner 38
Sport and the Spirit of Play in Contemporary American Fiction 24, 54–56, 156, 159, 162, 173

Star Wars 15
Stone, Natalie 103
substitute mothers 11, 57–90, 169
Sullivan, Silky 102
The Sun Field 43, 102, 116
The Sunlit Field 102
Sunshine, Linda 11, 71–72, 90, 94, 107–113
Suzanne, Jamie 101
The Sweetheart Season 4, 11–12, 23, 45, 71, 73, 150–152, 167–173
Swigart, Jane 61, 66, 71, 112
Szemanski, Annie 104–105

"Take Me Out to the Ball Game" 4, 12
Taves, Isabella 100–101
Tennenbaum, Silvia 12, 150–152, 159–167
"terrible mother" 77, 86
Thayer, Ernest L. 37–38, 50
Things Invisible to See 12, 45, 101, 150–159, 169
Thomas, Frank 35
Thoreau, Henry David 39
A Ticket for a Seamstitch 6, 59
Tlachtli 125–132
transformational goddesses 2, 12, 115–149
Traphagen, Berwyn "Red" Phillips 72, 96–99, 112
Tucker, Grandmother 80–84
Tucker, Roy 11, 66, 71–72, 80–84, 89, 94
Tunis, John R. 11, 43, 71, 80–92, 95
Twain, Mark 61
Tyler, Judith Winthrop 43
Tyler, Tiny 43

The Universal Baseball Association, Inc., J. Henry Waugh, Prop. 8, 70

The Venus of Willendorf 24
Von Tilzer, Albert 4

Walker, Alice 21–22, 25
Wasserman, Earl R. 10, 15, 46–47, 49, 77, 86, 115, 139

Index

Waugh, Henry 8
Webster, Aaron 72, 96–99, 112
Welty, Eudora 121
Westbrook, Deeanne 1, 10–11, 15, 46, 51–52, 57–58, 60, 69, 75–76, 107, 144, 156–158
Westling, Louise 121
What Hearts 52–54
When Women Played Hardball 5, 26
White, Bridget 4, 6, 12
Wiggen, Henry "Author" 6–7, 9, 20, 46, 50, 59, 70–73, 83, 90–100, 125, 132–137, 147
Wiggen, Holly Webster 6–7, 9, 11–12, 20, 45–46, 49, 51–52, 54, 71–72, 91–100, 119, 132–137, 147
Wiggen, Pop 72, 95–99, 112
Will, George F. 149
Willard, Nancy 12, 45, 101, 150–159

Williams, Ted 35
Wilson, August 7, 9, 11, 45, 52, 69, 75, 113, 118–125
"Women" 42
Women at Play: The Story of Women in Baseball 5, 26
women athletes 56, 173–174
Women in Baseball: The Forgotten History 5, 26
Wong, Hertha D. 62
Wong, Shirley Temple 74
Woodley, Richard 102
Woolf, Virginia 41
World Series 83

You Know Me Al 18, 43, 75, 107

Zeus 133

www.ingramcontent.com/pod-product-compliance
Ingram Content Group UK Ltd.
Pitfield, Milton Keynes, MK11 3LW, UK
UKHW042008140426
5217IPUK00015B/1055